Barbados

3rd Edition

Lynne M. Sullivan

HUNTER

HUNTER PUBLISHING, INC.
130 Campus Drive
Edison, NJ 08818-7816
☎ 732-225-1900 / 800-255-0343 / fax 732-417-1744
www.hunterpublishing.com
E-mail hunterp@bellsouth.net

IN CANADA:
Ulysses Travel Publications
4176 Saint-Denis, Montréal, Québec
Canada H2W 2M5
☎ 514-843-9882 ext. 2232 / fax 514-843-9448

IN THE UNITED KINGDOM:
Windsor Books International
The Boundary, Wheatley Road, Garsington
Oxford, OX44 9EJ England
☎ 01865-361122 / fax 01865-361133

ISBN 1-55650-910-3
© 2001 Lynne M. Sullivan

All rights reserved. No part of this publication may be reproduced, stored in a retrieval system, or transmitted in any form, or by any means, electronic, mechanical, photocopying, recording, or otherwise, without the written permission of the publisher.

This guide focuses on recreational activities. As all such activities contain elements of risk, the publisher, author, affiliated individuals and companies disclaim any responsibility for any injury, harm, or illness that may occur to anyone through, or by use of, the information in this book. Every effort was made to insure the accuracy of information in this book, but the publisher and author do not assume, and hereby disclaim, any liability for loss or damage caused by errors, omissions, misleading information or potential travel

Cover: Tony Arruzza Photography

Maps by Kim André & Lissa Dailey, © 2001 Hunter Publishing, Inc.

4 3 2 1

From the Author

Adventure is my favorite subject, and my goal is to give readers something extra to make a destination real and exciting. I'm an avid walker and backroad biker who always wants to see what's around the next corner and over one more hill. Beaches, forests and mountaintops draw my attention, and I never keep a remote discovery secret. As a certified scuba diver, I often opt for destinations that offer underwater excursions and sign on for trips to the best sites with a variety of guides.

Since shopping is the favorite activity of many travelers, I spend days hunting for one-of-a-kind treasures and outstanding bargains in artists' studios, craft workshops and unique stores. I tour all the attractions and evaluate the museums, peek into off-limits studios behind dusty windows, follow the locals to out-of-the-way sites, eat in comfy family-run joints as well as the best restaurants, inspect quaint little inns as well as upscale resorts, and stay out late to hit the trendiest nightspots.

In the end, I've discovered the best places to shop, visit, eat, sleep and hang out on a stingy budget as well as on unlimited funds. I've seen sites and visited places that aren't usually mentioned in travel guides and talked to experts and average citizens who know the destinations well. Then, I write it all down for you.

Travel guides are ever-evolving projects, and I welcome your commments and suggestions. Updated information appears regularly on my website, www.travelynne.com, where you can also ask me questions by e-mail.

www.hunterpublishing.com

Hunter's full range of guides to all corners of the globe is featured on our exciting website. You'll find guidebooks to suit every type of traveler, no matter what their budget, lifestyle, or idea of fun.

Adventure Guides – There are now over 40 titles in this series, covering destinations from Costa Rica and the Yucatán to Tampa Bay & Florida's West Coast, New Hampshire and the Alaska Highway. Complete information on what to do, as well as where to stay and eat, *Adventure Guides* are tailor-made for the active traveler, with a focus on hiking, biking, canoeing, horseback riding, trekking, skiing, watersports, and all other kinds of fun.

Alive Guides – This ever-popular line of books takes a unique look at the best each destination offers: fine dining, jazz clubs, first-class class hotels and resorts. In-margin icons direct the reader at a glance. Top sellers include: *The Cayman Islands, St. Martin & St. Barts,* and *Aruba, Bonaire & Curaçao.*

The ***Hunter-Rivages Hotels of Character & Charm*** books are top sellers, with titles covering France, Spain, Italy, Paris and Portugal. Originating in Paris, they set the standard for excellence with their fabulous color photos, superb maps and candid descriptions of the most remarkable hotels of Europe.

Our ***Romantic Weekends*** guidebooks provide a series of escapes for couples of all ages and lifestyles. Unlike most "romantic" travel books, ours cover more than charming hotels and delightful restaurants, with a host of activities that you and your partner will remember forever.

Contents

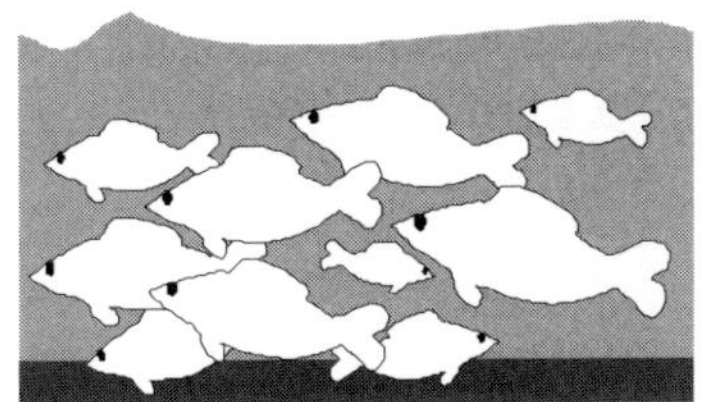

Introduction

Visitors are lured to Barbados by year-round sunshine, miles of splendid palm-fringed beaches, a bounty of excellent places to stay, world-class cuisine, and enticing activities to occupy unhurried vacation days.

The same could be said about many other tropical islands, but don't make the mistake of thinking Barbados is just another gorgeous piece of Caribbean paradise.

Nah, mon – she be mo' den dat.

For starters, the island doesn't fit neatly into the archipelago that curves gracefully, like a backward C, between the Caribbean Sea and Atlantic Ocean. It stands proudly to the east, like a brilliant star that's fallen from its constellation.

This arrant positioning puts the independent English-speaking island-nation entirely in the Atlantic Ocean – but residents refer to the west coast as the "Caribbean side." Almost 100 miles separate it from St. Vincent, its nearest neighbor to the west. Trinidad, off the coast of Venezuela, is 200 miles south, and Miami is 1,611 miles to the north.

In addition to being out of place, Barbados was created differently than other islands in the southeastern Caribbean and has a distinct appearance. Some islands are heaps of magnificently disguised volcanic debris, but Barbados is made of coral. Gentle plains wrap around the western and southern shore. Dramatic ocean-carved cliffs dominate the east coast. Diverse natural wonders fill the rolling green hills of the interior countryside.

Parts of Barbados are densely populated. Approximately 268,000 Bajans live on 166 square miles. The island is shaped somewhat like a distorted pear that measures 21 miles north to south, and 14 miles east to west between the widest points. Most of the population is concentrated in the south, around **Bridgetown**, the lively west-coast capital.

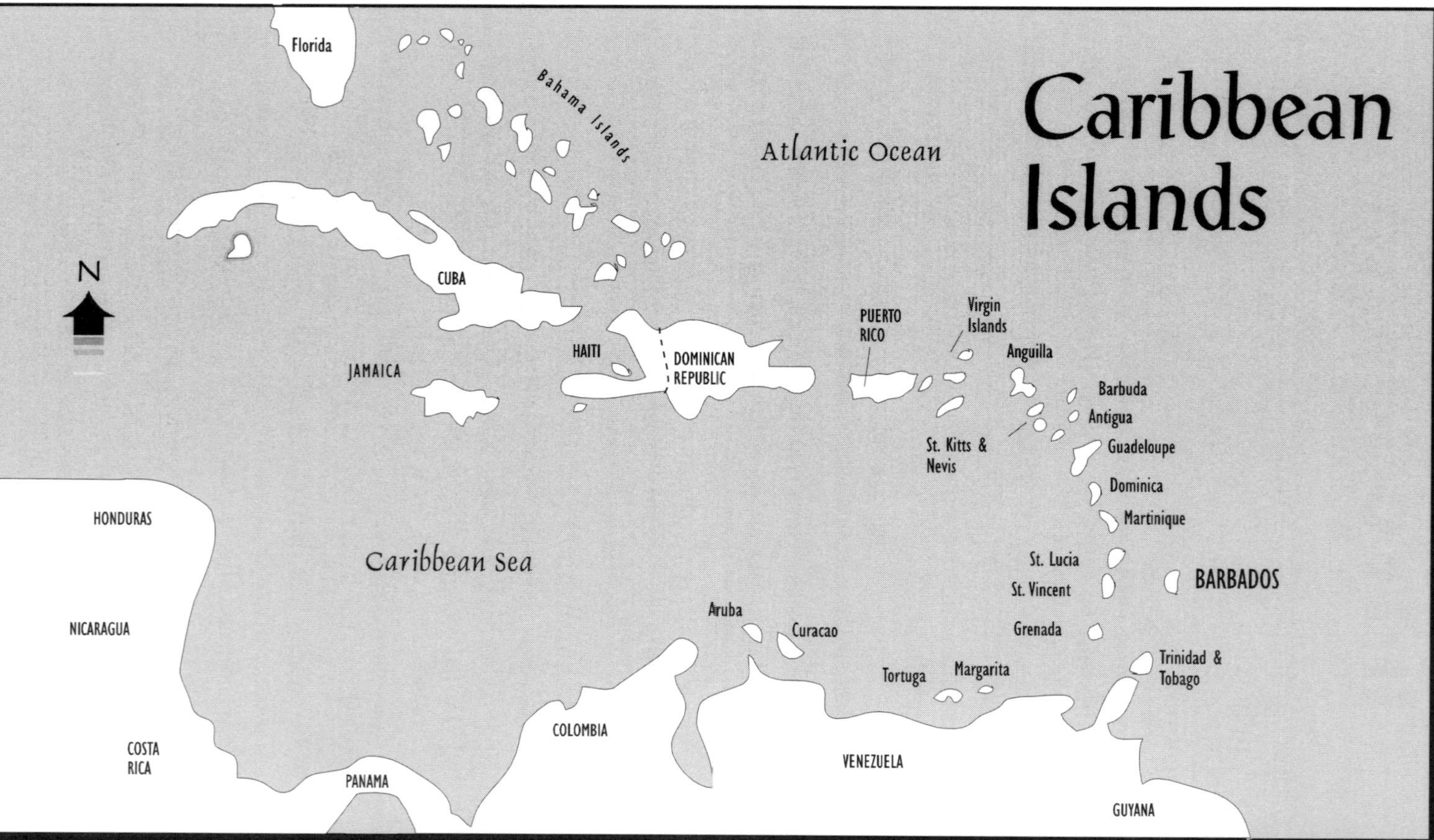
Caribbean Islands
Florida
Bahama Islands
Atlantic Ocean
N
CUBA
HAITI
DOMINICAN REPUBLIC
JAMAICA
PUERTO RICO
Virgin Islands
Anguilla
Barbuda
Antigua
St. Kitts & Nevis
Guadeloupe
Dominica
Martinique
St. Lucia
St. Vincent
BARBADOS
Grenada
Trinidad & Tobago
HONDURAS
NICARAGUA
COSTA RICA
PANAMA
Caribbean Sea
Aruba
Curacao
Tortuga
Margarita
COLOMBIA
VENEZUELA
GUYANA

Bajan (say bay jun) is a contraction or alteration of Barbadian, which was first shortened to Badian. Now, say Badian quickly with a lazy tongue. You may use either Barbadian or Bajan to refer to anything that is indigenous to the island, including both black and white citizens.

The island retains traces of the three centuries it spent as a British colony, but its soul is undeniably West Indian. Calypso music floats in the air over cricket fields, *cou-cou* (a thick mush-like island favorite made of cornmeal and okra) and flying fish show up on the menus of sleek Euro-style restaurants, and Bajan slang dominates conversations among the highly educated population.

Barbados doesn't pretend to be crime-free, but it appropriately presents itself as a *safe* tourist destination. Travelers are warmly welcomed by the proper, but easygoing, Bajans, and visitors rarely encounter harassment or rudeness. Beach vendors and street hawkers are scarce and politely retreat when told "No, thanks."

The People & Their Culture

■ Language

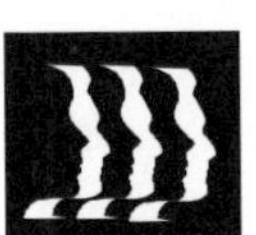

The official language of Barbados is English, and the well-educated residents use perfect grammar and smooth diction – when they want to.

Visitors often notice that the hotel staff and tour guides, both blacks and whites, speak pure, lightly accented English when speaking with tourists, but a completely different language when chatting with other Bajans. This unique hybrid jargon developed over more than two centuries as people from many African tribes mixed with various ethnic groups from Europe.

At first the Africans from different tribes struggled to learn English so that they could communicate with their field bosses and owners as well as each other. Not surprisingly, the language they learned in the fields wasn't always the King's English since overseers were often poorly educated working-class people or indentured servants.

The Bajan Dialect

As this Africanized and adulterated English was passed around and taught to children, it developed consistent patterns. For example, Bajans began to habitually substitute the letter *d* for the diphthong *th,* so that *this* became *dis*, and they contracted common English contractions even further, so that *isn't* became *en*. Bajans also confused English pronouns and verb tenses, so that subject pronouns were used as possessive or object pronouns, plural endings were omitted, and the present tense served just as well for the past or future. Instead of using comparative or superlative forms of adjectives, they simply repeat the descriptive word.

He en sleepin' late late dis mornin'. He be cookin' up she brekfas'.

It be we bag o fish? Dem big big big.

We good good good musik gine mek yuh dance like a nest o snakes.

Most Bajan sentences are made up of English words used in a different way. Tourists will find it fascinating to listen to Bajans chatting on the street or calling to one another from their cars. However, most residents will switch seamlessly to proper English when they speak to visitors. Those who don't may be making a statement, demanding respect for their culture, or simply displaying a little good-natured Bajan humor.

■ Architecture

Three Centuries of Style

Many examples of Barbados' early architecture remain as either renovated masterpieces or neglected ruins. As you drive around the island, watch for grand stone structures, overgrown windmills, preserved Victorian homes, and humble chattel houses. Their architectural styles and building materials are excellent reminders of an intriguing history with diverse influences.

Chattel Houses

These prefab mobile homes are a colorful part of Bajan heritage. You see them everywhere – small, wooden structures painted in bright tropical colors. The first *chattels* (the word means "moveable property") were constructed by slaves and indentured servants on their boss's plantation. The pre-cut pine came from North America, and Bajans could put them up on stone foundations with few tools and little building experience. When the worker was sold, fired, or evicted from the landowner's property, he could disassemble his house in sections and move it, along with his family, to the next location.

All the houses looked alike right out of the box, but as Bajans earned a little money, they added to the basic plan that consisted of a tiny two-room structure topped by a corrugated metal roof. The front of the house usually had a central door flanked by two windows. Gradually, the homes took on individual personalities. When Bajans began to earn enough money to buy their own land, they added real foundations and floors, attached rooms to the back, built covered front porches, put canopies over the windows, and decorated with bright paint and elaborate fretwork.

Today, some Bajans with enough money and land to build any type of home they want still prefer a chattel-style house. Several of the island's tourist attractions, restaurants, and bars are located in or designed after these original workers' homes. The simple design has an amazing ability to withstand storms and hurricane-force winds.

You'll find the quaint, attractive homes all around the island, but particularly handsome chattel-house shopping villages are located in St. Lawrence Gap on the south coast, at Sunset Crest on the west coast, and at Tyrol Cot, northeast of Bridgetown.

Don't expect the flamboyant styles seen on many Caribbean islands. With very few exceptions Barbados is, and always has been, strictly, uniformly, and properly, British. No Spanish flair. No

French folderol. Just magnificent designs inspired by **Jacobean** (from the reign of James I of England, 1603-1625), **Georgian** (pertaining to the reigns of the first four Georges of England, 1714-1830), and **Victorian** (associated with the reign of Queen Victoria, 1837-1901) notions of elegance. The most conspicuous exceptions are the lowly chattel houses that brighten the countryside with eye-catching colors.

Most of Bridgetown's first structures were built of wood taken from the island's dense virgin forests, which was unfortunate for two reasons. The forests were quickly obliterated; and most of the buildings were destroyed by fires that broke out in 1688, 1766, and 1860. The city has been rebuilt over the centuries in a mix of architectural styles, with most buildings constructed of stone.

Speightstown, the second largest town on Barbados, is small compared to the capital, and has declined since its heyday as a major seaport during the peak of the sugar boom. However, its sleepy streets are lined with old shops and houses that feature jalousie windows, wrought-iron gates, and overhanging balconies. The parish church has been renovated, and the post office and library are appealing examples of the Georgian style favored by early British settlers. More renovation and preservation is expected during the next few years through programs fostered by the National Trust.

Many of the finest historical structures on the island are the parish churches, military forts, and rural plantation houses, built primarily of stone – cut either from the native coral or from the ballast used in shipping. The **Savannah Hotel** in the Garrison area south of Bridgetown is a good example. The main building is actually two historic houses, with the eastern portion being the more interesting. It is built of brick that had been used as ballast, and features ornate, New Orleans-style wrought-iron balconies.

Drax Hall and **St. Nicholas Abbey** were built around 1650 in the popular Jacobean style; they are two of the three remaining mansions in that style in the western hemisphere (the third is Bacon's Castle in Virginia). Drax Hall is still a private residence and is open to the public only once a year, during the Open House program sponsored by the National Trust (see page 34; for information ☎ 246-426-2421). The house is surrounded by trees and sits secluded at the end of a long driveway off Highway 4B in eastern St. George Parish, out of view from the road.

Visitors are welcome at St. Nicholas Abbey near CherryTree Hill, off Highway 1 in St. Peter Parish (see page 109). This grand plantation house was never an abbey; it was built as a residence for Colonel Benjamin Berringer during the early phase of the English Renaissance.

The Georgian period followed the Jacobean, and the style that became popular in the 18th and early 19th centuries is dominant in many government buildings, churches and private homes dating from that time. Distinguishing features of the style include regal arcades, open courtyards and grand staircases in the Palladian style (named for Italian Renaissance architect Andrea Palladio, 1508-1580, and made popular during this period by English builder Inigo Jones).

The Garrison area, off Highway 7 to the south of Bridgetown, has several good examples of Georgian-era military structures. **Pavilion Court**, originally Hastings Hospital, was built in 1780; the **Barbados Museum**, once a military prison, was constructed in sections from 1817 to 1853; and the **Savannah Club**, an old guard house, has a clock tower that bears the date 1803.

Romantic Victorian features show up in both plantation mansions (greathouses) and chattel houses scattered about the island. Many of these homes have survived in excellent condition because they were never subjected to damage from the kinds of territorial conflicts that took place on most Caribbean islands.

The Barbados National Trust lists more than 300 houses of historic interest that merit notice.

Tyrol Cot Heritage Village is centered around the accurately restored former home of the late statesman Sir Grantley Adams. The lovely house was built in 1854 by Bajan builder William Farnum. While the house is considered to be of Georgian design, it has some atypical features, such as a roof fashioned to catch rainwater. A replica of a 19th century slave hut sits nearby, and a museum on the property holds relics from a typical island home at the beginning of the 20th century.

Tyrol Cot also has several newly constructed buildings designed to look like old, uniquely Bajan, chattel houses.

See *Exploring the Island*, page 87, for more information about Tyrol Cot.

The New Building Wave

Building is booming on Barbados. Several large residential developments are in the works; both Bridgetown and Speightstown have redevelopment plans; and new or renovated hotel complexes are opening continually.

One of the most exciting projects is the huge, traffic-stopping, multimillion-dollar renovation at **Sandy Lane Resort and Golf Club**, on the west coast. Reopening dates have been set and reset, and still the work goes on. When it is complete, Sandy Lane is expected to be a fabulous resort with world-class golfing (see page 140; or keep track of their progress by calling ☎ 800-225-5843 (in the US and Canada) or 246-432-1311, fax 432-2954.

The new **Royal Westmoreland** and **Port St. Charles**, both sprawling, multi-use developments, and **Millennium Heights** and **Sugar Hill**, which are residential compounds, are open – but still expanding or improving. All four complexes are raising the standards of Bajan-style design, which traditionally features steep roofs, roomy verandas, and wooden jalouise doors and windows. The newer buildings incorporate air conditioning, plenty of shaded glass, updated constructin materials and high-tech electronics.

More than a million square feet of new office space is under construction or recently completed in response to demands from international businesses. Much of this development is planned for the waterfront area of Bridgetown, but multi-use industrial parks are springing up in strategic locations along major highways connecting the capital with Speightstown and St. Lawrence. A project at **Apes Hill** is expected to bring a resort, a conference center, offices and villas, and a championship golf course to the currently undeveloped Scotland district in the northeast.

The chattel house motif is featured at **Kings Beach Village** and **Little Good Harbour** on the west coast. Both developments incorporate traditional Bajan looks with modern amenities, while preserving the natural surroundings. At Little Good Harbour, developers have taken special care to restore 300-year-old Fort

Rupert, and to maintain the distinct character of the local fishing community.

While all of this development is welcome, Barbadians are ever mindful of the need to preserve their past and protect their irreplaceable natural resources. Visitors may rightly assume that the island paradise will change, but only in a controlled and environmentally responsible manner.

■ Art

Barbados has produced some incredibly talented artists. Many are influenced by their African roots and island culture, which results in colorful creations with diverse themes. Art lovers, collectors, and souvenir hunters will want to visit several of the island's museums, galleries, and studios to see the variety of works by local artists and craftsmen.

As you tour the island, watch for the kaleidoscopic murals painted on the exteriors of buildings. These life-size paintings are brilliant creations depicting everyday life, and the **National Cultural Foundation** (☎ 246-424-0909) assists local artists who wish to paint these lifescapes on public buildings.

The **Barbados Arts Council** (☎ 246-426-4385) runs a respected gallery at Pelican Village (☎ 246-427-5350) on Hincks Street in Bridgetown. Nearby, the **Barbados Investment and Development Corporation** (☎ 246-426-7802) oversees the island's handmade crafts industry, with outlets at the airport, Harrison Cave, and selected hotels, as well as Pelican Village.

The Controversial Pelican

A large, rusting, avant-garde sculpture called *Pelican in Flight* is on dislay in the courtyard. The controversial piece is loved by some and detested by others; stop by to take a look.

Fine art is on exhibit at **The Barbados Gallery of Art** on Bush Hill in the Garrison area south of Bridgetown. Permanent collections include paintings, sculpture, prints, and mixed-media works by Barbadians as well as artists from other Caribbean islands and South America. Visitors may arrange tours through the museum office or explore on their own; the gallery is open Tuesdays-Saturdays, 10-5. Admission is B$10 on weekdays and B$4 on Saturdays for adults; B$4 on weekdays and free on Saturdays for children (☎ 246-228-0149, fax 228-5371).

Renowned Bajan Artists

Among the old-timers of the Bajan art world, **Fielding Babb** and **Karl Broodhagen** stand out. Babb's early works are watercolors, but for more than 20 years he has painted traditional island scenes in brilliant oils. He is credited with playing a key role in the growth of fine art on the island. Broodhagen's most famous work is *Freed Slave*, a sculpture (also known as *Bussa*) that stands in the center of the traffic circle on the ABC Highway where St. Michael Parish meets St. George Parish. Broodhagen also created the bronze figure of Sir Grantley Adams that is displayed in the Government Headquarters building on Bay Street in Bridgetown.

Whether you're buying or simply admiring, look for works by these highly touted Bajan artists and craft designers.

Goldie Spieler and her son **David Spieler** work from their studio/workshop/store, **Earthworks Pottery** (☎ 246-425-2334), turning out functional and artistic Caribbean-style pottery.

Geoffrey and **Joan Skeete** and their son and daughter-in-law, **John** and **Monica Skeete**, carve and draw birds of the Caribbean.

Winston Kellman's simple watercolors and charcoals are easily recognized and respected by Caribbean art fans.

Courtney Devonish, a Chalky Mount native, now works from his gallery/studio on Anguilla and is internationally recognized for his abstract sculptures.

Michael Adams creates hand-pulled silkscreens from his wildly colorful paintings.

Neville Legall is an award-winning painter who works in oils and watercolors.

David Alleyne is known for his oversized paintings that depict everyday Bajan life.

Ireka's unique woven pieces are identified by the shells, seeds and beads woven into the straw.

Amica, a Rastafarian, turns out splendid utilitarian products made of leather.

Errol Watson uses the hide of native blackbellied sheep to create exquisite handbags and wallets.

Wayne Wells carves intricate boxes from unique pieces of "found" wood.

See *Shopping*, page 147, for additional art and craft resources.

■ Music

Nothing of any significance can take place on Barbados without music. It's an essential part of everyday life and a requirement for all gatherings, big and small.

For most of the past decade, the island has celebrated each new year with the **Barbados Jazz Festival**, a week-long event that features some of the best musicians in the world. Past festivals have highlighted Gladys Knight, Nancy Wilson and Spyro Gyra. Concerts are held at various locations such as Farley Hill Park, Sunbury House, Sir Garfield Sobers Sports Complex, and the Royal Westmoreland. For schedule and ticket information, contact the promoter, GMR Tours International, Inc., ☎ 246-437-4537, fax 437-4538, e-mail bdosjazz@caribsurf.com.

Old Favorites

One of the oldest and most traveled Bajan groups is **The Merrymen**, who began drawing crowds in Europe, Canada and the United States back in the 1960s, with original songs that set folk lyrics to a Caribbean beat. Three members of the original band, Emile Straker, Chris Gibbs, and Robin Hunte, still schedule special appearances together and have plans to release a new CD with original songs written by Straker.

Tony Carter grabbed attention as the **Might Gabby** in 1968 when he won the music competition at the annual Crop Over Festival. He went on to become a well-known Calypso musician with hits such as *Miss Barbados*, which scoffs at the idea of a white Canadian representing Barbados as its official beauty queen in an international pageant; *Needles and Pins*, a jab at a local politician who tried to limit public access to Bajan beaches; and *Hit It*, a song about a cricket match betwen himself and a young lady.

New Trends

Many Bajans still consider calypso to be the only real music of the people, and several entertainers currently draw fans with sassy social commentary set to its catchy beat. **Red Plastic Bag** won the title of Calypso Monarch in 1982 and again in 1997, and went on to earn international recognition with hit songs that mix satire, double meanings, and mockery. In *Holes*, he sings of the embarrassment of taking his friend from the US on a tour of the island along roads riddled with potholes.

Other popular stars include **Adonijah**, a Rastafarian calypso singer; **Grynner**, a musician with a great sense of comedy who often appears with the Mighty Gabby; and **Romeo**, a charming entertainer whose songs were banned from radio because of their controversial lyrics.

Despite calypso's hold on the island, many musicians are moving toward other styles. In *Too Sexy*, Edwin Yearwood, the lead singer for the award-winning group **Krosfyah**, claims to be "too sexy for winter, but never too sexy for soca," which is a more soulful, heavy-bass style of calypso. The group's lead singer, Tony Bailey, goes even further by writing original music influenced by the French Caribbean and by old, upbeat dance tunes. In *Love Walks Alone*, the duo comes up with a blues-style ballad.

Bajan singer **David Kirton** captured attention in 1998 with his reggae/pop CD, *Stranger*, which has had tremendous crossover appeal to an international market. He records in Jamaica, and rejects the idea that it is unusual for a Bajan to become famous performing reggae. He sees the Caribbean as one region, and thinks his perspective is the wave of the future.

Square One, with popular lead singer Alison Hinds, is a Barbados-based group that also has international crossover appeal because of its fusion of several Caribbean music styles. Hinds sings chart-busting hits in French, Portuguese, and Caribbean patois, and the group has drawn large crowds on tours of the US, Canada, Europe, and other Caribbean islands.

A five-member Bajan group called **4D People** (formerly IV Play) is a rhythm-and-blues band featuring lead singer Tony Norville. The band writes its own imaginative music and continues to gain popularity on the island and elsewhere, despite their break with calypso and other typically Caribbean sounds – further evidence that Bajan music is becoming Caribbean music, which is becoming universal music (see *Bajan Music* in the *Nightlife* chapter, page 203).

■ The Spirit of the People

Some say that the game of cricket is the religion of Barbados. Others say music is the heart and soul of the people. Still others will insist that more Bajans worship in rum shops than in churches.

All these scoffers would be wrong. Religion is the religion of Barbados and, as proof, the island boasts more than 100 different denominations or sects worshipping in more than 300 separate churches. Every Sunday morning, Bajans parade to services in their finest clothes, and melodic hymns pour from open church windows.

In the Beginning

In order to understand Bajans' dedication to religion, it's necessary to look back more than 300 years to a time when the first English settlers were devoted equally to a heavenly God and to an earthly king. In 1652, the island's founders proclaimed religious tolerance a basic right, even though religious freedom was suppressed in England. However, as the island's population grew, it became obvious that religious tolerance actually meant Anglican tolerance.

The Anglican church was the official church of England and, as a result, the first religion to establish churches on the island. When Catholic priests arrived to minister to the Irish indentured servants working in the sugarcane fields, Anglican authorities showed no tolerance whatsoever, and subjected the clergymen to unusually cruel treatment. Likewise, when slaves were brought from Africa, the church leaders maintained that the practice of African religions interfered with the conversion of the black heathens. This policy allowed the white landowners a clear conscience about enslaving their fellow men.

To increase their control over the African population, plantation owners held their Anglican services behind closed doors, a practice that created superstitious fears among the slaves. Since people from different regions of Africa did not always share a common religion, they developed new customs on Barbados based on a combination of the beliefs brought with them and practices glimpsed in the "secret" Christian ceremonies.

Superstitious Beliefs

When an African died on Barbados, fellow slaves held a long, elaborate funeral to guarantee that the recently departed would not return to haunt the living. Ghosts were very real in many African traditions, and a belief in spirits, called *duppies*, persists to some extent even today.

Duppies

Some older black Bajans may occasionally be heard blaming bad luck on a duppy, and accidents are sometimes attributed to an unfriendly ghost.

Likewise, fortunate occurrences may be brought about by good spirits who are encouraged to act by gifts or through rituals. Some islanders continue to believe that certain herbal mixtures attract love, guarantee success at a job, or prevent extra-marital affairs. People claiming to be witches, or *obeahs*, profess to speak with the dead and perform good – or evil – magic.

Indigenous Religion

The only religious sect truly original to Barbados is the Spiritualist Baptist Church, founded in 1957 by Archbishop Granville Williams. Members of this energetic denomination tie colorful cloths around their heads, a practice that earns them the nickname "tie heads." Their services are flamboyant and emotional, with jubilant singing and rhythmic dancing.

New memebrs are baptized, attend a series of indoctrination classes, and then withdraw to a section of the church to meditate in seclusion for a week. Once they are renewed in the sirit, they come forth to sing praises, clap their hands, and dance with joy. On Saturday nights the congregation meets in Heroes Square in Bridgetown for a vigil, and on New Year's Eve they parade through the streets holding lighted candles. Three Spiritualist Baptist Churches on the island claim around 10,000 members.

Rastafarianism

The religion known as Rastafarianism has its roots in Africa and its origin in Jamaica. It was introduced to Bajans in 1975 and has gained many followers over the years.

The name comes from the Ethiopian Ras Tafari, who was crowned Emperor Haile Selassie I in 1930. Followers of Ras Tafari believe that he was the fulfillment of a prophecy made by Jamaican nationalist leader Marcus Garvey, who had told a congregation in 1927 that a great black leader would soon be crowned in Africa.

Haile Selassie, which means Mighty Trinity, claimed to be "King of Kings, Lord of Lords, the Conquering Lion of the Tribe of Judah," and a direct descendant of King David. True followers of Ras Tafari wear their hair in dreadlocks, abstain from alcohol, eat a vegetarian diet, and live quiet and faithful lives with few material possessions. Many Bajan Rastafarians work in the Rasta Craft Market complex at Temple Yard in Bridgetown (see *Shopping*, page 148) creating high-quality crafts and artwork.

Religion Today

About half of all Bajans, both black and white, practice the Anglican Religion, and some of the oldest buildings on the island are Anglican churches. However, numerous other religions also draw devoted congregations, and their pews and choir lofts are equally full on Sunday mornings. In addition to the various Christian denominations, there are groups of Jews, Hindus and Muslims.

Every parish has its parish church, and every town has a variety of storefront churches. Choral groups appear on the Sunday afternoon TV show, *Time to Sing*; weekly performances by local gospel groups are listed in the newspapers; schools begin the day with prayer; and radio stations devote time to spiritual programs.

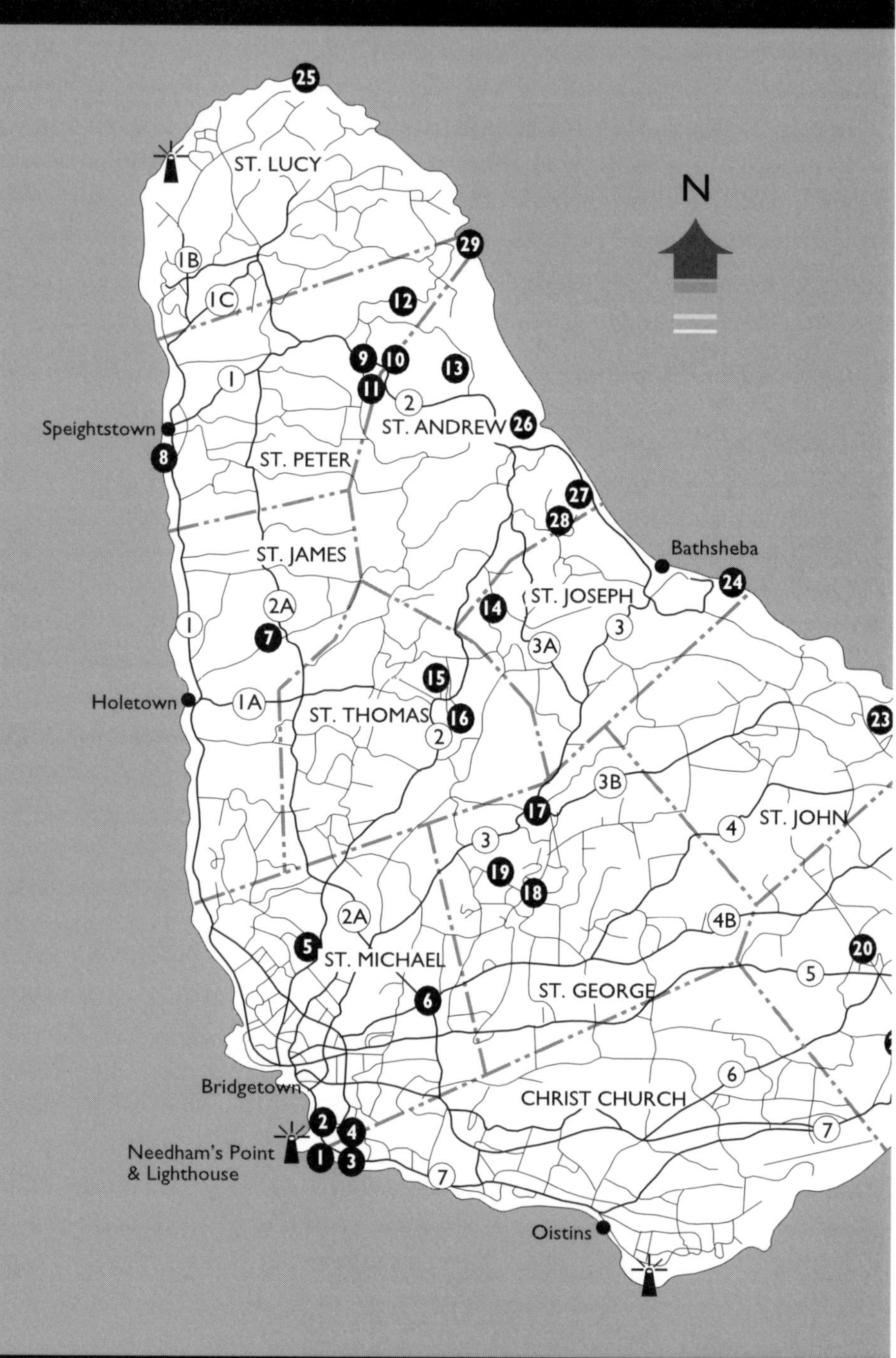
N
ST. LUCY
ST. PETER
ST. ANDREW
ST. JAMES
ST. JOSEPH
ST. THOMAS
ST. JOHN
ST. MICHAEL
ST. GEORGE
CHRIST CHURCH
Speightstown
Holetown
Bathsheba
Bridgetown
Needham's Point
& Lighthouse
Oistins

Historical, Natural & Cultural Sights

1. Charles Fort
2. St. Anne's Fort
3. Barbados Museum
4. Barbados Gallery of Art
5. Tyrol Cottage Heritage Village (Tyrol Cot)
6. Bussa Roundabout (Emancipation Monument)
7. Portvale Sugar Factory & Sir Frank Hutson Museum
8. Arbib Nature & Heritage Trail Kiosk
9. Barbados Wildlife Reserve
10. Grenade Hall Forest & Signal Station
11. Farley Hill National Park
12. St. Nicholas Abbey
13. Morgan Lewis Sugar Mill
14. Flower Forest
15. Welchman Hall Forest Reserve
16. Harrison's Cave
17. Orchid World
18. Gun Hill Signal Station
19. Francia Plantation House
20. Sunbury Plantation
21. Heritage Park & Foursquare Rum Distillery
22. Sam Lord's Castle
23. Codrington College
24. Andromeda Botanic Gardens
25. Animal Flower Cave
26. The Spout
27. Barclay's Park
28. Chalky Mount Village Potteries
29. Pico Teneriffe

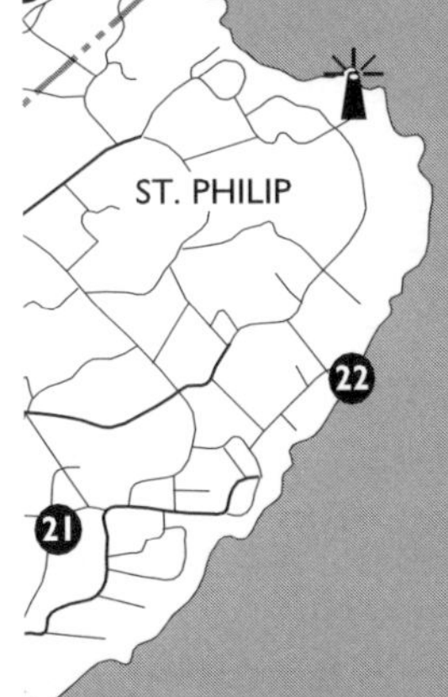

History

Archaeological discoveries reveal that stone age civilizations inhabited Barbados almost 4,000 years ago. Shell tools found on the northwest coast have been carbon dated at 1630 BC and identify these first Bajans as hunters and gatherers of the pre-pottery or Archaic Period. By 400 BC, tribes from South America who spoke a language known as Arawak had set up well-organized villages on the island.

■ Island-Hopping Amerindians

The **Arawaks** built 90-foot dugout canoes that carried people, animals, crops, fresh water, and religious icons across the sea and up the Caribbean archipelago. A narrow, swift-flowing sea channel known as The Dragons Mouth allowed them to make it from the north coast of South America to the nearby island of Trinidad. From there, they moved northward island by island.

Evidence of their advanced civilization has been unearthed in various locations and include a calendar system, materials for making pottery, and carved stones used to imprint designs on their bodies.

It's amazing that Arawak tribes ever found Barbados, which is flat and lies 100 miles east of the main island chain. Columbus sailed past without a clue on all four voyages to the West Indies.

Historians and archeologists say Arawaks were short people with olive-colored skin who often decorated their bodies with paint. The tops of their heads were pointed due to the tradition of tightly wrapping newborns' skulls. Adults wore nose rings and other jewelry to signify their authority within the tribe.

Each Arawak village had a chief (*caique*) who lived in a rectangular hut (*bohios*), while other members of the tribe lived in round huts called *caneyes*. The dwellings were simple structures made of wooden frames topped by straw roofs, but they were sturdy enough to withstand hurricanes

Villagers worshiped gods, whose likenesses, called *zemis*, were made of bits of wood, stone, and bones. These icons were thought to protect deserving humans from illness and storms, so the villagers offered gifts and food to them. A village and its chief were ranked in importance among the tribes by the number of *zemis* in their possession.

Arawaks were successful farmers and produced cassava (used in tapioca), maize, potatoes, peanuts, peppers, beans, and arrowroot using the slash-and-burn method of cultivation. They had simple tools made of sticks, called *coas*, and may have used ash or feces as fertilizers. In addition, they hunted and fished with baskets, nets, and sharp sticks. Large fish were sometimes caught by attaching sharpened sticks to *remoras*, small sucking fish that fastened themselves to larger sea creatures, such as sharks and turtles.

Food was cooked on hot stones or over an open fire, using peppers, herbs, and spices for flavor. Villagers preserved some foods with spices, but most was eaten fresh since the tropical climate allowed year-round farming, hunting, and fishing.

Arrival of the Caribs

Around 1200 AD, the Arawak population began to dwindle, and historians think it was because a hostile tribe arrived on Barbados. These late arrivals were called **Caribs**, and were a less advanced clan of hunters and fishermen. They managed to dominate Barbados for about 300 years through savage aggression and brute force.

The Caribs were more mobile and less ceremonial than the Arawaks. Their villages were smaller, sometimes made up of only extended family members with the head of the family acting as village leader. They lived in little wooden huts arranged around a central fireplace, which was probably used for community meetings.

Village leaders supervised fishing, done by the men, and farming, done by the women. In addition, they mediated disputes among the people and led raids into neighboring settlements to capture wives for the young men in the village.

Wives were often taken from Arawak tribes, most likely so that the women could raise the new generation of Carib-fathered children with the more polished Arawak skills and manners.

Raids and combat were important activities for Carib men, and their reputation as feared warriors is legend in the Caribbean. They attacked in long canoes that could carry up to 75 men, and used poisoned arrows, javelins, and clubs to subdue their foes. Reports spread that captured women were used as slaves or slave-wives, and that seized men were cooked over ceremonial fires and eaten by their captors.

Europeans who came to the West Indies in the 1500s returned home with tales of Carib cannibalism, but historians are not convinced they were true. Serious scholars insist the Indians didn't depend on human flesh for routine nutrition, but occasionally may have shared a slice or two of their captured foes to boost morale.

■ Europeans Leave Their Mark

Christopher Columbus never saw flat little Barbados as he sailed through the West Indies, so the island wasn't officially discovered by Europeans until 1536 when Portuguese explorer **Pedro à Campos** stopped by on his way to Brazil. He didn't encounter any Indians during his visit, which leads some historians to think that Spaniards may have stumbled onto the island a few years earlier and killed or captured the inhabitants. (Spanish law permitted such treatment of "savages" until 1542.)

Campos didn't stay on Barbados long, but he did record his discovery and leave a few pigs to fatten into a food source for his return voyages. He called the island *Los Barbados*, the bearded ones, and since he didn't report encountering any inhabitants, it's assumed he chose the name because of beard-like aerial roots that hung from fig trees growing along the shore.

The English arrived in May 1625, when British sea captain **John Powell** made a navigational error and bumped into *Los Barbados.* He liked what he found and claimed the pristine, uninhabited island for King James I. Two years later, Powell's brother, Captain Henry Powell, returned with 80 countrymen and some slaves (captured from a Spanish trading ship during the crossing) to colonize the island. The small group of settlers landed at a site on the west coast now known as Holetown on February 17, 1627, and began a 339-year stretch of continuous British control on the island they called Barbados.

Barbados celebrates the landing of Captain Powell during the ***Holetown Festival,*** *an annual event held in February that features special church services, music, dancing, parades, and a street market offering Bajan foods, arts, and crafts. Contact the* ***Barbados Tourism Authority*** *for this year's date;* ☎ *800-744-6244.*

Englishmen with the right social connections were granted parcels of land by the king, and the island's population quickly grew to 2,000. These early settlers stripped the island of its native forest (much of the timber was shipped back to Europe for furniture) so that tobacco, cotton, and food crops could be planted in the fertile soil. Since all of this clearing and cultivating required intense labor, white indentured servants were sent to the island. Many of these laborers were convicted criminals who were given the choice of being "Barbadosed" or going to the gallows.

■ Sweet Success

By 1637, the struggling colonists were looking for a big cash crop to supplement or replace their meager farm efforts. Dutchman **Pieter Blower** introduced them to sugarcane, a crop he learned to grow and process in Brazil, and in less than 10 years, the island was booming. Cane grew everywhere. The population count spiraled upward. Land values soared.

At first, sugarcane juice was used to make rum, a profitable product. But, soon, crystallized sugar became popular in Europe, and

Barbados couldn't keep up with the demand. Once again, Dutch expertise was sought, and plantation owners took their advice to import slaves from West Africa to work the fields and tend to household drudgeries.

Sugar production increased with slave labor, and as the landowners' profits grew, they brought in more laborers from Africa. Over a short period of time, the black population grew tremendously, while less efficient white indentured servants were phased out. Soon, a small number of white plantation owners dominated an island filled with overworked, underfed, ill-treated black slaves.

■ The Charter of Barbados

While Barbados was busy establishing the first large sugar plantations in the Caribbean, British royalty was contending with **Oliver Cromwell**. The island had always been pro-monarchy while enjoying local rule under their own House of Assembly, which was set up in 1639 as the second parliament established in a British colony (Bermuda's was the first.) When King Charles I was executed in 1649, Barbados declined to accept the authority of Cromwell.

Not one to accept rejection, Cromwell eventually sent a military fleet to seize control of the island. Barbadians defended their island for six months, until finally The **Articles of Agreement** (or Articles of Capitulation) were signed in Ye Mermaid Tavern in the town of Oistins on January 11, 1652. These Articles formed the basis of the **Charter of Barbados** and guaranteed an administration overseen by an appointed governor and a freely elected assembly. In addition, the island was granted freedom from British taxation without local consent.

Soon after the Articles of Agreement were signed, a large group of Jewish families emigrated from Brazil to escape persecution by ruling Portuguese. The immigrants' knowledge of Brazilian sugar production and business management was put to good use on their adopted island. Profits from sugar sales increased, and Barbados entered an enhanced period of prosperity.

■ The Good Life

During the mid-1600s, Barbados became Britain's wealthiest colony, elegant greathouses were built on large plantations, and elaborate stone churches were constructed in each parish. At the same time, slaves, who outnumbered white landowners 30 to one, endured bleak lives in makeshift stick-and-brush shacks with no floors.

Today, visitors can tour the elegant Jacobean (a style associated with the reign of England's King James I, 1566-1625) mansions of ***St. Nicolas Abbey*** *and* ***Drax Hall*** *(built in the 1650s), and the impressive* ***Gothic church*** *in St. John Parish (built around 1660).*

Well-educated whites from Europe and North America visited and moved to the island in order to enjoy the climate and improved living conditions. They brought with them the highly developed skills, talents, and principles common to the upper classes, which further smoothed the rough edges associated with life in the tropics. As a result, Barbados gained an international reputation for healthful, genteel conditions, and blacks benefited from the whites' enlightened humanitarian concerns. In general, for most people, life was good – or as good as could be expected for the slaves.

Barbados' reputation as a healthful tropical retreat is long-lived, and had an indirect impact on the history of the United States. When Lawrence Washington, brother to then-19-year-old George Washington, became infected with tuberculosis in 1751, his doctors recommended a therapeutic stay on Barbados. Young George accompanied his brother, and the two boarded at Bush Hill House on the Garrison Savannah. While Lawrence rehabilitated, George spent his time watching British troops training on the grounds outside his temporary residence – a pastime that no doubt aided his future military career.

Unfortunately, George's vacation turned sour when he came down with smallpox, a common peril on the island. This misfortune was a disaster at the time, but turned out to be an historical stroke of good luck, since Washington developed an immunity to smallpox as he recovered. Years later, when his army became ill with the disease while fighting in the American Revolution, Washington remained healthy, established himself as an outstanding leader and war hero, and went on to become the first president of the United States.

The house where the Washington brothers resided during their stay on Barbados now serves as a business office and is not open to the public. Have a look at the outside of the building, located just east of Highway 7 next to the watermill and bath house on Bush Hill Road, across from the northwest side of the Garrison Savannah.

■ Emancipation & Beyond

The slave trade was officially abolished by the British Parliament in 1807, but it was still not illegal to keep slaves who were already owned. In 1815, England passed a bill requiring all slaves in the West Indies to be registered so that compliance with the 1807 decree could be monitored. Barbadian slave owners objected to this violation of their right to self-government, and refused to inventory their slaves.

Ironically, at that time, most slaves on Barbados were on good terms with their owners and were treated better than anywhere else in the world. Food was plentiful. Working conditions were good. Housing had improved. However, blacks still were not free. When they heard about the new English law, they misunderstood its intent, and thought the bill offered them freedom rather than merely registration. Naturally, they were furious that their owners would not comply.

After months of planning at island-wide weekend parties, slaves and freed mulattos staged an all-out revolt on Easter Sunday, April 14, 1816. **Bussa's Rebellion**, named for the slave who led the uprising, caused the death of one white and 176 slaves, destruction of a fifth of the island's sugar crop, and damage to many plantation houses. Although the rebellion was quickly put down by the militia, damage was significant enough to get the attention of white slave owners, who tried to forestall the inevitable with new laws to restrict the privileges of blacks.

A statue of the slave called Bussa, sculpted by Bajan Karl Broodhagen, stands in the center of a traffic circle at the intersection of Highway 4 and the ABC (Errol Barrow) Highway, east of the capital.

Total emancipation did not occur until 1834, when slaves entered a four-year apprentice program designed to ease them into independence. When this transition period was over, a new black middle class grew quickly, and a law was passed granting anyone who earned 50 pounds sterling per year the right to vote. This enabled enough blacks a political voice so that, in 1843, Samuel Jackman Prescod became the first black member of the House of Assembly. The Franchise Act of 1884 eased voting restrictions even more, and within a few years blacks took political control of the island.

As the political and social conditions changed, foreign control diminished, and the British military removed their last troops from Barbados in 1905. When a worldwide economic depression caused sugar prices to plunge in the 1930s, unemployment and reduced wages hit blacks hard. **Clement Payne**, a resident of Trinidad, seized this time of discontent to bring the idea of trade unions and labor parties to Barbados. Whites panicked and deported Payne, which started a three-day riot that resulted in 14 deaths and hundreds of arrests.

Many black Bajans spoke out against rioting as a means of creating change, but most agreed that decisive measures were needed to bring about improved conditions for workers. The **Barbados Progressive League** was formed in 1938 to promote and protect the rights of poor Bajans. **Grantley H. Adams** quickly proved himself a great leader within the League, which became the **Barbados Labour Party**, and worked to legalize trade unions and win voting rights for all Bajans. In the 1951 election, the BLP won five seats in the House of Assembly, and Adams became the Prime Minister. Seven years later, he was appointed Prime Minister of the short-lived Federation of the West Indies, which was created to promote and protect the interests of the Caribbean region. (The Federation was disbanded in 1962.)

Erroll Walton Barrow, a member of the **Democratic Labour Party** that was founded in 1956, became prime minister in the 1961 election and led Barbados' push for independence. Finally, on November 30, 1966, with Barrow still in office, the island became an independent nation and a sovereign state within the Commonwealth of Nations.

Important Dates in Barbados History

- 1529 – Barbados first appears on a map.
- 1625 – The first English ship, the *Olive Blossom*, arrives.
- 1627 – The first settlers arrive at Holetown.
- 1639 – Parliament is established.
- 1651 – Barbados is invaded by British forces under Oliver Cromwell.
- 1652 – The Articles of Capitulation (the basis of the Charter of Barbados) are agreed to at the town of Oistins.
- 1731 – The first newspaper, the *Barbados Gazette*, is published.
- 1807 – British Parliament abolishes the slave trade.
- 1816 – Rebellion is led by a slave named Bussa.
- 1818 – Gun Hill Signal Station is built to convey military messages.
- 1831 – "Free coloured men" are allowed to vote.
- 1834 – Slavery is abolished.
- 1838 – Slaves gain complete freedom.
- 1881 – Women gain the right to vote.
- 1905 – The British military withdraws from the island.
- 1924 – Charles D. O'Neal founds the Democratic League.
- 1938 – Grantley Adams, founder of the Barbados Labour Party, is elected to the House of Assembly.
- 1951 – Universal adult suffrage begins.
- 1954 – Ministerial government is instituted, and Grantley Adams becomes the first premier.

- 1958 – Barbados becomes part of the West Indies Federation.
- 1961 – Barbados achieves the right to full self-government.
- 1962 – The West Indies Federation dissolves.
- 1966 – Barbados becomes an independent nation within the British Commonwealth. Errol W. Barrow becomes the first Prime Minister.
- 1967 – Barbados joins the Organization of American States.
- 1973 – The Barbados dollar replaces the East Caribbean dollar as the official currency.
- 1976 – Tom Adams elected Prime Minister.
- 1985 – Prime Minister Tom Adams dies in office.
- 1986 – Errol Barrow becomes Prime Minister for the second time.
- 1987 – Barrow dies in office; L. Erskine Sandiford becomes Prime Minister.
- 1994 – Owen Arthur becomes Prime Minister.

Government & The Economy

At the turn of the new millennium, the independent nation of Barbados is considered one of the most stable and progressive islands in the Caribbean region. The government is led by the elected Prime Minister, The Right Honourable **Owen Arthur**, member of the Barbados Labour Party. Queen Elizabeth II is the titular head of state, and appoints a governor general to represent her on the island. Government is based on the British parliamentary system, which includes an elected House of Assembly and an appointed Senate. Civil grievances and criminal appeals are heard by a Privy Council appointed by the governor.

Barbados enjoys one of the highest standards of living of all the Caribbean islands, and its prosperity is on an upward course. Tourism has replaced sugar as the major economic force, and foreign investment is a significant part of the island's financial security. Tax incentives attract outside insurance, banking, and data-processing firms, and sugar still accounts for half of the island's agricultural earnings. With the cash flow provided by more than a half-million non-cruise-ship visitors each year, Barbados initiates new golf courses, hotels, restaurants, and residential developments, which, in turn, draws more visitors.

Bajan Facts

Barbados' parliament was established in 1639; it is the second oldest in the Caribbean and the third oldest in the world.

The island's government was under English rule from its original settlement in 1627 until its independence in 1966.

The Barbados dollar has never been devalued.

The United Nations' quality-of-life index lists Barbados among the top 20 countries in the world.

The population of Barbados is approximately 260,000.

The island has a literacy rate of 98%, one of the highest in the world.

More than 350 churches, representing more than 100 religious groups, are located on the island.

■ The Flag of Barbados

Barbados' official flag features three vertical panels of equal size. The center panel is gold, symbolizing the color of sand, and bears a black trident representing the three-pronged spear carried by Neptune, the mythological god of the sea. The center panel is flanked by two ultramarine panels which represent the colors of the Caribbean sea and sky.

■ The Coat of Arms of Barbados

Below the golden shield of the Bajan coat of arms is the country's motto, "Pride and Industry." The shield itself depicts an indigenous bearded fig tree, similar to those that grow wild in the island's ravines and which some historians believe to be the basis for the island's original Portuguese name, *Los Barbados*, "the bearded ones." Two red Pride of Barbados flowers sit in the top corners of the shield above the fig tree. A pelican holds the right side of the shield with his extended web foot. A scaly fishlike dolphin balances on his tail and clutches the left side of the shield between his flippers. The dark arm of a worker holding two sugar canes rises from a red and gold laurel on the top of the shield.

The Barbados National Anthem

In plenty and in time of need,
When this fair land was young,
Our brave forefathers sowed the seed
From which our pride has sprung;
A pride that makes no wanton boast
Of what it has withstood,
That binds our hearts from coast to coast –
The pride of nationhood.

***Chorus*:**

We loyal sons and daughters all
Do hereby make it known:
These fields and hills beyond recall
Are now our very own.
We write our names on history's page
With expectations great;
Strict guardians of our heritage,
Firm craftsmen of our fate.
The Lord has been the peoples' guide
For past 300 years;

With Him still on the peoples' side
We have no doubts or fears.
Upward and onward shall we go,
Inspired, exulting, free,
And greater will our nation grow
In strength and unity.

Irving Berlin wrote the lyrics for the National Anthem of Barbados. He was born in New York in 1926 of a Barbadian mother and an American father. His other musical work include *Island in the Sun* and *Ballad of Bimshire*, and he was founder of the Irving Burgie Literary Award for writings by Bajan school children.

The Land

Barbados is in the tropical Atlantic, 100 miles east of the Caribbean island chain known as the Lesser Antilles. This isolated positioning earns the tiny nation recognition as an incomparable singular island and sets it apart from its Caribbean neighbors.

Unlike the mountainous Antilles, which resulted from volcanic outbursts, Barbados is the comparatively flat outcome of a mighty collision of two of the earth's structural plates more than 600,000 years ago. This geological wreck between the Atlantic plate and the Caribbean plate caused an uplifting of sedimentary rock from the ocean floor, which was gradually covered by an accumulation of coral. As the coral polyps manufactured limestone, deposits built up and formed a coral island with a limestone cap and a sedimentary base.

The visible aftermath is a mixed landscape of low central hills that slope to flat coastal land in the west and rise to craggy 1,000-foot-high cliffs in the east. Rainwater has filtered through the island's soft-coral cap, creating limestone caverns and steep-sided gullies, and causing a lack of surface water. Less than a foot of topsoil blankets the coral cap, but dense tropical forests thrived on the island before much of the interior growth was cut down to make room for agricultural production.

Fun Facts

Harrison's Cave and **Welchman Hall Tropical Reserve** are popular tourist attractions created by rainwater.

The island's pure, delicious **drinking water** is pumped up from a vast structure of underground springs and reservoirs.

Swamps in the south provide a habitat for plants and animals that serve as a food source for fish and birds.

Mt. Hillaby, at 1,105 feet, is the highest point on the island.

Ghost crabs, sea roaches, and juvenile fish live in **tidal pools** along the south and southwest coast.

Climate

Barbados has one of the best year-round climates in the Caribbean. The average daytime high temperature is 83°F in the winter and 86°F in summer. Nights average 10° cooler. Northeast trade winds keep even summertime afternoons comfortably cool.

January, February, and March are the driest months, with days averaging 10 hours of sunlight. June, July, September, October, and November average only eight hours of sunlight each day.

Most of the rain falls in quick, air-freshening showers from June through November. Since the island is covered by a porous cap of soft coral, rainwater quickly drains into underground reservoirs, and outdoor activities return to normal.

Dramatic tropical storms sometimes occur during the Caribbean hurricane season, which runs from June through October. Since Barbados is outside the main Antilles chain, most hurricanes skip over the isolated landmass and swing 100 miles to the north. However, hurricanes did hit the island in 1955, 1898, and 1831.

Hurricane Facts

- Most hurricanes occur from mid-August through mid-October.
- Often, hurricanes originate off the west coast of Africa and skip from landmass to landmass through the Caribbean.
- A hurricane's winds flow counterclockwise in the Northern Hemisphere and clockwise in the Southern Hemisphere.
- Any wind faster than 75 mph is considered "hurricane force."
- Hurricanes form only over tropical oceans, and their force weakens quickly when they move over land or cold water.
- Typhoons and hurricanes are basically the same type of storm. They are called typhoons in the western part of the north Pacific. In the eastern part of the north Pacific, as well as the Atlantic, Caribbean, and Gulf of Mexico, they are called hurricanes. In the rest of the world, they are known as tropical cyclones.
- No hurricane has ever hit California, but they occasionally do hit Mexico's west coast.
- A small hurricane is about 100 miles wide; a large one may be 300 miles across.
- Some hurricanes last only a few hours before they weaken, while others maintain their strength for two weeks.
- Forecasters began naming hurricanes in 1950. At first they used words from the international phonetic alphabet: Able, Baker, Charlie, etc. Women's names common to English-speaking countries were first used in 1953. Beginning in 1979, forecasters began alternating French, English, and Spanish male and female names.

Hurricane Tips

Give your home phone number to the airline, hotel, and travel agent so you can be notified if your trip will be canceled or delayed because of a hurricane.

Ask if you may change your travel dates at no charge if a hurricane threatens your vacation.

Before you make a hotel reservation, find out if the establishment has a hurricane warning and escape plan, a working generator, an adequate fresh water supply, and a safe area for guests.

If you're buying cancellation insurance to protect you from weather-related problems, read the fine print carefully. Most policies do not cover Acts of God.

Plants

At one time, thick woodlands covered Barbados, but soon after colonization began, indigenous trees were cut down to provide fuel and building materials for settlers. Cedar and other durable woods were harvested for export to Europe. Vast forests were cleared to make room for sugarcane fields.

*Today, **Turners Hall Woods** in St. Andrew Parish is the only remaining primeval forest in Barbados. (See* Exploring the Island.*)*

Still, the countryside and gardens yield 700 native and imported flowering plants, the sandy shores are lined with coconut palms and sea grapes, and natural ravines are micro forests teeming with tropical vegetation.

Most likely, Barbados' original flora came from nearby volcanic islands, South America, and Africa – lands that are geologically older and more bio-diverse. Seeds were carried by winds, ocean currents, sea creatures, and birds. Later, man brought in various species that quickly adapted to the favorable climate and spread wildly throughout the island. Soon, non-native plants were so prolific and vigorous that they were commonly assumed to be indigenous.

Barbados has excellent public parks and gardens as well miles of untended gullies where dense vegetation flourishes. Private gardens are open to the public during the **Barbados National Trust's Open Houses Programme** (☎ 246-436-9033 or 426-2421, fax 429-9055, e-mail natrust@sunbeach.net) and the **Barbados Horticultural Society's Open Gardens' Programme** (☎ 246-428-5889). Both events are held annually and feature some of the most beautiful homes and gardens on the island.

Plants & Trees To Watch For

Bougainvillea – a native of Brazil that has a woody vine and brilliantly colored petal-like bracts.

Century plant – a native Bajan species that looks like a cactus with a tall central stalk that produces a yellow flower. It takes 10 years, not 100, for the plant to bloom and die.

Flamboyant tree – the royal poinciana tree from Madagascar that puts out a blazing display of large red or orange flowers.

Tamarind, mango, guava, breadfruit, and grapefruit trees – some of the deciduous fruit trees that grow wild in rural areas as well as in backyard gardens.

Mahogany tree – from Honduras, this hardwood tree produces reddish-brown lumber that is used for making furniture.

Casuarina tree – a native of Australia, is called a "mile tree" and routinely grows to 150 feet. Look for it along the roadsides.

African tulip tree – a native of western Africa, it produces red blooms each spring.

Pride of Barbados – probably from South America, this plant produces clusters of bright red or yellow flowers surrounding a long, center stamen.

Hibiscus – a crowd-pleasing bush with abundant flowers. It originated in Hawaii and became a symbol of the tropics.

Frangipani – an American tree that puts out a showy display of fragrant flowers in multiple colors.

Orchids – the best place to see the multiple varieties of this delicate flower that grows well on Barbados is **Orchid World** in St. George Parish, ☎ 246-433-0306. (See *Exploring the Island.*) Examples include *Vanda*, *Ascocendas*, *Phalaenopsis*, *Cattleyas*, and *Oncidiums*.

Bearded fig tree – an indigenous tree with aerial roots that hang from overhead branches, giving it the appearance of an ancient man with an unmanageable beard.

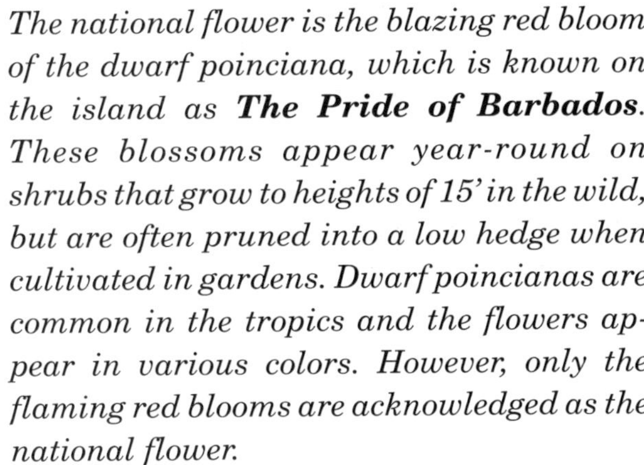

The national flower is the blazing red bloom of the dwarf poinciana, which is known on the island as ***The Pride of Barbados****. These blossoms appear year-round on shrubs that grow to heights of 15' in the wild, but are often pruned into a low hedge when cultivated in gardens. Dwarf poincianas are common in the tropics and the flowers appear in various colors. However, only the flaming red blooms are acknowledged as the national flower.*

■ Medicinal Plants

Herbal medicines and potions are popular folk-cures on Barbados. While modern medicines are readily available, many Bajans commonly depend on natural remedies that have been used since the island's earliest settlers arrived. Arawak and Carib Indians undoubtedly used native plants for medicine, African slaves brought their knowledge of folk cures with them during the island's plantation days, and Rastafarians recently have rekindled a lagging interest in nontraditional treatments.

Barbadian Home Remedies

If alternative medicine appeals to you, try the following:

- For motion sickness – chew or make a tea with ginger root or mint leaves.
- For bladder or kidney problems – eat ground coconut or drink coconut water.
- For diarrhea – make a tea with bark from the sea grape tree.
- For constipation – eat paw paw fruit.
- For sunburn – apply the gel found inside the stalks of aloe plants.
- For flu-like symptoms – eat baked or boiled prickly pear cactus.
- For general good health – enjoy peanuts.

Wildlife

Barbados doesn't have much in the way of spectacular wildlife. Too many people. Too little wilderness.

However, there are over 10,000 **green monkeys,** or vervets, living on the island. They belong to a family known as Old World (*Cercopithecoidea*) monkeys and were brought here from Africa over 300 years ago as pets of slave traders. The vervets have olive-brown fur, long legs, and a long tail. Your best chance of seeing them is at the **Wildlife Reserve** in St. Peter Parish, ☎ 246-422-2286. (See *Exploring the Island*, page 106.)

Although they're no longer wild, **black-bellied sheep** are considered indigenous by livestock experts who believe the breed developed on Barbados from hair sheep brought to the island from West Africa by slave traders during the 1600s. These hair sheep mated with European wool sheep and produced a breed that became known as Barbados sheep when they were imported into the United

States and Canada in the early 1900s. On Barbados, they are known as **blackbellies**. The sheep range in color from light tan to dark reddish-brown with black bellies and black points on their faces and legs. They don't require shearing and are parasite and heat resistant.

You'll see plenty of **mongooses** scampering across the roads and through the underbrush. These exasperating little squirrel-like critters were brought to Barbados from India via Jamaica in the late 1800s to kill poisonous snakes that lived in the sugarcane fields. Since they had no enemies in nature, they reproduced freely and became an annoyance – especially after the harmful snakes became extinct. Now they can't be eradicated and have become a threat to birds, beneficial reptiles, and newborn domestic animals.

You'll also hear, but rarely see, musical **crickets** and **whistling frogs**. Both are shy, but vociferous, and always serenade at night. While you're searching for the cricket or frog that's keeping you awake, you may spot a **bat**. Six types live on the island, and most live in caves and feed on insects or fruit. The only time you're likely to see one is just after sunset, when they sometimes glide over water looking for bugs.

Geckos dart up walls when you flip the light on at night, and **green lizards** do comical pushups on your patio to prevent you from napping. In all, Barbados is home to five species of lizard, a few rare or harmless snakes, and a breed of fat toads called **crapauds** or **cane toads**.

Cane toads were brought to the island in the early 1800s to eat insects that enjoyed munching sugarcane. Like the mongoose, the toads overproduced, and now hop all around the island, especially after a rain. They produce a mild toxin, so don't pick them up.

Birdwatching

Barbados is home to 24 species of birds, and more than 150 species of migratory visitors stop by each year. Even if you don't consider yourself a birdwatcher, consider a trip to **Graeme Hall Swamp**

Bird Sanctuary (see page 81), which is in the mangrove swamp on the south coast. You'll be able to watch a variety of birds.

The **bananaquit** is a small bird with dark feathers on its back and a bright yellow throat and breast. It loves sugar and fruit, and will make itself at home on your outdoor dining table.

The **golden warbler** is another yellow-feathered bird with dark streaks along its body.

Chubby **wood doves** have white or black sprinkles on their gray feathers. You'll recognize them by their chant-like cooing.

Blackbirds, or grackles, are common and are recognizable by their shiny ebony feathers.

Cattle egrets are sometimes called cowbirds because they are often sighted with cattle and like to sit on top of cows.

Magnificent frigate birds (magnificent is part of its name) are jet black except for their throats. Males have red necks, the females' throats are white. Both have wide wingspans that reach up to six feet.

Two types of **hummingbird** are found – the **Carib**, which has a purple throat and curved bill, and the **doctor booby**, a smaller bird with a straight bill.

Underwater World

Bajan waters harbor pristine reefs, endangered sea turtles, spiny lobsters, and a colorful collection of fish. The silvery-blue **flying fish** is considered both the unofficial national dish and the unofficial national fish. Seafarers have reported seeing huge schools of the seven-to-nine-inch fish vaulting from the ocean and "flying" through the air for 50-75 feet – a spectacular sight.

Scuba divers and snorkelers discover several types of creatures living and feeding in and around the reefs, rocks, and grasses on the ocean floor. Fishermen find first-rate conditions for snagging snapper, kingfish, tuna, dorado, and barracuda.

■ Creatures

Sea turtles are the most fascinating creatures in Bajan waters. Females come ashore at night to dig their nests and lay eggs. After burying the eggs under a thin layer of warm sand, the female returns to the ocean, leaving the eggs to incubate for about eight weeks. The youngsters hatch at night and instinctively turn toward the sea, where they grow to maturity.

Some females return to the beach where they hatched to lay their own eggs.

Leatherbacks, the largest turtles, are an endangered species. They have a leather-like skin over their backs instead of a shell and can grow to be six feet long, weighing up to 2,000 pounds. Poachers kill numerous leatherbacks, but many more die when they eat discarded plastic bags which they mistake for jellyfish, their favorite food. The plastic obstructs the turtles' intestines.

Hawksbills are named for their hawk-like beak; they grow to be three feet in diameter and weigh up to 100 pounds. They live around warm-water reefs and primarily eat other sea creatures, such as crabs and snails, but also dine on encrusted organisms that they scrape off rocks with their pointed noses.

Sea Turtle Nesting

If you're on Barbados between April and October, you may have the opportunity to watch a sea turtle nesting. The process always takes place at night and requires about an hour to complete. Once the turtle begins to dig a nest with her flippers, nothing distracts her, and you can observe from a fairly short distance if you are quiet and don't use any light, including flash cameras. Check with the **Belairs Research Institute** in Holetown (☎ 246-422-2087) for information, and be sure to report any nests or hatchlings you spot to the **Sea Turtle Hotline** (☎ 246-230-0142). Sea turtles are endangered and protected by law, so do not disturb the nests, eggs, or hatchlings.

Many types of crustaceans (lobsters, crabs, shrimp), mollusks (conchs, clams, scallops, cuttlefish) and echinoderms (sea urchins, sea cucumbers, starfish, sand dollars) also inhabit the underwater world.

Bajan **lobsters** are the spiny or rock type found in warm seas. They are actually marine crayfish and lack claws but have sharp spines on their carapace (the shell-like exoskeleton that covers their heads and thoraxes). You'll find them and other crustaceans listed on restaurant menus, but don't be surprised to learn that most are imported. Some restaurants have reliable contacts that keep them stocked with locally caught varieties, but customer demand far exceeds the supply. Imported North American lobster often is more available on the island, especially during the summer.

Your **shrimp** dinner may be imported, as well – from Guyana, on the north coast of South America. They're the large *Peneus* shrimp found in the alluvial area at the mouth of the Essequibo River. Barbados has several types of freshwater shrimp that breed in brackish water and are known as **crayfish.**

Several types of **crabs** live in or near the water, and many can survive long periods on dry land. One well-represented species is the **sand crab,** also called a land or ghost crab. They hang out on the beach, and you'll see them peeking from their underground homes and scurrying from burrow to burrow when they think nobody's around. **Hermit crabs** live primarily in the discarded shells of gastropod mollusks, but they will move into almost anything – even small jars – and call it home.

Beware of **sea urchins,** pesky little brutes with sharp barbs that puncture tender feet. These spherical-shaped echinoderms (an animal phylum of marine bottom-dwelling invertebrates) can show up in any type of ocean water, but they prefer to live in shallow water with a rocky bottom. Several varieties live in the ocean surrounding Barbados, and a dish, known simply as *sea eggs*, is made with the roe (an egg mass) of white sea urchins. The gold-hued roe is gathered from reefs, lumped into clean sea shells, covered with a leaf from the sea grape tree, and steamed. Since sea eggs have been over-harvested, the government now restricts collecting to certain seasons.

Sea cucumbers, **sand dollars,** and **starfish** are other echinoderms that you may see in the ocean or washed up on shore. Sea cucumbers have long bodies, a circle of tube-feet around their mouths, and a rather entertaining back-end. When they become irritated, they shoot out either a mass of tubes or part of their digestive tract through the anus. The eviscerated organs break off and the creature grows new ones. Sand dollars and starfish are far less amusing, but kids love to collect their washed-up bodies during strolls along the beach.

Conch (say "konk") is a favorite mollusk. The gastropod's heavy spiral shell is used as a decoration and as a horn at festivals. The meaty animal inside has been a fundamental food source in the Caribbean for centuries. You'll find conch soups, stews, and fritters among the more tasty offerings on many restaurant menus.

■ Plants

Most underwater plants are algae, a group of primitive vegetation without true roots, stems, leaves, or flowers. Some are so small that you'd need a microscope to see them. Others, such as **kelp**, grow to lengths of 100 feet. All are an important part of the earth's food chain since they serve as a major source of nourishment for aquatic wildlife. The simplest forms help to make up **plankton**, small organisms that float unnoticed in the water. **Sea grasses** and **seaweeds** that grow in shallow water have root-like basal disks and stem-like fronds. They help to clear the ocean of fine sediment, provide shelter for fish and other sea creatures, and prevent erosion of beaches and the ocean floor.

■ Coral Reefs

Most reefs are made up of **stony** or **soft coral polyps**, which are small marine animals related to the sea anemone. Others are created by limestone-secreting algae, mollusks, and echinoderms. However, any reef constructed by a living community is usually called a coral reef. All are formed in a delicate environment that must be covered by no more than 100 feet of saltwater that is warmed to at least 72°F.

Stony coral polyps secrete a calcium carbonate (limestone) skeleton around themselves that may reach a diameter of 10 inches, but usually measures less than an eighth of an inch. Soft coral polyps have a flexible skeleton made up of organic material. The skeletons of dead polyps are broken up by waves, and piled into an intricate heap that supports living corals, other animals, and plants.

Coral reefs are classified as **fringing reefs, barrier reefs**, and **atolls.** A fringing reef follows the line of an island's shore and is usually exposed at low tide. Barrier reefs are farther offshore and either are separated from an island by a wide, deep lagoon or encircle a lagoon with a central island. An atoll is a ring-like reef or reef-island that allows passage through the reef to the ocean and surrounds a lagoon without a central island.

A Dozen Reasons to Visit

- Sophisticated British niceties laid out in tropical sunshine.
- Sweeping pink-and-white sand beaches along a 70-mile coastline.
- Stately old plantation houses and lush botanical gardens that are open to the public.
- Tax-free bargains on luxury items, island-made rum, and fine local arts and crafts.
- Organized eco-hikes, a wildlife reserve, and protected natural wonders.
- A thriving underwater world filled with caves, blue holes, wrecks, and a variety of marine life.
- Ideal windsurfing and wave-riding conditions.
- Colorful festivals celebrating a rich culture and love of music, dance, theater, and art.
- No-wait marriages.
- Award-winning international chefs creating innovative cuisine with fresh island foods.
- Hundreds of rum shops and safe drinking water directly from the tap.
- Secluded coves, deserted woodlands, and get-away-from-it-all cliff tops.

Travel Information

Fun Things to Do

- Capture monkeys on film during a **photo safari** in the Wildlife Preserve.
- **Water-ski or sail** along the west coast to check out all the resorts and villas.
- **Shop** for an exquisite piece of local art.
- **Picnic** on a hillside in the Scotland District.
- Get to know the chefs at your favorite restaurants so they will share their recipes.
- Go *caf crawlin'* (**bar hopping**) along Baxters Road or in St. Lawrence Gap.
- **Buy a monkey jar** (to keep water cool) directly from one of the potters at Chalky Mount Village.
- **Pet a hawksbill** sea turtle in Alleynes Bay.
- Collect your prize at the end of the **Banks Beer Trail**.
- Explore the vast limestone caverns of **Harrison's Cave.**

When to Visit

Barbados, like most Caribbean islands, is most popular and most expensive during the winter. If you plan to visit between mid-December and mid-April, make airline and hotel reservations early. Flights and accommodations for the most desirable dates often sell out a year in advance.

Savvy travelers know that there is little difference between winter and summer temperatures in the tropics, and prefer to avoid high prices and big crowds by visiting the islands during the low or shoulder seasons. Often, hotel rates drop 25% to 50% after April 15, and some of the best festivals take place during the spring and summer. Also, winds are calmer, the ocean visibility is clearer, and every plant and tree is in full bloom.

September and October can be sticky-hot. But, if you're planning to spend half your time stretched out on the beach and the other half inside an air-conditioned resort, these slow-paced months offer excellent bargains.

Still, there is something to be said for heading to Barbados when icy winds drop temperatures below freezing in your part of the world. If that's your preference, you'll find the island warm, sunny, breezy, dry, and ready to entertain you.

What to Bring

- Swim wear and coverups.
- Shorts and lightweight tops.
- A windbreaker or lightweight sweater for cool evenings.
- Elegantly casual evening wear: long pants and sports shirts for men; sun dresses or pants outfits for women. Dress shorts are acceptable in casual restaurants at dinner.
- Shoes and gear for recreation (diving, horseback riding, golfing, tennis, hiking, biking, etc.)
- Small binoculars.
- All medication in original bottles. Customs officials get nervous when they see loose pills in a bag. If you want to take a small amount from a large bottle, bring a copy of the original prescription or bottle label. You're unlikely to need it, but it could speed your way though customs if you're questioned.
- A camera, extra batteries, and more film than you think you'll use.
- Sun hat or visor.
- Sunglasses.
- Sunscreen with a high protection factor.
- Insect repellent.

Festivals & Holidays

Barbados is a nation of festivals, and almost any historical or current happening is cause for celebration. Because it's determined to be a year-round world-class destination, the island schedules events for every season and includes entertainment from throughout the Caribbean and across the globe.

For exact dates, contact the individual committee for each listing below, the Barbados Tourism Authority (☎ 800-221-9831) or search for festival information on the Internet at www.insandouts-barbados.com.

■ January

The **Barbados Jazz Festival** is held annually on Martin Luther King, Jr.'s holiday weekend during the second week of January. The event draws popular performers and music enthusiasts from around the world. Arturo Tappin and Nicholas Brancker, two highly acclaimed Bajan jazz musicians, have been featured during recent festivals, along with well-known personalities such as Ray Charles, Roberta Flack, Lou Rawls and Najee. Indoor and outdoor settings are used for a variety of shows during the festival weekend. For tickets and information, ☎ 246-429-2084, e-mail jazz@axses.net.

■ February

In February of 1977, a group of Bajan citizens organized a festival to celebrate the 350th anniversary of the day in 1627 that 80 English pioneers and 10 African slaves stepped onto Barbados soil to set up the island's first European colony. The original **Holetown Festival** was so popular that it became an annual seven-day event held the last week of February. Vendors set up stalls to sell local arts and crafts, island food specialties, and drinks. Entertainment includes parades, folk dancing, sports competitions, and open-air concerts featuring music by gospel, calypso, classical, and reggae groups. For information about this year's festival, ☎ 246-430-7300 (ask for John Kidd at Holders House).

■ March

Holder's Season is a chic international performing arts festival that takes place annually on the majestic grounds of Holders Plantation House. Members of the Holder family were among the early settlers of Barbados, and the lovely greathouse now owned by John and Wendy Kidd was built by William Holder in 1680. Holder's Season features a variety of performances and has a reputation for encouraging new works. Recent Holder's Seasons sponsored by Virgin Atlantic Airlines included a world premier opera, a concert by Luciano Pavarotti with the Royal Philharmonic Orchestra, and a staging of Shakespeare's *The Tempest*, staring David Calder and incorporating Caribbean music. For details about upcoming Holder's Season events, contact the box office at ☎ 246-432-6385, fax 432-6461.

Around the same time that Holder's Season takes place on the west coast, **Oistins Fish Festival** starts up on the south shore. A more casual crowd turns out in Oistins to celebrate fish and the people who catch them, clean them, sell them, and cook them. Most celebrants just want to eat them. Vendors' stalls sell freshly caught fish cooked in a variety of methods and laced with an assortment of sauces. Parades, concerts, and competitions round out the schedule of events. For details on this year's festival, ☎ 246-428-6738.

■ April

The highlight of **Congaline Festival** is *De Human Congaline,* the Caribbean's longest string of conga dancers. Locals, visitors, kids, and old folks ignore color and class distinctions to join in the vibrant dance of unity that proclaims one love, one people, one destiny. This love fest started in 1994 and is held annually from the last weekend in April through May Day. *De Congaline Village*, set up on the Dover Athletic Field in the St. Lawrence Gap area, is the center of activity. Musicians and other performers provide daily and nightly entertainment while dozens of stalls sell food, drinks, arts, and crafts. On the first of May, T-shirt bands parade through the streets to kick off the final day, which is called *Congaline Carnival*. Check with the National Cultural Foundation for more information at ☎ 246-424-0909, fax 424-0916.

■ May

Gospelfest, held eight weeks after Easter on Whitsun weekend, is a three-day gala featuring international and local gospel musicians. The event, which began in 1993, pays tribute to the island's strong spiritual ties and includes uplifting soul, reggae, jazz, and calypso music. For a schedule of concerts and information about this year's performers, ☎ 246-430-7300 (ask for Adrian Agard at Holders House).

The two-week **Celtic Festival,** held annually at the end of May, applauds the role of Celtic countries and Celtic people in the development of the Caribbean. This inter-cultural event hosts choirs, musicians, dancers, and actors with true Celtic spirit from all over the world. Past festivals have featured Welsh choirs, Scottish dancers, and Irish poets. On the final day, the celebration peaks with an authentic Celtic wedding. ☎ 246-426-3387.

■ July & August

The biggest fête of the year is **Crop Over**, an all-out affair that celebrates the end of the sugar crop harvest. At one time, individuals and communities held parties and fairs to mark the end of harvest, but now the occasion has become an island-wide extravaganza. Throughout history, sugar has driven the island's economy, and Crop Over serves as a reminder of its importance to Bajan culture.

Activities start in mid-July with the ceremonial Delivery of the Last Canes, and ends on the first Monday in August with Grand Kadooment Day, a national holiday. Many events are scheduled during the three-week celebration, including street fairs, art exhibitions, concerts, and parades.

Kadooment is a Bajan word that means something like "big deal" and refers to a happening of major significance.

Calypso musicians compete throughout Crop Over for the coveted title of Calypso Monarch, an honor bestowed at the Pic-O-de-Crop Finals. An elaborate variety show known as Cohobblopot stars the newly crowned Calypso Monarch, the King and Queen of Costume

Bands and the Junior Monarch, along with the island's best performing artists in dazzling costumes.

Barbados throws the biggest party of the year on Grand Kadooment Day. All Bajans dress in colorful garments and pour into the streets of the capital to "jump up" to the lively music of popular bands. Visitors can dress up and dance along with a costume band, or simply watch from the sidelines. Either way, it's a crowded, joyful, clamoring, kaleidoscopic good time. Check with the National Cultural Foundation for a schedule of events, ☎ 246-424-0909.

■ October & November

November 30 is Barbados Independence Day, a national holiday, and the final day of the **National Independence Festival of Creative Arts**. The festival and holiday commemorate the date in 1966 when the island became an independent nation. All types of performing and visual artists vie for bronze, silver, and gold medals during competitions that run through October and November. The winners are recognized during Independence Day events that include a dignified ceremony at the Garrison Savanna. Call the National Cultural Foundation for more information on either the Festival of Creative Arts or the Independence Day celebration, ☎ 246-424-0909.

Public Holidays

January 1	New Year's Day
January 21	Errol Barrow Day
March/April	Good Friday and Easter Monday
May 1	Labor Day
May/June Whit Monday	(eighth Monday after Easter)
1st Monday in August	Grand Kadooment Day
1st Monday in October	United Nations Day
November 30	Independence Day
December 25	Christmas Day
December 26	Boxing Day

Documents

Citizens of Britain, Commonwealth countries, the European Union, the United States, Canada, Australia, and New Zealand may enter Barbados with a valid passport and proof of onward travel, but no visas, for stays up to 90 days.

Canadian and US citizens staying less than six months also may enter by showing a birth certificate plus valid picture identification and a return airline ticket.

Be prepared to tell the immigration officer where you will be staying on the island. You may also be asked to prove that you have sufficient funds to cover expenses during your stay, and immigration has the right to turn away anyone who has no visible means of support.

Customs & Duty-Free

■ Entering Barbados

You may enter Barbados with the following duty-free items:

- 200 cigarettes or 100 cigars or 250 grams of tobacco
- 1 liter of wine or spirits
- 50 grams of perfume

You may *not* enter Barbados with the following:

- agricultural products
- firearms
- narcotics
- pornography

Questions regarding allowable goods may be directed to the Barbados Customs Department, ☎ 246-427-5940.

When you return home, you will be required to present an official customs form listing all merchandise acquired while you were away. Be prepared to show sales receipts to verify the value of the listed goods.

■ Leaving Barbados

Adult citizens of the **United States** may bring back the following duty-free purchases:

- US$600 worth of goods
- 1 liter of spirits
- 200 cigarettes and 200 cigars
- unlimited items made on Barbados

For more information, contact US Customs Service, ☎ 202-927-6724. The website is www.customs.ustreas.gov.

Adult citizens of the **United Kingdom** may bring back the following duty-free purchases:

- UK£145 worth of goods
- 200 cigarettes or 100 cigarillos or 50 cigars or 250 grams of tobacco
- 1 liter of alcohol or 2 liters of fortified or sparkling wine or 2 liters of liqueur, plus 2 liters of still table wine
- 50 grams of perfume and 250 ml of toilet water

For more information, contact H.M. Customs and Excise Office, ☎ 0171 2-024227. The website is www.open.gov.uk/customs/c&ehome.htm.

Adult citizens of **Canada** may bring back the following duty-free purchases:

- C$300 worth of goods
- 200 cigarettes, and 50 cigars, and 200 grams of tobacco
- 40 imperial ounces of alcohol

For more information, contact Revenue Canada, ☎ 613-993-0534. The web site is http://rc.gc.can.

Customs regulations change and some countries base exemptions on the amount of time a citizen spends outside their own country. Therefore, it's wise to contact the appropriate government agency for up-to-date regulations.

Getting Here

■ By Air

The main North American gateway cities for nonstop flights to Barbados are New York, Miami, and Toronto. In addition, passengers may book direct or connecting flights through Puerto Rico or Jamaica from other cities.

Air Canada provides daily nonstop service from Toronto during the winter season, and weekly nonstop service from Montreal year-round. Flights from Toronto become less frequent during the summer. **BWIA** also flies nonstop from Toronto to Barbados once a week.

American Airlines, BWIA, and **Air Jamaica** offer daily nonstop service from New York. **BWIA** and **American Airlines** also have nonstop flights from Miami.

Air Jamaica flies nonstop to its hub in Montego Bay, with service on to Barbados, from Los Angeles, Atlanta, Chicago, Baltimore, New York, Newark, Philadelphia, Phoenix, Orlando and Miami. **American Airlines** flies to San Juan, Puerto Rico, with connecting flights to Barbados on **American Eagle**, from many US gateway cities.

Passengers from the UK fly nonstop from London to Barbados on **British Airways, BWIA,** and **Virgin Atlantic.**

Charter operations and tour packages usually offer the lowest fares. European citizens often find that connecting through a US gateway is the least expensive way to go, but probably not the most convenient.

Delta Air Lines, Virgin Atlantic, American Airlines, and **British Airways** are a few of the carriers that fly from major cities in Europe and the UK to US cities with nonstop service to Barbados.

If you're coming from another Caribbean island, **LIAT** and **BWIA** can help. **LIAT** flies directly from Antigua, St. Lucia, Grenada, and St. Vincent. **BWIA** has nonstop service from Antigua and Trinidad. In addition, **Air Jamaica** has flights from Montego Bay. Another option is to fly from any island to San Juan, then connect with an American Eagle flight to Barbados.

***LIAT** and **BWIA** offer air passes that allow multiple stops during a fixed time period. This may be the least expensive way to go if you plan to visit more than one island during your vacation. Be certain to read the restrictions carefully before you buy.*

Travel time to Barbados from San Juan is 1½ hours; from Miami it is three hours and 40 minutes; from New York, count on four hours and 20 minutes; coming from Montreal or Toronto, you'll be in the air five hours; and if you start out in London, the flight will take eight hours.

Airline Contact Numbers

Air Canada . ☎ 800-776-3000 (US); 428-5077 (Barbados)

Air Jamaica . ☎ 800-523-5585 (US); 420-7361 (Barbados)

American Airlines, ☎ 800-433-7300 (US); 0345-789789 (UK); 428-4170 (Barbados)

British Airways, ☎ 800-247-9797 (US); 0345-222111 (UK); 436-6413 (Barbados)

BWIA, ☎ 800-538-2942 (US); 426-2111 (Barbados)

Delta Air Lines, ☎ 800-221-1212 (US); 0800-414767 (UK)

LIAT, ☎ 800-468-0482 (US); 246-436-6224 (Barbados)

Virgin Atlantic, ☎ 800-862-8621 (US); 01293-747-747 (UK)

***BWIA**, British West Indies Airline, is a privately owned airline based in Trinidad. **LIAT** is based in Antigua, but co-owned by 11 Caribbean islands.*

Package Tours

Package tours that wrap the cost of transportation and accommodations into a neat bundle are usually a good choice, financially. Airlines and hotels contract to give customers a break on cost in order to tie tourists into using their joint services. Also, independent tour operators buy airline seats and hotel rooms in bulk at lower than standard rates and resell them as a package for less than consumers would pay if they bought each segment separately. However, take the time to check out the hotel that's included with the great airfare to guarantee that you aren't signing up to stay in a hotel that doesn't meet your standards. (See *Vacation Packages* in the *Where to Stay* section.)

Several airlines offer vacation packages through their tour department. Some to try are **American Airlines Fly-Away Vacations,** ☎ 800-321-2121 (in the US), ☎ 0345-789789 (in the UK); **Delta's Dream Vacations** ☎ 800-872-7786 (in the US), ☎ 0800-414767 (in the UK); **Air Jamaica Vacations,** ☎ 800-622-3009 (in the US); and **BWIA Vacations,** ☎ 800-780-5501 (in the US).

Air-Travel Tips

- Buy a round-trip ticket. Barbados requires an ongoing or return ticket for everyone entering without a visa.
- Pack important articles and essential comforts in a small, lightweight carry-on bag, so you'll have everything you need at all times.
- Make three copies of your passport, airline ticket, travelers' check numbers, itinerary (including flight times and numbers, and confirmation numbers for hotels and rental cars), and credit cards. Leave one copy with a trusted relative or friend; you and your traveling partner each put a copy in a secure place. If the important documents are lost or stolen, you will be able to replace them more quickly. If

someone needs to contact you in an emergency, the friend or relative will know how to find you at any time.

- When you buy a First Class or Business Class airline ticket you will receive a special stamp on your boarding pass that entitles you to process through one of two special immigration desks and the Fast Track customs area.
- Leave expensive jewelry at home.

At the Airport

Grantley Adams International Airport is modern and efficient, but high-season crowds can overwhelm immigration officials and baggage handlers. You'll avoid delays if you fill out your immigration card, which is distributed in flight, and have it in hand along with your passport, return ticket, and baggage-claim stubs when you deplane.

After you clear through, put your stamped immigration card, passport, and return ticket, together with the required B$25 departure tax, in a secure place where they can be found easily at the end of your vacation.

Be sure to take either your immigration card or your passport plus your airline ticket when you go shopping. You must present them to buy tax-free merchandise.

A currency-exchange bureau is located in the arrival area near baggage claim, and is open daily, from 8 am-midnight.

It's a good idea to exchange a small amount of US currency for Barbados dollars while you wait for your luggage. You can use US dollars to pay the taxi to your hotel, and US dollars are accepted as tips and for the departure tax, but don't expect Bajans to make change in US currency.

The arrival area also has a post office, rental car kiosks, and a duty-free shop. A sufficient number of porters will be on hand to help you collect your luggage and get it into a taxi or rental car. Plan to tip US 75¢ per bag.

If you plan to rent a car during your stay on Barbados, consider picking it up at or near your hotel rather than at the airport, especially if you're not accustomed to driving on the left. This will allow you time to acclimate a bit after your flight before you get behind the wheel of a strange car in an unfamiliar environment.

Taxi Fares

Taxis are plentiful and regulated fares from the airport to various hotels are posted in the arrival area. From Grantley Adams International Airport to:

Bridgetown	B$30
Crane Beach	B$20
Holetown	B$38
Rockley	B$22
Speightstown	B$48
North of Speightstown	B$55

Divide Barbados dollars by two to get the US equivalent and by three to get the equivalent in pounds sterling.

■ By Sea

Approximately 500,000 visitors arrive in Barbados each year by cruise ship. A recently renovated terminal on the outskirts of the capital is considered one of the finest in the Caribbean. A tourist information office, car and bike rental kiosks, ATMs, and a communications center are located inside the huge facility.

Shoppers never have to leave the port, since 19 duty-free shops, 13 local retail stores, and a dozen vendors are set up to resemble a chattel-house village right at the dock. However, most cruise-ship passengers want to tour the island, spend time on a beach, or shop in town. All of these things are possible in a single day, but only on a very limited scale.

Visitors who really want to explore the island usually don't come by sea. Barbados is set apart from the main Caribbean chain, and the closest neighbor is 100 miles away. There's no scheduled inter-island boat service, and no chartered day-tripping.

A cargo line called **Windward Lines Limited** takes passengers on its 180-foot boat that stops at Barbados, St. Lucia, St. Vincent, Trinidad, and Margarita Island. You can take the boat one-way from any of its stops for about US$60. To book passage or reserve a sleeping berth, which costs an additional US$10 per night, contact Windward Agencies, ☎ 246-431-0449, fax 246-431-0452.

Cruise Lines

If you want to book a cruise that makes a stop at Barbados, you have many options. Cruise lines change itineraries and rotate ships from season to season, but the following regularly include Barbados in their routes.

Carnival Cruise Lines . . . . ☎ 800-327-9501

Celebrity Cruises . . . . ☎ 800-437-3111

Club Med Cruises . . . . ☎ 800-453-7447

Cunard . . . . ☎ 800-221-4770

Holland America Line . . . . ☎ 800-426-0327

Norwegian Cruise Line. . . . . ☎ 800-327-7030

Premier Cruises . . . . ☎ 800-990-7770

Royal Caribbean. . . . . ☎ 800-327-6700

Windstar Cruises . . . . ☎ 800-258-7245

One of the following cruise specialists can help you compare various ships, individual lines, itineraries, and costs.

Cruise.com . . . ☎ 800-303-3337 (Omega World Travel), www.cruise.com

The Cruise Web . . . ☎ 800-377-9383, fax 202-333-8401, e-mail office@cruiseoutlet.com

The Cruise Outlet . . ☎ 800-775-1884, fax 203-248-8390, e-mail naba@ix.netcom.com

World Wide Cruises . ☎ 800-882-9000, www.preferr.com

Getting Around

■ By Taxi

Taxis are abundant and point-to-point rates are government regulated. You'll find rates posted and cabs waiting outside the cruise-ship terminal, airport, and large hotels. Identify them by the letter "Z" on the license plates. If you don't see an available taxi, contact one of the companies listed below.

All drivers carry a list of standard rates, but if you're making several stops or are going out to the countryside, establish the fare – and the currency it's quoted in – before you get into the cab. Bajan taxi drivers have a reputation for being knowledgeable, friendly, and honest. Many are happy to take you around the island to see exactly the sites you wish to visit. Expect to pay about B$8-B$10 per hour for this type of customized tour, but up to five passengers can share a cab and the cost.

Barbados Taxi Companies

Aquatic Taxi Services	☎ 246-436-9432
Barbados International Transportation	☎ 246-425-5427, 424-8078, 231-1136
Casuarina Taxi Service	☎ 246-428-9827
Divi Southwinds Taxi Service	☎ 246-428-5941
King's Vere Transport Services	☎ 246-422-2459
RDH Enterprises	☎ 246-422-4099
Southern Palms Taxi Service	☎ 246-428-7713

■ By Car

Cars, vans, mini-mokes (a small open-sided convertible), and four-wheel-drive vehicles can be hired by the day or week from one of the island's many car rental agencies. You'll need an International Driver's License or a valid driver's license from your home country plus a visitor's temporary permit (issued at a cost of B$10 for a period of one year at any police station and by most car rental agencies). Also, expect to show a major credit card for the security deposit.

Remember that driving is on the left. If you come from a country that drives on the right, you may feel uncomfortable or utterly dangerous behind the wheel – especially if the vehicle has a manual transmission that requires shifting with the left hand.

Otherwise, driving is rather pleasant on the generally well-maintained roads. Be cautious of occasional potholes, narrow roadways, unfenced farm animals in the countryside, and school kids in the towns. Drive slowly and stay alert. You may find it easier and safer to travel by taxi on unfamiliar roads at night.

Expect to pay about US$55 per day for standard cars rented from agencies that offer unlimited mileage, free delivery and pick-up, and unlimited liability and third-party personal injury insurance. Check before you leave home to see if your credit card or insurance company covers you for collision damage to rented vehicles. If not, take the additional insurance from the rental company at a cost of US$8-US$10 per day.

Some Bajan rental agencies have the same name as major international companies, even though they are not associated with the well-known firms. At publication, no major international companies had affiliates on Barbados. Don't assume that you are dealing with a familiar agency.

AUTO RENTAL COMPANIES	
Auto Rentals, Ltd.	☎ 246-228-1520 or 228-1528; fax 426-1583 caddy@sunbeach.net, www.skyviews.com/autorentals
Coconut Car Rentals	☎ 246-437-0297; fax 228-9820 coconut@caribsurf.com, www.coconutcars.com
Corbins Car Rentals	☎ 246-427-9531; fax 427-7975 rentals@corbinscars.com, www.corbinscars.com
Courtesy Rent A Car	☎ 246-431-4160; fax 429-6387 courtesy@goddent.com
Direct Rentals, Ltd.	☎ 246-420-6372 or 420-6391; fax 420-6383 direct@sunbeach.net, www.barbadosrental.com

Drive-A-Matic	☎ 800-223-6510 (US), 800-268-8354 (Canada), 0181-402-2277 (UK), 422-3000 or 434-7670 (Barbados); fax 422-1966 or 435-7535 bernmar@caribsurf.com
Johnson's Stables & Garage	☎ 246-426-5181; fax 429-3528 toursbgi@caribsurf.com
Mangera	☎ 246-436-0562; fax 436-0562; cell 230-0212
National Car Rentals	☎ 800-550-6288 ext. 2424 (US & Canada), 0870-6006666 (UK), 422-0603, fax 422-1966 (Barbados) edwards@caribsurf.com www.barbados.org/tours/national
Regency Rent-A-Car	☎ 246-427-5663 or 427-0909; fax 429-7735
Sunny Isle Motors	☎ 246-435-7979, fax 435-9277 sunisle@caribsurf.com
Top Class Car Rental	☎ 246-228-7368 or 228-7369 or 436-5564; fax 429-3485 akab@caribsurf.com
P&S Car Rentals	☎ 246-424-2052 or 424-2907

Travel Tips

Driving Tips

- Drive on the left.
- A quick toot on the horn means anything from "whaz hap'nin'?" to "I'm about to pass you." A long honk is a warning – heads up.
- Drivers at an intersection may quickly flash their headlights to signal that they are allowing you to go first.
- Yield to cars on your right at traffic circles.
- When you enter a traffic circle, stay in the left lane to take the first exit, take any lane to continue straight ahead, and move to the right lane for all other exits.
- Expect heavy traffic on most main roads during the rush hours of 7 am-9 am and 4 pm-6 pm. Highways into and out of Bridgetown are especially crowded during these hours.
- The speed limit is given in kilometers (km) per hour. Remember that 0.621 miles equal one kilometer. The in-town speed limit is 35kmh and the countryside speed limit is 60kmh, unless posted otherwise.

- Watch for unguarded and unmarked rocky projections and drainage ditch drop-offs along the sides of roads.
- A blue "P" identifies parking areas in Bridgetown.
- Be alert for one-way streets in Bridgetown.

■ By Bus & Minivan

It's possible to go anywhere on the island by bus. Barbados has an extensive public transportation system that includes both privately owned vehicles and a government-owned system under the control of the **Barbados Transport Board** (**BTB**).

BTB buses are blue with a yellow stripe. In Bridgetown, buses leave the main terminals approximately every 30 minutes for destinations in all directions. Buses also leave less frequently from a terminal in Speightstown for Bathsheba, on the east coast, and for Oistins, on the south coast. Destinations are clearly identified by signs over the front windshield.

The fare is B$1.50 per trip, and you are expected to have exact change. For a schedule or other information, ☎ 246-436-6820.

Bus Information		
TERMINAL / PHONE	**LOCATION**	**DESTINATION**
Fairchild St. ☎ 246-427-8795	East of Independence Square in Bridgetown	South & East
Lower Green ☎ 246-426-5695	Near Cheapside Market & St. Mary's Church in Bridgetown	North along West Coast Rd.
Princess Alice ☎ 246-426-2832	Near Pelican Village in Bridgetown	North along West Coast Rd.
Speightstown ☎ 246-422-2410	North of town near bypass	Bathsheba & Oistins

You can board buses at any of the round red-and-white signs posted along the main roads. They are marked either *To City* or *Out of City* depending on whether the bus will be going into or away from Bridgetown.

You must raise your hand to signal the bus to stop. Simply standing beside the sign means nothing.

Privately owned minibuses are painted bright yellow with a blue stripe. They travel short routes with quick turnarounds and charge B$1.50 per trip. Drivers usually will make change, but the exact fare is appreciated. Destinations are displayed on the lower corner of the windshield. In Bridgetown, you'll find these easily identifiable minibuses traveling along River Road, Temple Yard, Cheapside, and Probyn Street. Raise your hand to signal them to stop.

White minivans displaying a "ZR" on their license plate are privately owned route taxis that travel select circuits. Most often you will recognize them by the unbelievable number of passengers they have packed inside. You can flag them down along most main streets, and the charge is B$1.50 per trip.

Getting Married

Recent changes in Barbadian laws make the island a popular wedding destination. Couples can now say "I do" on the same day they arrive, because residency and advance notice requirements have been eliminated. All you need is an easily obtainable license and someone to perform the ceremony.

The first step is to decide between a civil ceremony officiated by a magistrate and a religious ceremony conducted by a minister. A letter of consent is provided by the marriage officer and presented when the couple applies for the license. This can be arranged in advance by the couple or a representative on the island.

When the couple arrives on Barbados, they may apply immediately for their marriage license by appearing together with the required documents at the office of the **Ministry of Home Affairs**, located in the General Post Office Building on Cheapside in Bridgetown. Once you get the license and pay the fees, the marriage can take place immediately. The office is open Monday-Friday, 8:15 am-4:30 pm, ☎ 246-228-8950, fax 437-3794.

In addition to the letter of consent from the marriage officer, both the bride and groom must present the following documents:

- Return airline tickets.
- A valid passport or the original or certified copy of their birth certificate.
- Divorced applicants must bring an original *decree absolute* or a certified copy of the final judgement.
- Widowed applicants must provide the previous marriage certificate and a death certificate for the deceased spouse.
- (All documents that are not written in English must be accompanied by a certified translation.)
- If neither the future bride nor the future groom are citizens or residents of Barbados, the couple must pay a B$125 fee in cash for a wedding license and revenue stamp. When either the bride or groom is a citizen or resident, the charges are B$45 for a license and stamp.
- Ceremonies performed by a magistrate require a B$100 court fee. Church ceremonies require a B$200 church fee.

Roman Catholic Ceremonies

Roman Catholic ceremonies require a few extra steps. Couples must complete and sign a pre-marital inquiry form, provide baptismal certificates, submit a Statement of Freedom to Marry form signed by the home-parish priest, and provide a certificate proving participation in a marriage preparation program. If neither the bride nor groom are Catholic, the home Bishop must send a letter giving permission for the couple to marry or signifying dispensation from disparity of cult. Anyone who was previously married must also provide copies of documents declaring the earlier marriage ended in annulment or death of a spouse. The couple's home bishop sends all of the above documents along with a testimonial letter to the Bishop of Bridgetown well ahead of the wedding date.

■ Wedding Packages

Many major hotels offer wedding packages that include the services of a coordinator who will plan every detail of any type or size wedding you can imagine. Independent wedding consultants also provide these services for couples staying at private villas or hotels without wedding packages. Couples who dream of getting married at an historical or natural location can arrange a ceremony at **Andromeda Botanic Gardens**, **Tyrol Cot Heritage Village**, **Gun Hill Signal Station**, or **Welchman Hall Tropical Forest** by contacting the **Barbados National Trust**, ☎ 246-426-2421 or 436-9033, fax 429-9055, e-mail natrust@sunbeach.net.

Independent Wedding Coordinators

Island Weddings, Cave Hill, St. Michael, ☎ 800-945-3289 or 424-7181, fax 424-6209, e-mail islandweddings@caribsurf.com

St. James Travel and Tours, Sunset Crest, St. James, ☎ 246-432-0774, fax 432-2832, e-mail stjames@sunbeach.net

Tropical Weddings, Hastings, Christ Church, ☎ 246-228-9868, fax 228-9869, e-mail ies@caribsurf.com

Precious Memories, Atlantic Shores, Christ Church, ☎/fax 246-420-4832, e-mail isla@caribnet.net

Destination Mgmt. Services, Hastings, Christ Church, ☎ 246-429-6016, fax 429-6024, e-mail dmsi@sunbeach.net

Weddings in Barbados, Warners Gardens, Christ Church, ☎/fax 246-437-2280, e-mail mwood@sunbeach.net

---

Exploring the Island

Barbados offers great diversity in a compact space. Cruise-ship passengers and visitors on a tight schedule can see many of the best attractions in a single day, but two days of touring is better, and a week allows you enough time to linger at your favorite spots.

Organized Tours

If you want to see the island with someone who knows it well, consider joining an organized tour. Most large hotels and resorts offer full-day and half-day sightseeing excursions, or you can contact one of the companies listed below. Expect to pay around US$55-$60 for a typical full-day tour, including lunch, and about US$20-$30 for a half-day tour that includes drinks. Children typically pay half price.

Independent guides, usually taxi drivers who were born on the island, charge about the same price, but sometimes are willing to negotiate, especially during the low season. Even if you pay more than the price for a standardized tour, you'll be able to structure the itinerary to your special interests and spend as much time as you wish at each location. In addition, the driver/guides are full of entertaining local lore.

Contact the **Barbados Tourism Authority** on Harbour Road in Bridgetown, ☎ 246-427-2623 (see *Barbados A-Z* for other locations), or check with the activities desk at your hotel, for recommended guides. The following operators offer a variety of group tours.

■ Tour Operators

Boyce's Tours, ☎ 246-425-5366, fax 424-1455. Customize your own excursion or join a scheduled tour run by this experienced family-owned company. Vans, taxis, and buses transport visitors on combination or interest-specific tours. Eco-tours are a specialty.

Adventure Land, ☎ 246-429-3687. This company takes you off the beaten track in their open-air four-wheel-drive vehicles. Some tours include hiking and lunch. You can also rent your own vehicle with a driver for the day.

Island Safari, ☎ 246-432-5337 or 436-6424. Customized open-air Jeeps take you to the island's most scenic out-of-the-way places. Full-day land-and-sea excursions include snorkeling, sightseeing, lunch, and drinks.

Highland Outdoor Tours, ☎ 246-438-8069, fax 438-8070. Call Highland for details on their uniquely adventurous tour options that include hiking, mountain biking, horseback riding, and tractor-drawn jitney trips.

E.L. Scenic Tours, ☎ 246-424-9108 or 230-1519, fax 427-8715. This well organized company uses air-conditioned buses take you on a variety of land tours.

L.E. Williams Tour Company, ☎ 246-427-1043, fax 427-6007. You'll get in-depth information on a tour of the island's top attractions with this experienced company. Drinks and a Bajan-style lunch are included in the all-day excursions.

VIP Tour Services, ☎ 246-429-4617 or 432-0774. Settle into the air-conditioned comfort of a Mercedes when you book a private tour with this luxurious company.

Topaz Tours, ☎ 246-435-8451, fax 435-6444, e-mail topaz@sunbeach.net. Beach stops, drinks, and snacks are part of this company's well-priced five-hour tours.

Bajan Helicopters, ☎ 246-431-0069, fax 431-0086. Jump aboard an air-conditioned six-passenger Astar jet helicopter for a scenic flight over the coasts. Choose *Discover Barbados* for a 20-minute ride that includes Bridgetown, the Flower Forest, the Scotland District, and Bathsheba. A slightly longer tour adds a look at the south coast beaches, Sam Lord's Castle, and most of the scenic east coast.

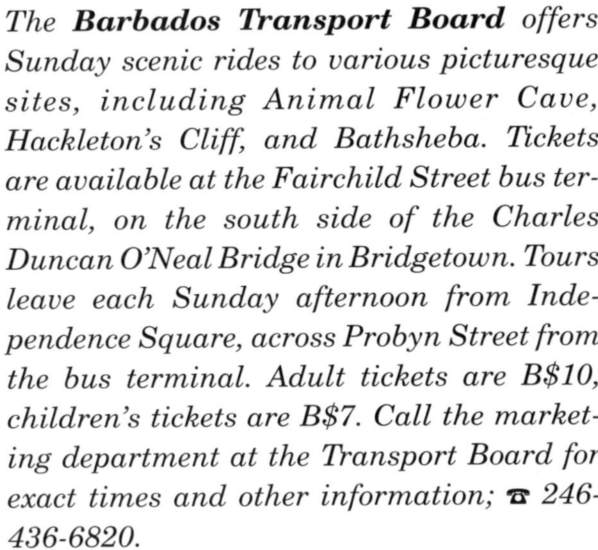

*The **Barbados Transport Board** offers Sunday scenic rides to various picturesque sites, including Animal Flower Cave, Hackleton's Cliff, and Bathsheba. Tickets are available at the Fairchild Street bus terminal, on the south side of the Charles Duncan O'Neal Bridge in Bridgetown. Tours leave each Sunday afternoon from Independence Square, across Probyn Street from the bus terminal. Adult tickets are B$10, children's tickets are B$7. Call the marketing department at the Transport Board for exact times and other information; ☎ 246-436-6820.*

Touring on Your Own

The **Barbados National Trust**, which promotes the island's cultural heritage and fosters environmental concerns, puts out a pocket-size pamphlet called *Barbados Heritage Passport*. Copies are available at hotels, restaurants, and tourist-oriented locations, or you can request one online at natrust@sunbeach.net. The booklet gives a brief description of eight of the Trust's historical sites, along with phone numbers and hours of operation. When you visit four of the sites and have your passport stamped by the ticket office, you may visit the other four sites without charge. This will save you about US$20, if you see all eight attractions. Even if you don't visit every location, the stamped passport makes a fine souvenir.

Armed with the Passport, a detailed map (see *Barbados A-Z* for resources), and a reliable vehicle, set off to scout the island.

Any plan for orderly sightseeing is quickly defeated by the complicated network of roads that loops and crisscrosses the island's countryside. The proposed circuits that follow are structured geographically with landmarks near either Bridgetown or

Speightstown as the point of departure, and the *Barbados in a Nutshell* map as a reference. These maps are available free at Esso gas stations and many tourist-oriented businesses including hotels. Use the maps in this guide as an additional resource.

Side trips are mentioned when they are located near major attractions so that you can make a leisurely stop at sites that interest you.

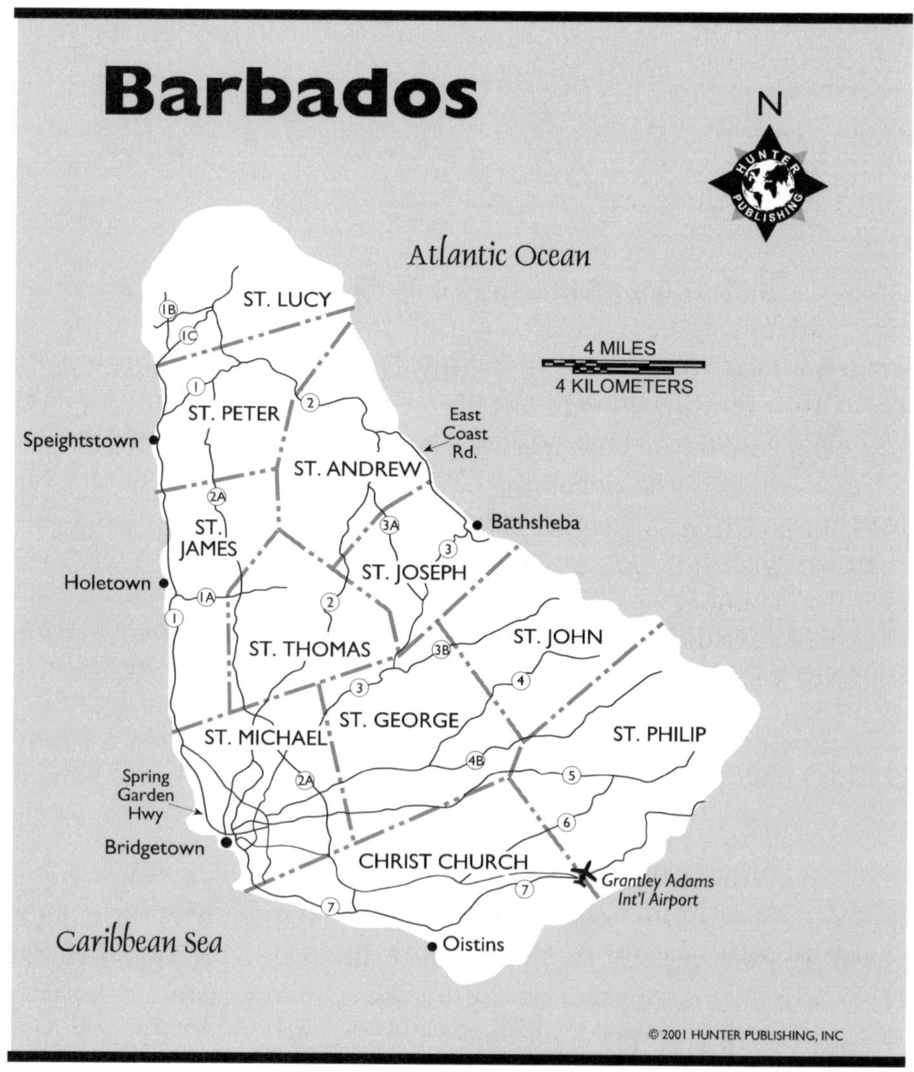

■ The Parishes

Barbados is divided into 11 districts known as parishes. It's possible for visitors to be oblivious to these divisions and never know when they leave one parish to enter another. However, each of the small sections is unique in some ways, much as neighborhoods vary within a city. When you take the time to notice, you'll find that the island as a whole is greatly enhanced by the distinctive characteristics of its 11 parts.

When the island was divided in 1645, each of the 11 parishes was allowed to send two representatives to the legislative assembly, which was set up in 1639 and composed of landowners who answered to the head of the local churches. This Vestry form of government lingered more or less unchanged for 300 years. During the 20th century, the system gradually evolved into the current mode of centralized government.

Bridgetown, the capital and only true city, is in **St. Michael Parish**, the densely populated center of Bajan government, business, history and culture. Within its borders on the southwest coast, you'll find duty-free shopping, the Barbados Museum, Tyrol Cot Heritage Village, the Garrison Savannah parade grounds, and numerous sites of architectural and historical interest.

Farther south, in busy **Christ Church Parish**, budget-conscious tourists find abundant hotels, restaurants, nightclubs, and shops scattered among traditional island-style homes, schools, and churches. Grantley Adams International Airport, the bustling nightlife of St. Lawrence Gap, and a string of white sand beaches, make this the island's most popular parish for visitors.

A more luxurious tourist district runs north of Bridgetown along the western Gold Coast in **St. James Parish**. The island's most lavish resorts stretch along this picturesque shore where calm Caribbean waters meet miles of soft white sand. Lushly landscaped golf courses, elegant restaurants, upscale nightspots and chic shops make this area the destination of choice for sophisticated travelers.

St. Peter Parish extends from the glitzy west coast, just north of St. James, to the pastoral east coast. Within its borders lie the sleepy village of Speightstown, historical St. Nicholas Abbey, the

Barbados Wildlife Reserve, Grenade Hall Signal Station and Forest, and Farley Hill National Park.

At the top of the pear-shaped island, **St. Lucy Parish** curves along the northern shore from the Caribbean side, where elegant residences overlook yachts in the new Port St. Charles Marina, to the Atlantic side, where windswept cliffs are battered by a steady surf. Animal Flower Cave, North Point, and The Spout at River Bay are among this rustic region's most majestic sites.

Like St. Lucy, **St. Andrew Parish** is rustic and sparsely populated. Adventuresome visitors who take the time to explore its treasures find remote beaches, the fully restored Morgan Lewis Mill, spectacular views from Cherry Tree Hill and Mount Hillaby, traditional potters at Chalk Mount Village, and the island's only remaining original forest in Turners Hall Woods.

St. Joseph Parish is nicknamed Little Scotland because of its resemblance to the rolling hills and coastal landscapes of that country. World-class surfers favor the waves off the cliff-lined beach in the east coast fishing village of Bathsheba, and amateur horticulturists spend blissful hours among the blooms at Andromeda Botanic Gardens and the Flower Forest.

Hackleton's Cliff, a 1,000-foot-high ridge that parallels the east coast, dominates **St. John Parish**. Villa Nova, a renovated plantation house that recently opened as a luxury hotel; St. John's Parish Church, a stunning hilltop structure; and Codrington College, set in a beautifully landscaped campus, are among the most interesting historical buildings on Barbados.

St. Philip Parish is home to Sam Lord's Castle and Crane Beach Resort, but because of its distance from Bridgetown and its Atlantic-side setting, it has been ignored by big developers. However, the sugarcane fields and isolated hilltops are beginning to attract the attention of international investors, so things may change rather quickly. Currently, the best attractions are Sunbury Plantation and Foursquare Heritage Park and Rum Factory.

Fascinating sites are scattered among the sugarcane fields of landlocked **St. George** and **St. Thomas Parishes**. Francia Plantation, Gun Hill Signal Station, and Orchid World provide a full afternoon of sightseeing in St. George. In St. Thomas, Welchman Hall Tropical Forest Reserve and Harrison Cave are two of the island's best natural attractions, while Earthworks Pottery and Bagatelle Great House draw artists, collectors and shoppers.

■ The Capital

Bridgetown is not a beautiful city, but it does have a few attractive areas and many interesting sites. History and architecture fans will find more to admire than others, but most visitors enjoy at least a quick stroll through the center of town. Spend a few hours at the stores suggested in the *Shopping* section of this book and glance at the attractions mentioned below, then get out of town. Bridgetown is the heart of Barbados, but the countryside is its soul.

Since the roads are usually clogged with traffic, consider taking a bus or taxi into town. If you do decide to drive, arrive after the 7-9 am rush hour and before the afternoon heat sets in.

The best places to park are at Independence Square, off Bay Street on the south side of the Careenage, or in the multi-level garage on the east side of St. Mary's Church between Suttle Street and Lower Broad Street.

Bridgetown was founded in 1628 and called **Indian Bridge** because of a makeshift log crossing built by Caribs. The bridge spanned the waterway that branches inland from the island's only natural harbor and connects with the Constitution River. Early documents refer to the settlement as **Town of St. Michael**, but by 1654 the official name was recorded as Bridgetown, in honor of a new bridge that replaced the original.

The Bridges of Bridgetown

Two bridges now connect north and south sections of Bridgetown across the mouth of the Constitution. The **Chamberlain**, an old swing bridge that once swivelled out of the way to allow schooners to sail into the **Inner Basin**, is to the west. It is named for Joseph Chamberlain, a British Statesman who supported financial aid for Barbados' sugar industry in the early 1900s. **Independence Arch** is on the south side of the bridge. It was dedicated in 1987 to celebrate the 21st anniversary of the nation's independence. The **Charles Duncan O'Neal Bridge** is a block inland. It is named for the founder of the Democratic League, the island's first political party to represent the common man.

The city that began with a small group of British settlers now claims about 100,000 residents, almost 50% of the island's population. Historical records show that the early settlement suffered from mosquito infestation due to its proximity to swamplands, but businessmen overlooked this health hazard because of the excellent harbor in Carlisle Bay.

Throughout the island's economic boom, sugar, rum, and slaves were traded from large warehouses built along the waterfront. Numerous storms and a devastating fire in 1860 destroyed most of the warehouse and graceful balconied colonial buildings, and most of Bridgetown today is made up of modern office complexes. However, you'll spot several survivors of the colonial era as you make your way along the city's busy streets.

The Careenage

Start your city tour at the Careenage, an active area around the lower part of the Constitution River. Formerly a safe harbor for inter-island clipper ships, the Careenage now serves as a marina for sleek yachts, scruffy fishing vessels, and tourist-packed catamarans. Walk along the Boardwalk on the north side, then cross the bridge and enjoy a drink at an outdoor table in front of **The Waterfront Café** (see *Where to Eat*). The trendy boutiques, bars, and restaurants in this area were once warehouses and are some of the oldest structures in the city. In late morning, you're likely to see fishermen, both real and tourist-fakes, returning to the pier with their catch.

The name Careenage comes from the word "careen," meaning to lean to one side, which is what workmen once did to a ship when its bottom needed to be cleaned.

From your table on the waterfront, you'll have a good view of **National Heroes Square** (called Trafalgar Square until 1999), which is dominated by a statue of **Lord Nelson**. This likeness of the famous admiral of the British fleet has gazed out over the bustling city since 1813 and is older than the Nelson Column in Trafalgar Square, London. Bajans raised funds for the monument, sculpted by Sir Richard Westmacott (creator of monuments in Westminster Abbey), after they learned of Nelson's death off Cape Trafalgar in 1805. The islanders had been awed by the admiral when he steamed into Bridgetown Harbour shortly before his death in pursuit of the French fleet, which had broken through his blockade at Toulon in the Mediterranean. However, future Bajans questioned the appropriateness of a white English hero standing watch over an island-nation that is inhabited predominantly by blacks. Many demanded that the statue be removed, but a compromise was reached in 1925 when a memorial honoring Bajans who served in World War I was constructed nearby. (A bronze panel listing WWII heroes was added in 1953.)

The **Dolphin Fountain**, adjacent to Nelson, celebrates the arrival of fresh water to the town in 1861 by pipe from a spring on the east side of the island.

The 19th-century **Public Buildings** are across St. Michael's Row from the square, and are the seat of Barbados' **Parliament**. The appointed Senate and publicly elected House of Assembly were established in 1639, and constitute the third-oldest parliamentary body in the English-speaking world after Britain and Bermuda. Parliament meets in the east wing, a stone neo-Gothic structure with island-style green shutters and an eye-catching red roof. Stained-glass windows depict English notables, including Queen Victoria and Oliver Cromwell. The west wing, with the church-like clock tower, houses offices and many of the island's public records.

St. Michael's Row

Two blocks east, at the corner of St. Michael's Row and Spry Street, you'll find **St. Michael's Cathedral**, which was consecrated in 1825 when Barbados got its first Anglican Bishop, William Hart Coleridge. A small stone church was built on this site in 1665, but was destroyed by fire in 1780. The present red-roofed structure replaced the original and is a mix of architectural styles, including Gothic Revival and Georgian. It's worthwhile to step into the sanctuary, which is open to the public daily, from 9 am-4 pm. Beautifully

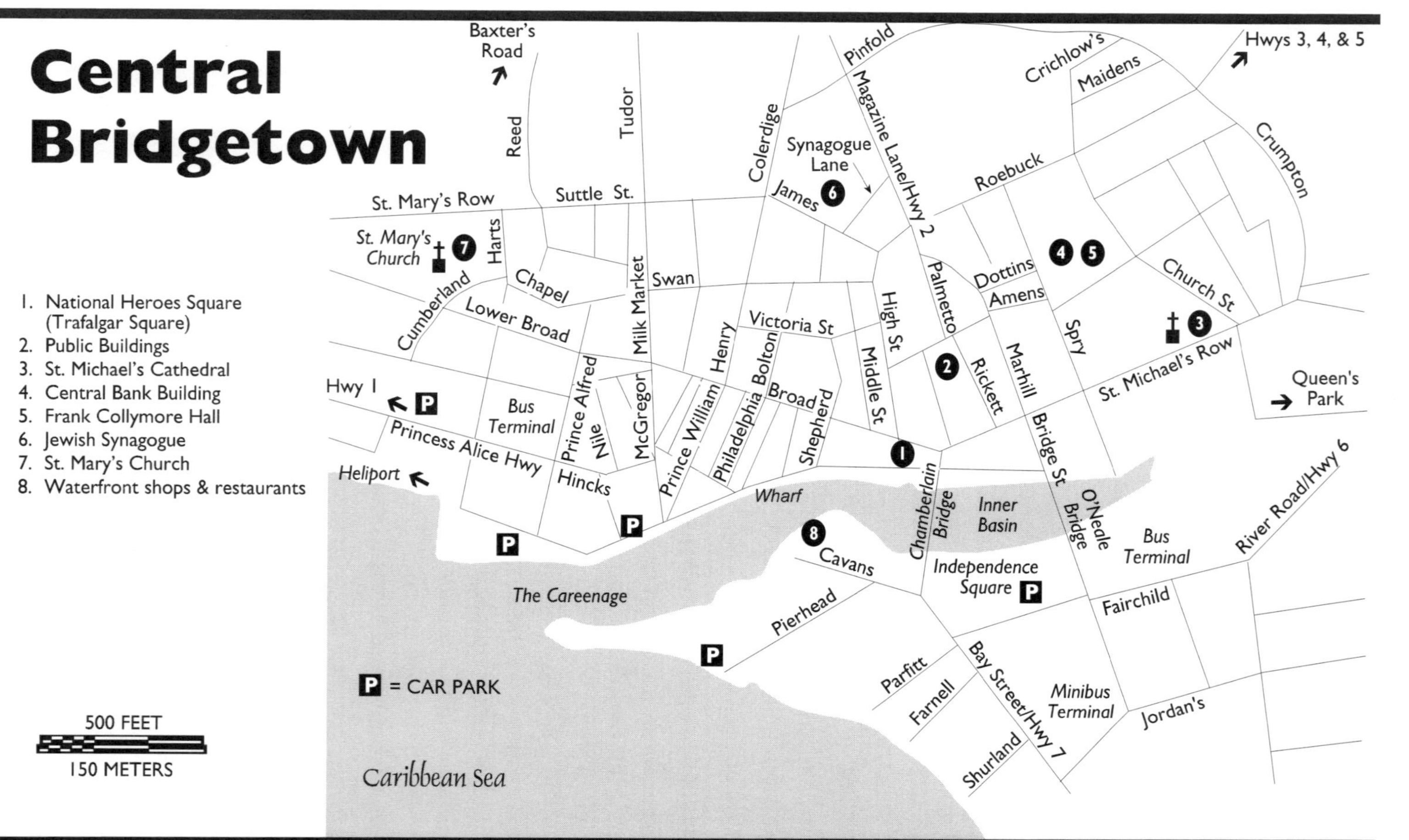
Central Bridgetown
1. National Heroes Square (Trafalgar Square)
2. Public Buildings
3. St. Michael's Cathedral
4. Central Bank Building
5. Frank Collymore Hall
6. Jewish Synagogue
7. St. Mary's Church
8. Waterfront shops & restaurants
500 FEET
150 METERS
P = CAR PARK
Caribbean Sea
The Careenage
Baxter's Road
Reed
Tudor
Coleridge
Pinfold
Crichlow's
Maidens
Hwys 3, 4, & 5
Crumpton
Synagogue Lane
James
Magazine Lane/Hwy 2
Roebuck
St. Mary's Row
Suttle St.
St. Mary's Church
Harts
Chapel
Milk Market
Swan
Cumberland
Lower Broad
Victoria St
High St
Palmetto
Dottins
Amens
Church St
Spry
Henry
Bolton
Middle St
Rickett
Marhill
St. Michael's Row
Queen's Park
Hwy 1
Bus Terminal
Prince Alfred
Nile
McGregor
Prince William
Philadelphia
Broad
Shepherd
Bridge St
Princess Alice Hwy
Heliport
Hincks
Wharf
Chamberlain Bridge
Inner Basin
O'Neale Bridge
Bus Terminal
River Road/Hwy 6
Cavans
Independence Square
Fairchild
Pierhead
Parfitt
Farnell
Bay Street/Hwy 7
Minibus Terminal
Jordan's
Shurland

carved mahogany is used throughout, several fine sculptures decorate the walls, and the church's namesake, Michael the Archangel, is depicted with sword in hand in a lovely stained-glass window over the altar. An adjacent cemetery is the final resting place of many of the island's former dignitaries, including the airport's namesake, Sir Grantley Adams (see page 87).

The Central Bank Building, the tallest structure on the island at 11 stories, towers above the Cathedral. A side building houses **Frank Collymore Hall**, a theater, art gallery, and cultural center where the National Independence Festival of Creative Arts is held in November (see page 48 for details). **Roebuck Street** (Highway 3), on the north side of the bank, has a jumble of shops and produce stands selling fresh fruit and homemade goodies.

A couple of blocks to the east, St. Michaels Row leads to **Queen's Park**, which surrounds **Queen's Park House**, an 18th-century home built for the commander of the British armed forces assigned to the West Indies. Currently, the house is managed by the National Conservation Commission (☎ 246-425-1200) and serves as a theater and art gallery with rotating exhibits. You may visit the Georgian home free of charge daily, from 10 am-1 pm, and from 2-6 pm.

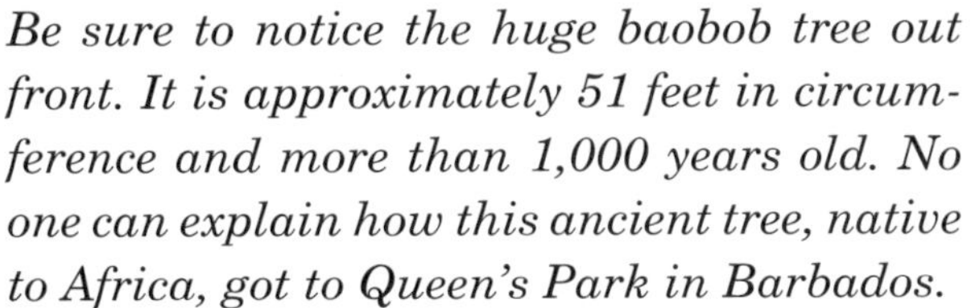

Be sure to notice the huge baobob tree out front. It is approximately 51 feet in circumference and more than 1,000 years old. No one can explain how this ancient tree, native to Africa, got to Queen's Park in Barbados.

West of the Central Bank Building, **James Street** will bring you to a side street leading to the old **synagogue**. Jewish settlers arrived in Barbados in the early 1600s, and the original building dated from that time. The Barbados National Trust rescued the synagogue from neglect and decay and renovated it to its present beauty. It's open Monday-Friday, 9 am-noon and 1 pm-4 pm; ☎ 246-432-0840. There's a small admission fee, but you can visit free of charge if you have a fully stamped Heritage Passport (see page 67 for details).

Most of the synagogue's original treasures have been sold, stolen or moved to the Barbados Museum, since the congregation was dissolved in the 1920s, but the lovely interior still features a marble floor, rich wooden railings, intricately carved prayer benches, and glass-and-brass chandeliers. Grave markers in the adjacent cemetery date back to the 1630s, when Jewish settlers begin arriving from Brazil. Their knowledge of sugarcane cultivation and business greatly influenced the island's prosperity.

Return to James Street, where architecture buffs will want to turn right and walk west until the road becomes Suttle Street and passes **St. Mary's Church**, built in 1827, a fine Georgian-style building surrounded by gardens in an otherwise rundown neighborhood. Shoppers may prefer to wander south past the outdoor markets and street-corner entrepreneurs along Swan Street (one-way running east) and Boulton Lane (a narrow road running north-south), which leads to the major shops on **Broad Street**. The **Rastafarian Market** is on Temple Yard, just past the bus station (see *Shopping*).

■ South of the Capital

Take **Bay Street** (H7) out of the city, around the curve of **Carlisle Bay**, past the early Gothic-style **St. Patrick's Catholic Cathedral**, which was built in 1897, to an area known as **The Garrison**. It was the first military post in the West Indies, and the 150-acre base for the British Windward and Leeward Islands Command. Today, it has a race track, sports fields, amazing old cannons, and a dynamic museum.

Needham's Point, the tip of a rugged peninsula that juts into the ocean at the south end of Carlisle Bay, about two miles from central Bridgetown off H7, has an excellent beach that is popular with locals on weekends. A lighthouse, built on the point in 1865, is the smallest of four found on the island. Nearby **Charles Fort,** originally called **Needham's Fort**, was the first fortification built by the British around 1650. Its ruins are incorporated into the grounds of the **Barbados Hilton Hotel**, which is being renovated and may reopen by the time you read this book.

St. Anne's Fort, bordering H7 east of the lighthouse, was begun in 1704 to serve as a backup to Charles Fort, but grew into a 1.5-acre stone bastion. The structure was never completed, but the main walls survived. Today, the striking Georgian-style Main Guard Building serves as headquarters for the Barbados Defense Force and the Garrison Committee. Visitors aren't allowed inside, but an information center is located on the wide veranda, and antique cannons are set up the lawn.

The impressive **National Ordnance Collection**, outside the Main Guard building, includes the world's largest collection of 17th- to 19th-century iron cannons. Major Michael Hartland of the Barbados Defense Force is overseeing a project to gather the extraordinarily large number of old weapons discarded on the island. To date he's found more than 400 centuries-old English, Dutch, Swedish, and French firearms left behind by the British military. You can see 26 of the most important cannons displayed on the lawn, and Major Hartland welcomes interested visitors to see other pieces by appointment. ☎ 246-426-8982, fax 429-6663.

The Iron Legacy

The plethora of antique military weapons in the **National Ordnance Collection** is testimony to the importance of Barbados as a British military base in the 17th, 18th, and 19th centuries. During the American Revolution, 1775-1783, and the Napoleonic Wars, 1803-1815, the island was a strategic defense center for England's interests in the Caribbean.

The oldest of the abandoned cannons recently discovered on the island was cast in 1620. One of the most remarkable is the Victoria Gun, which weighs more than three tons. The collection also includes ponderous cannons made during the reigns of King George II (1727-1760) and King William IV (1830-1837).

Perhaps the rarest and most important find is one Commonwealth Cannon bearing the coat of arms of Oliver Cromwell, Lord Protector of England from 1649 until his death in 1658. Another is on display in the Tower of London. These two cannons are the only known artifacts that survived after King Charles II mandated that all evidence of Cromwell's rule be obliterated (British history buffs will remember that Cromwell was leader of the contingent that beheaded King Charles I, the father of Charles II, in 1649).

While no dollar value can be assigned to the National Ordnance Collection, auction houses have sold antique cannons for more than US$20,000. Using that measure, the Barbados display is worth millions of dollars. Locals, however, find the cannons make priceless seating for viewing the horse races at the track on nearby Garrison Savannah.

Across the way, the **Garrison Savannah** parade grounds now serve as a horse-racing track, playground, and athletic fields. The **Barbados Museum** is on the northeast corner of the green, across Garrison Road, in the former military prison, which was built in sections between 1817 and 1853.

Prison cells hold artifacts from the Arawak and Carib Indian tribes; room displays from British Colonial times, including furniture, china, glass, and silver; rare historic maps; African, Creole, and European art; and archeological exhibits. If you're interested in working on an archaeological project, taking a look at rare West Indian artifacts dating back to the 1600s, or tracing your roots through genealogical research, check with the **Research Library**, which is open weekdays, 9 am-1 pm. The Museum Shop is stocked with books, maps, crafts, and jewelry, and the **Museum Café** serves lunch and tea in the adjoining shady courtyard. If you happen to be on the island on the first Saturday in December, stop by for the annual **Fine Craft Festival**. The museum is open Monday-Saturday, 9 am-5 pm, and Sunday, 2 pm-6 pm. Admission is B$11.50 for adults and B$5.75 for children 12 and younger. ☎ 246-427-0201 or 436-1956, fax 429-5946.

The **Barbados Gallery of Art,** located on Bush Hill, across the Savannah from the museum, houses a permanent collection of Bajan and Caribbean art. Visiting exhibits rotate through the gallery and a small selection of prints is available for sale. The building is open to the public, Tuesday-Saturday, 10 am-5 pm. Admission Tuesday-Friday is B$5 for adults and B$2 for children 18 and younger. On Saturdays, the fee drops to B$2 for adults and children are admitted free of charge. Call for information about tours and temporary exhibitions; ☎ 246-228-0149.

Don't leave the Garrison area without visiting the captivating assortment of vintage cars at **Mallalieu Motor Collection**, in the Barbados Car Museum at Pavilion Court, one of the historic military buildings that surround the Savannah. Bill Mallalieu will take you on a guided tour of his private collection, which includes a rare Vanden Plas Princess, once used to transport members of the Brit-

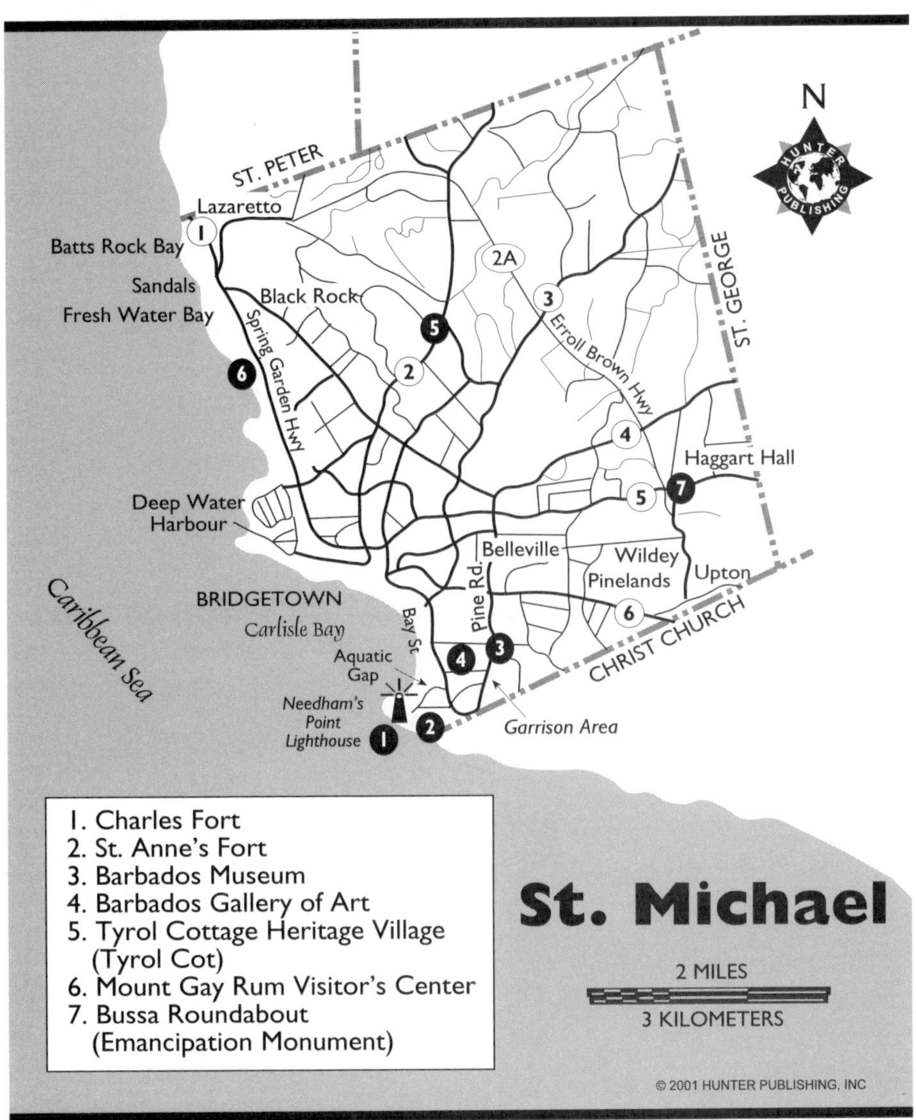

ish royal family during their visits to the island. Another one-of-a-kind treasure is a 1947 Bentley MK VI Vanden Plas Drophead that was custom designed for the Netherlands' Prince Bernhard and raced by him in the 1947 rally at Monte Carlo. Some of the cars are immaculately restored old favorites that are of interest simply because so few people take the time to preserve them. The museum is open Monday-Friday, 8-5, and on weekends by appointment. Admission is B$10; ☎ 246-426-4640.

Christ Church Parish

Leaving the Garrison Savannah area, travel south along the coast on H7 to the touristy **Parish of Christ Church**. Cool off at **Accra Beach** in Rockley or **Sandy Beach** in Worthing. The soft white sand is excellent for lounging or strolling, the water is perfect for swimming, and you'll find plenty of casual bars, open-air restaurants, and watersports centers. (See *Beaches* for more information.)

The most popular spot on the south coast is a district called **St. Lawrence Gap**, a mile-long stretch of road known for it's trendy restaurants, unique shops, and vivacious nightlife. Find the Gap by turning right, toward the water, off H7 at Little Bay, just past the police station. Halfway down the narrow road, you'll come to **Dover Beach**, a wide sash of white sand that draws windsurfers and beach bums.

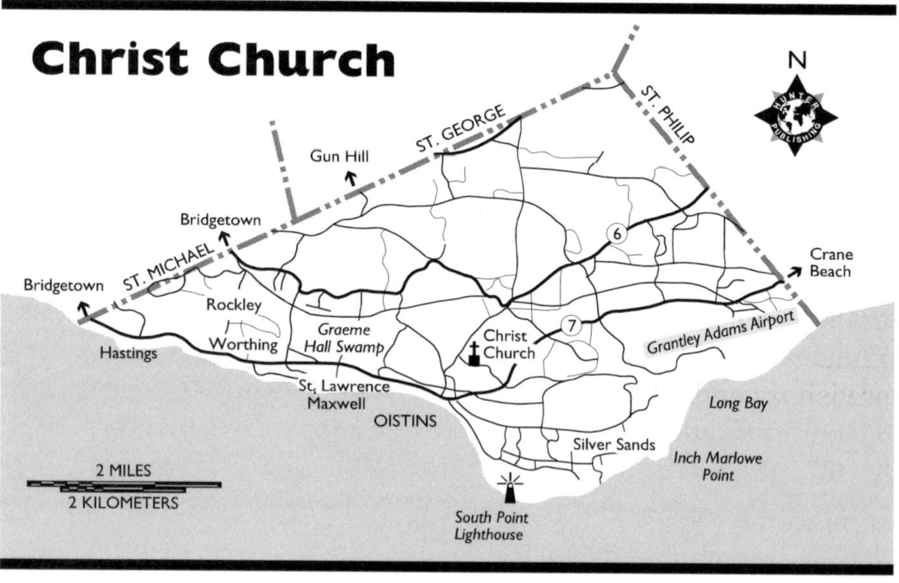

The Dover Athletic Field in St. Lawrence Gap is the site for Congaline Village, the focal point of De Congaline Festival, an island-wide carnival held annually at the end of April. The village features stalls selling food, drinks, and local arts and crafts. Entertainment includes calypso, gospel, and reggae music played by some of the best bands in the Caribbean.

A short distance farther east, H7 runs through the mostly residential town of **Maxwell**. It, too, has a touristy coastal road with a nice beach and some attractive, medium-priced accommodations, and the atmosphere is pleasantly relaxed. (See *Where to Eat* and *Nightlife* for information on restaurants and clubs in St. Lawrence and Maxwell.)

Graeme Hall Swamp

Graeme Hall Swamp is a 40-acre bird sanctuary within a 100-acre mangrove swamp surrounding a network of peaceful lakes. It is located a short distance north of the towns of Worthing and Dover on the south coast of Christ Church Parish. The swamp is being revitalized with funds donated by a retired Canadian lawyer, Peter Allard, who now lives on Barbados. Much of the wetlands is off-limits to the public, and only scientist are allowed access in order to conduct research. However, several facilities have been constructed for visitors under the direction of Dr. Karl Watson of the University of the West Indies. Public sites include two walk-through aviaries, an interpretive center, and a boardwalk through the reserve.

At one time, thousands of native and migratory birds lived in the swamp, but an abandoned condominium project turned the marsh into a cluttered mess of dead trees, building debris, and trampled earth. Hunters illegally shot thousands of birds; hundreds of migratory species found winter homes in more pristine territories. Slowly, these disastrous conditions are being corrected. If the restoration is successful, the swamp will provide a managed habitat for many types of wildlife, including endangered birds that nest in the trees and fish that breed in the tangled underwater roots of the mangroves.

The sanctuary at Graeme Hall Swamp is open daily, 7 am-6 pm. Contact them at ☎ 246-435-6330, or by e-mail at sanctuary@barbadosbirds.com. Their website is www.barbadosbirds.com.

Oistins

The little fishing village of Oistins, about a mile east of Maxwell, is the third-largest town on Barbados. It was here, in 1652, that the Barbados Charter was signed by the Royalists, surrendering the island to Cromwell's Commonwealth Commissioners.

Originally called Austin's Bay, after a well-known local drunk who liked to drive wildly along the coast in his ostentatious carriage, the name was repeatedly mispronounced, perhaps by the drunk himself, until it officially became Oistins.

Every Friday night, the town hosts a fish fry with jump-up music, icy beer, and wooden stalls selling fresh-caught grilled and fried fish. Most days, you can find local fishermen at Oistins Bay squatting beside their colorful boats repairing their nets, or cleaning their catch inside the large modern fish market/terminal.

*Bajans love **flying fish**, a small species with long pectoral fins that make them look like overgrown dragonflies. The fish can't actually fly, but they do shoot out of the ocean going 30 miles an hour for up to 100 yards. Fishermen go 20 to 30 miles offshore to catch them in long nets covered at one end with fronds from a palm tree and baited with ground fish.*

Once a year, people from all over the island turn out for the **Oistins Fish Festival.** This huge celebration, held during Easter week, honors residents who work in the fishing industry. The festival's official opening is announced by the cacophonous blast of conch-shell horns, a noise historically used to alert villagers that fishing boats had returned with a fresh catch. Highlights of the event include a fish-boning competition that flaunts the amazing skills of the participants, *tuk* bands, which use a hollow log instead of a drum, pa-

The South Coast

1. Charles Fort
2. Stann's Fort
3. Gallery of Art
4. Garrison Savanna
5. Barbados Museum
6. Rockley 9-hole Golf Course
7. Graeme Hall Swamp
8. Fish Market

© 2001 HUNTER PUBLISHING, INC

rading through the streets followed by a long line of revelers, and a variety of kiosks selling Bajan food specialties and local crafts. For the exact date of this year's festival, ☎ 246-428-6738.

■ North of the Capital

Mount Gay Rum Visitors Centre

Leaving Bridgetown on the Spring Garden Highway (H1), you'll soon reach the Mount Gay Rum Visitor's Centre in Exmouth Gap. The distillery is farther north in St. Lucy Parish, but the fermented and distilled spirits are shipped to this southern plant for aging, and visitors are invited to tour the facility.

Mount Gay Rum has been in continuous production since 1703, making it the oldest rum in the world. Premium White, Extra Old, and Eclipse are three of the varieties made by the Bajan company that produces a total of 500,000 gallons of rum per year.

One of the best ways to sample the process is by taking a luncheon tour that begins at noon each day. You'll be transported to and from your hotel, enjoy a Bajan-style buffet at the on-site veranda restaurant overlooking lovely gardens, and see the plant with an informative guide. The price is B$55 for adults and B$27.50 for children.

A Spirited History

Sugar and rum are tightly woven into the history of Barbados, one of the first places in the world to distill cane into spirits.

The process began almost 400 years ago when sailors stationed in the West Indies brewed up a rough-edged liquor from sugarcane. They called their tonic *rum*, a shortened form of *rumbullion*, a word used in the 1600s to describe an intoxicated person. It became well-known as the beverage of choice for pirates and as a pacifier doled out to British sailors to prevent mutiny. Over the years, the quality of the drink improved, and its popularity boomed when foreign troops were again stationed in the Caribbean during the world wars.

Barbados got into the rum-making business back in 1637 when a Dutchman named Pieter Blower introduced sugarcane to the island. He had learned to grow and process the crop in Brazil. Before crystallized sugar became popular in Europe, cane was used to produce rum.

Rum-making is quite simple. All that is required is sugar, water, and yeast. Bajans soon discovered that the potent stuff could just as well be made from molasses, a black, sticky, sweet liquid that's left over after sugar crystallizes.

The Dutch, who dominated trade between Europe and the Caribbean during the 1600s, began bringing in large numbers of slaves to work in the cane fields on Barbados, and in turn offered high prices for the end product.

Sugar became so profitable that landowners were reluctant to set aside valuable land for the relatively unprofitable business of growing food. Rich planters had no trouble paying high prices for imported food, but small growers and slaves often did without proper nourishment. By 1650, most of the island's forests had been cleared so the land could be cultivated, black slaves outnumbered the white upper class by three to one, and Barbados was one of Britain's wealthiest colonies.

If you prefer to take the 45-minute guided tour without lunch and transportation, you'll see a video inside an air-conditioned rum shop that is built to resemble a traditional chattel house. A guide then takes you through the plant and explains the process of rum production from cane to bottle.

Fermented and single- or double-distilled spirits arrive from the northern distillery to be aged in oak barrels for two to 12 years. Over 4,000 casks are stacked in the warehouse that reeks of the heady aroma of rum evaporating into the closed atmosphere. About 7% of the original distillates escape into the air and become what is known as the "angels share" – a portion given up graciously to the spirits who guard the spirits.

You'll also have a chance to watch barrels being made in the same way that they have been crafted for centuries, and watch the modern bottling process. Then, it's on to the tasting. You'll be taught how to properly enjoy rum to the fullest and given the opportunity to buy bottles of your favorite type of Mount Gay. Cost of the tour and tasting is B$12 for adults, and children may accompany their parents without charge. Guided tours begin every half-hour Monday-Friday, 9 am-4 pm. Reservations are not necessary for regular tours, but you must call ahead for the luncheon tour. ☎ 246-421-9066.

The Sweet Story of Cane & Rum

Today, visitors who tour one of the Bajan distilleries will find that sugar becomes rum in a high-tech process that still follows the 400-year-old principle of mixing molasses, water, and yeast. Molasses, consisting of about 55% sugar, is combined with local water, which is considered to be some of the purest in the world because it is rainwater that is naturally filtered through the island's coral and limestone base.

This molasses and water blend is mixed with live yeast that has been grown in specially designed containers to produce distinct flavors in the rum. The yeast devours the nutrients and sugar in the mixture and uses up all the oxygen within 10 hours – a process known as aerobic fermentation. As fermentation continues an additional 36 hours, sucrose and glucose are converted to alcohol in a process called anaerobic fermentation. The result is a mash containing 9% alcohol.

In many modern distilleries, the carbon dioxide that results from fermentation is captured, compressed into liquid, and sold to soft drink manufacturers to add fizz to their products. This eco-friendly process replaces the old method of making carbon dioxide by burning fossil fuels.

After anaerobic fermentation is complete, the mash is continuously fed into a distillation vat, or still, similar to those designed by Irishman Aeneas Coffey early in the 19th century. Before Coffey's invention, mash was dumped into heated copper pots, which produced a vapor that was captured in another container. This process produced a coarse rum of unreliable quality. Stills such as Coffey's have two columns that allow continuous distillation. The first column takes in the fermented mash and condenses it to 55% alcohol. The second column heats the mix to the boiling point, which removes most of the oils and esters that cause hangovers, and produces a liquid that is 95% alcohol.

At this point, the alcohol content is reduced by adding demineralized water, and the immature rum is put into oak barrels for aging. After two to 10 years, the barrels' contents are sampled, and the aged rums are blended to give each brand its own characteristics and reduce the alcohol content to 43%.

Tyrol Cottage

Tyrol Cottage Heritage Village (Tyrol Cot) is a restored mansion and a chattel-house artists's community northeast of Mount Gay Visitors' Center on Highway 2. The least complicated way to get there is to take Spring Garden Highway (H1) south towards Bridgetown, then pick up H2 and proceed northeast. Tyrol Cot is on Codrington Hill, about a mile north of the capital.

The village is a must-see for all lovers of history, architecture, antiques, and art. The focal point is the former home of **Sir Grantley Adams**, the island's first elected official and, thus, the Father of Democracy on Barbados. He lived in the house, built in 1854 by William Farnum, for 60 years, beginning in 1929. (Tom Adams, his son and the prime minister of Barbados from 1976 until 1985, was born there.) The family's antiques and keepsakes are scattered throughout the home. One of the most interesting souvenirs is Sir Grantley's flag of the short-lived West Indies Federation.

Farnum added some unique architectural twists to the basically Georgian, single-story, coral-block house. The roof was designed to catch rainwater, and the windows have double shutters (one above the other) that keep out rain while allowing cool air to flow into the house. Inside, rooms are furnished with handmade mahogany furniture that was crafted on the island.

Colorful chattel houses containing artisans' studios and shops sit on three acres of landscaped grounds adjacent to the mansion. This **Heritage Village** includes a restored slave hut, a pottery workshop, a functioning blacksmith's shop, and stores offering basketry, wood carvings and paintings. The **Chattel House Museum** contains antiques and historical artifacts. **Old Stables Restaurant** is actually an old stable that has been converted into a café and now serves West Indian food at lunchtime. **Cockspur Rum Shop** is a traditional community bar serving liquid refreshments.

Tyrol Cot is managed by the **Barbados National Trust** (☎ 246-436-9033 or 426-2421, fax 429-9055, e-mail natrust@sunbeach.net) and open Monday-Friday, 9 am-5 pm. The entrance fee is B$11.50 for adults and B$5.75 for children. Contact Tyrol Cot directly for additional information at ☎ 246-424-2074.

■ The West Coast

Highway 1 follows the west coast from the bustling capital of Bridgetown in St. Michael Parish, north to the sleepy historic village of Speightstown in St. Peter Parish. In between is one of the wealthiest stretches of shoreline in the Caribbean. Understandably known as the **Gold Coast**, this dazzling strip is the site of elegant resorts, luxurious private homes, and splendid restaurants.

Holetown

Holetown, where the first settlers stepped ashore in 1627, is an attractive town with colorful chattel houses sitting across the main road from plush hotels.

Folkestone Underwater Park and Museum is open Monday-Saturday, 9 am-4 pm. Admission is B$1. ☎ 246-422-2314. The marine park makes an interesting stop. Located off the main road, it's run by the National Conservation Commission (Codrington House, St. Michael, ☎ 246-425-1200), and has a visitors' center, gift shop, and small marine-life exhibit. Seven-mile-long **Dottin's Reef** is just offshore, and the marine park protects two miles of it. Glass-bottom boats take passengers out to the reef, and scuba divers can boat about a half-mile out to dive the deeper portions. Visibility is typically 100 feet, and the reef's sponges, sea fans, gorgonians, and coral are a habitat for turtles, large fish, and rays. Snorkelers follow a marked underwater trail in the sheltered recreational waters near shore.

St. James

To Speightstown
ST. PETER
ST. ANDREW
Gibbs Bay
2A
Apes Hill
1
Alleynes Bay
Mount Steadfast
Endeavour
Porters
ST. THOMAS
2A
St. James Church
HOLETOWN
1A
1. Royal Westmoreland Golf Course
2. Folkstone Underwater Park
3. Portvale Sugar Factory
4. Sir Frank Hutson Museum
5. Sandy Lane Golf Course
Sandy Lane Bay
N
HUNTER PUBLISHING
Holder
Paynes Bay
1
2A
Fitts
ST. MICHAEL
2 MILES
2 KILOMETERS
To Bridgetown
© 2001 HUNTER PUBLISHING, INC

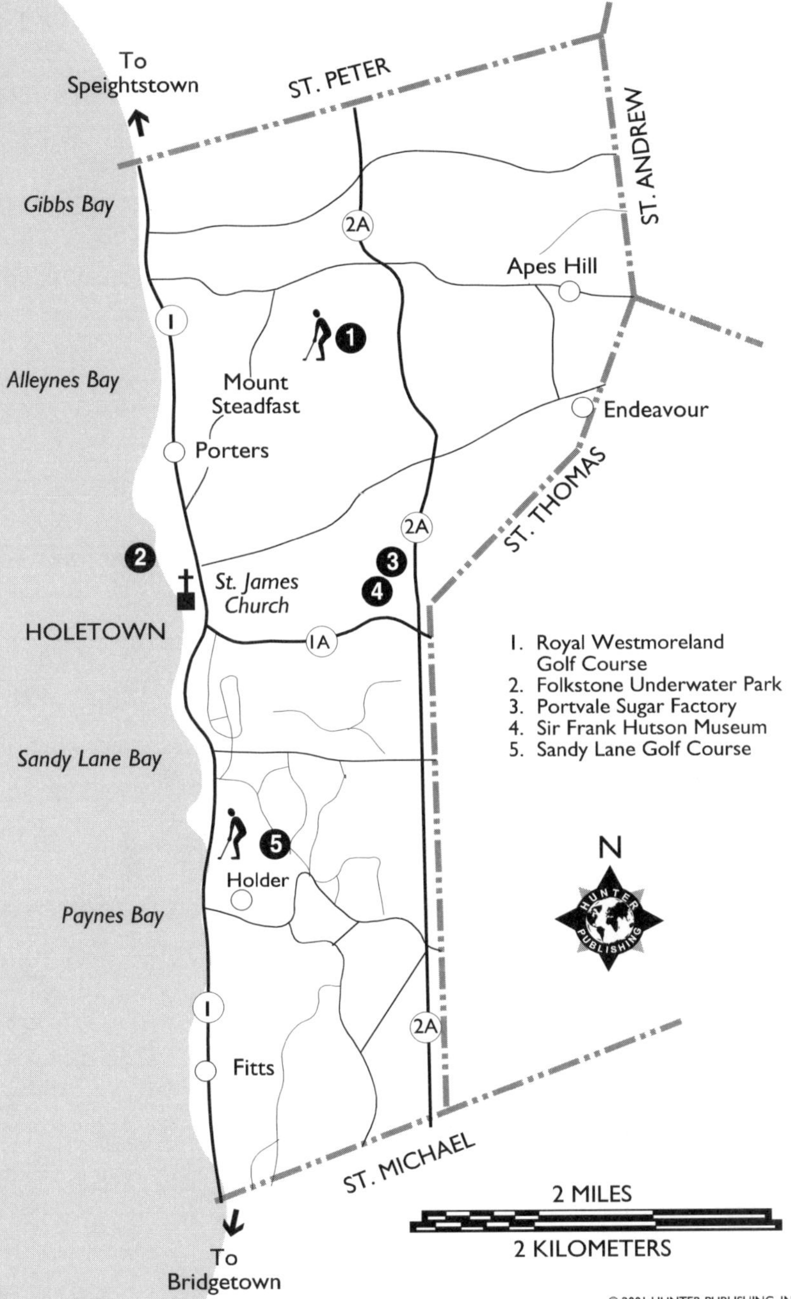

Portvale Sugar Factory and the **Sir Frank Hutson Museum** are between Highway 1 and Highway 2, a short distance east of Holetown. If you're on the island during harvest season, between February and June, you can take a combined tour of the museum and operating factory to view the entire process of making sugar. At other times, visitors tour only the museum, which explains the important role "King Sugar" has played on Barbados for more than 300 years. Sir Frank Hutson searched the island for old sugar-milling machinery and incorporated the cleaned pieces into an interesting exhibit inside a former boiling house on an old plantation. Visitors are welcome Monday-Saturday, 9 am-5 pm. Combined tours during the harvest are priced at B$15. Museum-only tours are B$8, and children visit for half-price. ☎ 246-426-2421.

Speightstown

Speightstown (pronounced *spikestown*), at the northern end of Highway 1, is in the midst of a redevelopment project meant to breathe fresh life into the old but captivating port town. The plan

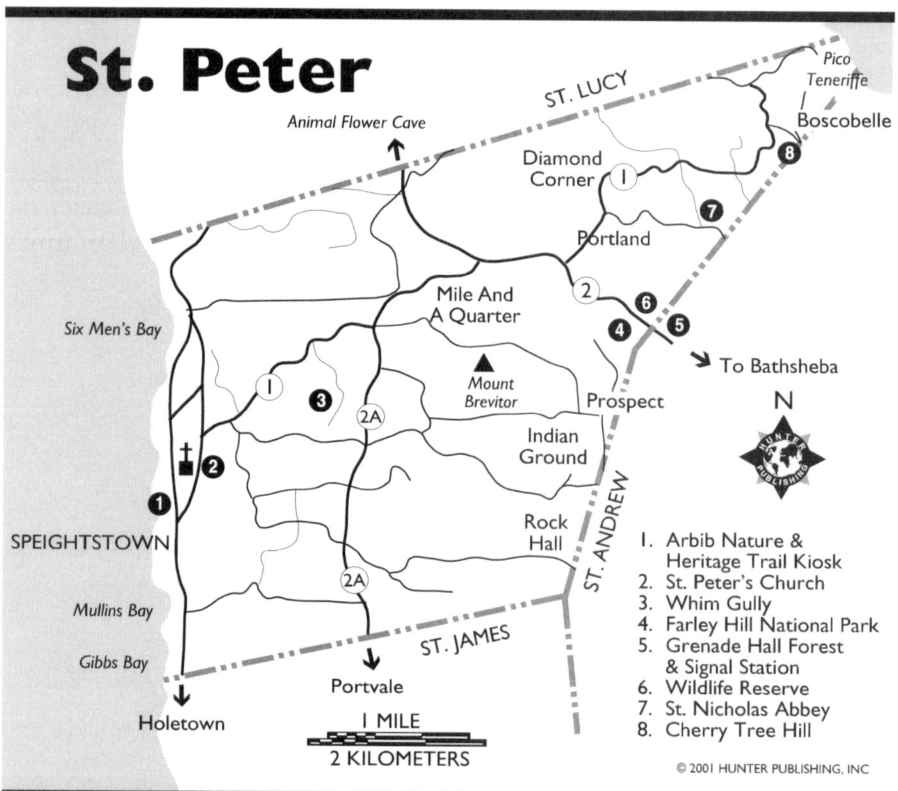

calls for subsidized individual refurbishing of the historic balconied buildings, and incentives to develop facilities to draw tourists. Already, you'll notice colorful new paint on some of the buildings at the south end of town, and the seaside **esplanade**, with its old cannons and mature tamarind trees, boasts a new kiosk that serves as a departure point for the award-winning eco-tour along the **Arbib Nature and Heritage Trail** (see *Hiking*, page 134).

Through-traffic now by-passes town, so walkers will enjoy strolling the pleasantly uncrowded old streets. **St. Peter's Parish Church,** at the corner of Church and Queen Streets, dates back to the 1600s. Its original architecture was Georgian, but the church was rebuilt in the Greek Revival style in the 1800s, after a hurricane wiped out much of the island. The church building was restored once again in the 1980s after a fire destroyed everything except the tower and exterior walls. Markers in the overgrown graveyard make interesting reading, and the shops across **Church Street** are good examples of what the town looked like when it was a thriving seaport.

■ The Southern Parishes & Up the Atlantic Coast

Begin your driving tour of southern Barbados at the intersection of H2A (the Errol Barrow Highway) and H5, east of the capital. Here, a statue called **The Freed Slave** stands watch over a traffic circle. The statue is a monument to a slave named Bussa who led an uprising in 1816, which resulted in the passage of the Slave Registry Bill. The traffic circle also is known as **Bussa Roundabout** and the statue is often called the Emancipation Monument.

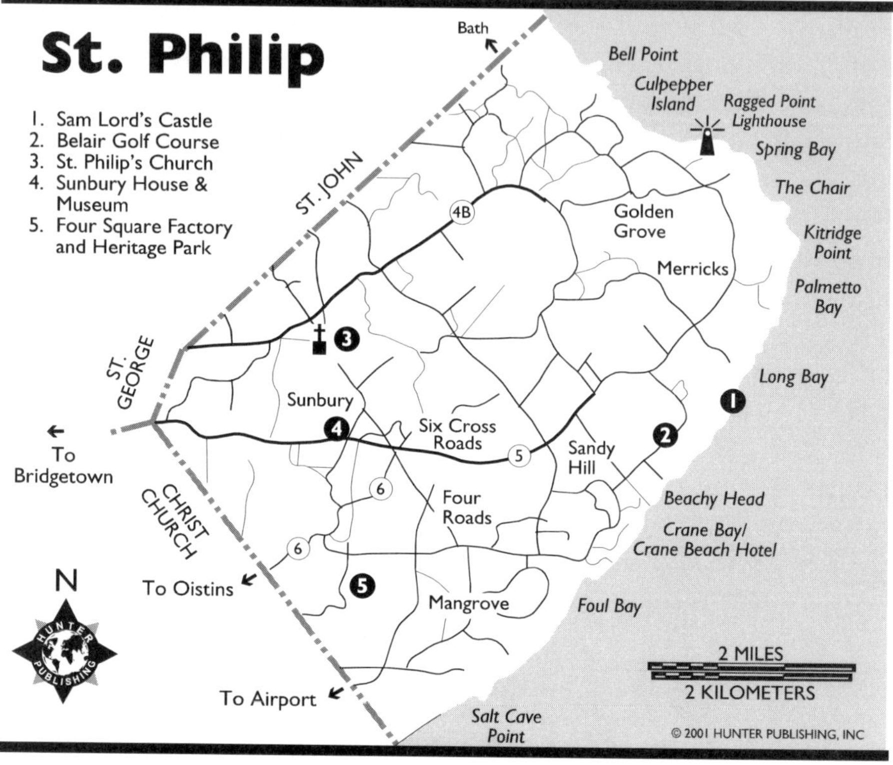

Locals often refer to roads and places by various unofficial names. A good example is the Errol Barrow Highway, which also is called the ABC Highway to honor three former Prime Ministers: Adams, Barrow, and Cummins. Residents frequently know a street or location only by landmarks and give directions such as "turn after the old banyan tree," or "it's near the big yellow house." The traveler's best defense is a detailed map!

Sunbury Plantation

Travel east on H5 past fields of sugarcane and other crops, through the southern portion of St. George Parish, to Sunbury Plantation in the Parish of St. Philip. A sign on the left, just before you reach the intersection at Six Cross Roads, indicates a driveway that leads to the island's only historic greathouse that opens all its rooms to the public.

Sunbury gives you a good idea of the elegant lifestyle enjoyed by plantation owners during Barbados' thriving sugar-boom days. A magnificent 18-place claw-footed table dominates the dining room, and carved four-poster beds furnish the upstairs bedrooms. Other antiques include a desk that's been in the house for more than 200 years, handmade dolls, and a collection of optometrist's tools that belonged to the island's first eye doctor. All the rooms are furnished and decorated to look as if the residents just stepped out for an afternoon buggy ride. In fact, the buggies are on display in the garden.

The house was built about 1660 by Matthew Chapman, son of Thomas Chapman, one of the island's first settlers. One hundred years later, brothers named John and George Barrow bought the property and named it after their ancestral home in an English town, Sunbury-on-Thames. John's son was living on the plantation with his wife when the cane fields and outbuildings were set on fire by rioters during the 1816 slave rebellion.

In 1835, Thomas and John Daniels, friends of the renowned Sam Lord (see *Sam Lord's Castle,* below), bought Sunbury. Their descendants owned the estate until 1981, when the greathouse was sold at auction and opened to the public three years later. A fire destroyed much of the house in 1995, but the two-foot-thick walls and some of the treasured antiques survived. Dedicated preservationists, including the current owners Angela and Keith Melville, carefully restored the structure to its former beauty, and the plantation reopened in 1996. Your visit starts with a tour of the greathouse led by an informative guide. Then you're free to wander around the landscaped grounds, and stop at the gift shop and small restaurant. Admission is B$12 for adults, B$6 for children, and the plantation is open daily, 10 am-4:30 pm. ☎ 246-423-6270, fax 423-5863.

Side Trip: Heritage Park

Heritage Park and **Foursquare Rum Distillery** make an interesting stop between visits to Sunbury Plantation House and Sam Lord's Castle. Signs at the Six Cross Roads roundabout, just east of Sunbury on H5, point the way. You take the fourth exit left out of the circle onto H6 going southwest toward Foursquare. The park and distillery are a short distance away.

Foursquare produces Old Brigand, Doorly's Rum, and E.S.A.F. White Rum, the island's top seller. The new distillery is a technological marvel touted as the most modern and environmentally friendly in the world. This computerized facility is the focal point of Heritage Park, an eight-acre landscaped village laid out on the grounds of a former plantation. Many of the original structures built during the 17th through 19th centuries have been restored, and now house museums, galleries, shops, and eateries.

The Art Foundry occupies a beautifully restored 250-year-old stone sugar factory designated as both an architectural and historical site by the National Trust. On the upper floor, galleries feature a variety of work in several artistic media. Some of the paintings, photographs, and sculptures are for sale, but others are on temporary loan from artists around the Caribbean. Several Bajan artists work in studios set up in the gallery area on the second floor, and visitors are encouraged to observe and ask questions. On the ground floor, a print-making studio makes bottle labels for Foursquare Rum and turns out posters and cards featuring the work of local artists.

An 18th-century restored sugarcane hoist towers over the **Cane Pit Amphitheatre**, which is tucked into a storage hollow that held cut cane when the sugar factory was operating. A canvas top covers the stage, dressing rooms, and 250 seats in the open-air theater, so that presentations by local performers are rarely canceled because of rain.

Heritage Park also encompasses a children's pet farm and pony-riding track, a wedding pavilion, a folk museum, and a food court. **The Sugar Cane Café** resembles a restaurant from a past era, and serves Bajan specialties. Crafts shops sell locally made baskets, pottery, leather, and jewelry. Antique machines and factory equipment are displayed around the grounds. Signs describe the use of each item so that visitors can take a self-guided tour of the sugar-making process.

During a 40-minute guided tour of the distillery, you'll get a glimpse of the most technologically advanced method of producing rum, a product that's been made on Barbados for over 350 years. The newest techniques allow Foursquare to distill rum at an ultra-low temperature, which results in a more consistent quality. Also, the company is able to turn molasses waste, a by-product of rum production, into concentrated protein (used in livestock feed) rather than dump it into the sea, where it pollutes the water.

Foursquare Rum Distillery and Heritage Park are open Monday-Friday, 9 am-5 pm; Saturday, 1-6 pm; and Sunday, 11 am-5 pm. Admission is B$12 for adults and B$6 for children. ☎ 246-420-1977, fax 246-420-1976, e-mail rumfactory@sunbeach.net.

Sam Lord's Castle

After touring Sunbury Plantation House, continue east on H5 to the traffic circle at Six Cross Roads. The second exit left out of the roundabout will put you back on H5, which leads to the gates of Sam Lord's Castle perched on a cliff above the beach at Long Bay. Several signs point the way.

The legend of Sam Lord is a favorite with Bajans, and his historic castle-like home is both a luxury hotel and a major sightseeing attraction. Fact and folklore have mixed over the years, and the guide who shows you through Lord's former home will tell you both.

The story begins in the early 1800s when Samuel Hall Lord decided to finance a lavish lifestyle with stolen money. He hung lanterns in the trees at Long Bay to lure ships toward the island over dangerous reefs. When the ships wrecked offshore, Lord and his corrupt buddies overtook the crew and plundered the ship.

Lord's pilfering brought in enough money to hire skilled European craftsmen to build a grand Barbadian mansion, which he filled with expensive furniture, paintings, silver, and china. You'll see many of these rare and costly items on display inside the castle. Rumors linger about treasure still buried on the estate grounds, but if Lord had money hidden away, why would he leave huge debts when he died in England in 1845?

Other scandalous details make Lord's story captivating, and you'll learn them all when you tour his former home, which is, of course, haunted. The 72-acre estate is open for tours daily, 8:30am-5 pm, and the admission fee of B$12 for adults and B$6 for children allows you to use the pool, beach, and restaurants. For additional information, contact the reception desk at Sam Lord's Castle, ☎ 246-423-7350 (see *Where to Stay*, page 182, for more details).

Bottom Bay to Ragged Point

Leave Sam Lord's Castle the way you came and take a right on H5 going east. This will take you to the turn-off for Bottom Bay, where steps lead down a cliff to a lovely white-sand beach. Craggy cliffs shelter the wide, shady, isolated beach that makes an ideal picnic spot. On most days, medium-size waves roll ashore, and there's a gentle undertow.

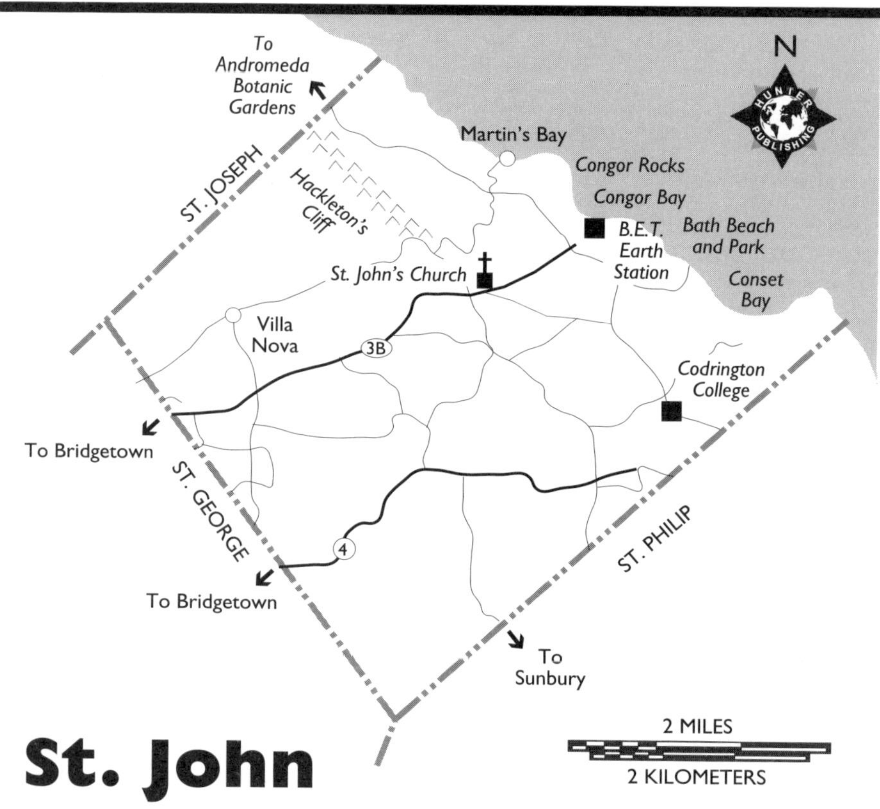

© 2001 HUNTER PUBLISHING, INC

A short distance north, the highway rounds the easternmost point of the island, and the lighthouse at **Ragged Point** comes into view. It was built in 1885 to warn approaching ships of dangerous offshore reefs. Visitors aren't allowed inside the lighthouse. However, the view from the point is spectacular. Atlantic surf pounds towering bluffs, and on a clear day you can see all the way up the coast to the shore of northernmost St. Lucy Parish.

Codrington College

When you leave Ragged Point, head north on the main highway toward Bayfield. Turn west onto Highway 4B, pass Three Houses Park, then follow the signs to Bathsheba (right, right, left), which puts you on Highway 3, parallel to the east coast . Watch for signs to Codrington College, a stunning campus opened in 1745 and now the oldest seminary in the Western Hemisphere.

A long lane lined on both sides by 100-year-old palm trees leads onto the college grounds, which overlook **Conset Bay** and offer panoramic views of the Atlantic coast. Today, it is part of the University of the West Indies, and students from throughout the Caribbean study here to become ordained Anglican ministers. When the school was founded by Christopher Codrington and The Society for the Propagation of the Gospel in Foreign Parts, it was meant to be an institution of learning for students living under monastic vows of poverty, chastity, and obedience.

An entrance fee allows you to walk through the peaceful campus and look into buildings that are not being used for classes. However, the most stunning view is free of charge. From the entrance road, you can look straight down the long line of palm trees, through the triple arches of the main building dating from 1743, to the Atlantic Ocean.

If you decide to pay the small price of admission, look into the beautiful chapel, wander past the pond filled with lily pads, and follow the self-guided nature trail through the woodlands on the northwest side of the campus. Visitors are welcome daily, 10 am-4 pm. Admission is B$5. ☎ 246-423-1274.

Conset Bay to Bathsheba

Before you proceed north toward Bathsheba, make a quick stop at historic **St. John's Church**, a turn to the west soon after leaving Codrington College. The current building, a lovely Gothic-style church with an attractive tower, was built in 1836. Note the 17th-century windows and doors salvaged from the original structure after the hurricane of 1831. Inside, notice the pulpit, which is made of six types of wood, and the sculpture by Richard Westmacott of St. John as an infant with Mary and Jesus.

The view from the graveyard behind the church is breathtaking.

Constantine's Coffin

One of the graves belongs to Ferdinando Paleologus, said to have been a descendant of the brother of Constantine XI, the last emperor of the Byzantine Greeks. Constantine died in a battle against the Turks in 1453, and the Imperial family moved to England, where Ferdinando was born many years later. Naturally, he was a Royalist during the English Civil War, and escaped to Barbados after King Charles I was killed and the monarchy lost power. His coffin was discovered in a vault during restoration of the church after the 1831 hurricane. Consistent with Greek Orthodox tradition, the head of his coffin was pointing west and his skeleton was embedded in quicklime.

When you leave the church, head back toward the East Coast Road where you'll turn to the north in the direction of Bathsheba by way of Martin's Bay and Foster Hall. This area, from the Parish of St. John into neighboring St. Joseph, is fabulous for anyone interested in photography, horticulture, hiking, surfing, or wide-eyed gawking. **Hackleton's Cliff** rises a thousand feet to the west, with sweeping views that encompass the entire eastern shoreline from the lighthouse at Ragged Point to Pico Teneriffe, far to the north. The tree-topped ridge was created millions of years ago when mighty ocean waves battered away the island's limestone covering. Between Hackleton's Cliff and the Atlantic lies a wild, unsettled terrain spattered with native plants and exposed rocks.

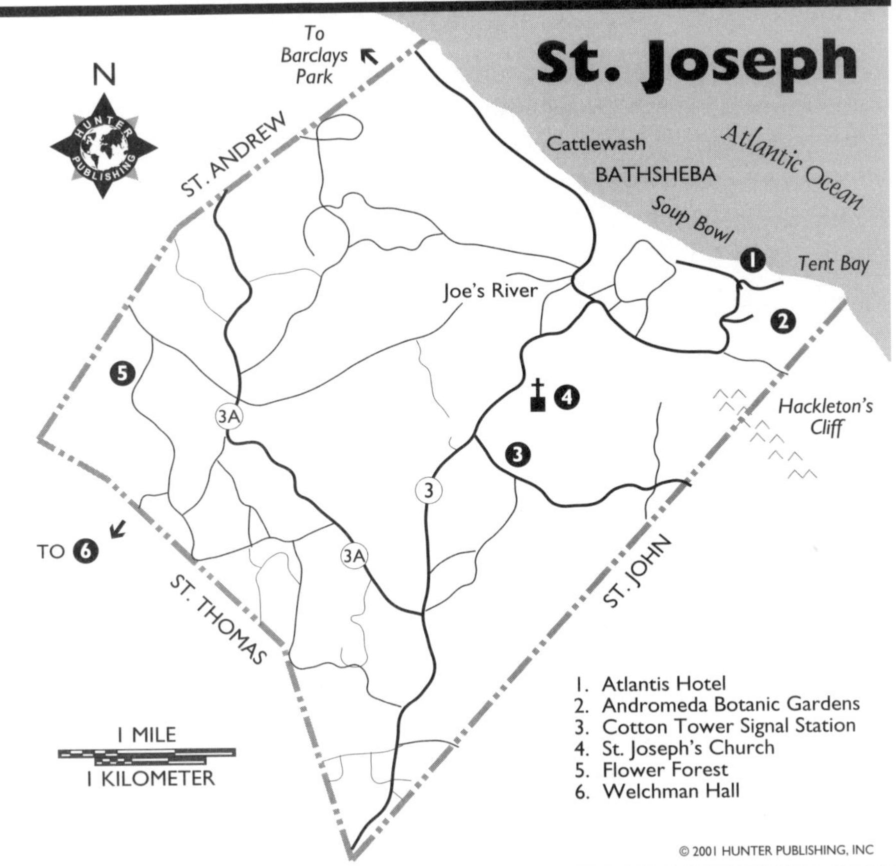

Andromeda Botanic Gardens

Just before Bathsheba, watch for signs directing you to the delightful Andromeda Botanic Gardens. This colorful floral park is the loving creation of the late **Iris Bannochie**, an internationally renowned Bajan horticulturist and the author of *Gardens of the Caribbean.* She traveled extensively during her lifetime and always returned home with samples of exotic species for her gardens.

Bannochie began her splendid garden in 1954 and named it after a character in Greek mythology who was chained to a seaside rock. Like the mythological enchantress, Bannochie's Andromeda appears to be tethered to coral boulders on the hillside above **Tent Bay**, a small fishing community.

Princess Andromeda

The mythological Andromeda was an Ethiopian princess, the daughter of King Cepheus and his wife/concubine, Cassiopeia. When Cassiopeia boasted to Poseidon, god of the sea and protector of all waters, that her daughter was more beautiful than any of the sea nymphs, he became furious and sent a vicious sea monster to terrorize Ethiopia.

The only way to appease the horrible monster was to sacrifice the king's daughter. Andromeda was chained to a rock on the seashore, but before she could be grabbed by the monster, Perseus, the son of Zeus, killed the beast and rescued Andromeda.

King Cepheus was so pleased that he allowed Perseus and Andromeda to marry. Their son was Electryon, the grandfather of Hercules. Cassiopeia, Cepheus, and Andromeda were all set in the sky as brilliant constellations.

Now managed by thc Barbados National Trust, the gardens recently underwent a half-million-dollar renovation, which included a new entrance, additional waterfalls, and expanded horticultural collections. Volunteer horticulturists lead tours on Wednesdays at 10:30am, but two self-guided circuits are laid out in a brochure for those who prefer to go it alone.

Hikes in the Gardens

If you have only a half-hour, take **Iris' Walk** which leads you past a "travelers tree" (thirsty travelers drink water trapped at the base of the leafs) to a tranquil pond filled with water lilies, water lettuce, and papyrus.

Other interesting highlights of this short tour include the mammee-apple, a native tree that bears a fruit used to make candy and liqueur; *Heliconia stricta Iris*, named for the gardens' founder; native Anthuriums, with eye-catching flower clusters that attract flies for pollination; and Agave, a useful plant used to make sisal rope and tequila.

John's Path is hilly and takes about 45 minutes – longer if you stroll slowly or stop often. It leads to breadfruit trees, descendants of plants brought from Tahiti to Barbados by Captain William Bligh of *Mutiny on the Bounty* fame; calabash trees, which produce a hard-shelled fruit that is used to make bowls; and aromatic frangipani, which is gorgeous but poisonous.

Trails along both John's Path and Iris' Walk criscross a natural stream that meanders through the gardens before it empties into the ocean below. These trails connect groupings of multicolored hibiscus that mingle with copious oleanders and profuse bougainvillea loaded with purple, pink, and red blossoms. Numerous varieties of orchids bloom year-round, and countless species of palms provide welcome shade for ferns, vines, and mosses.

Be sure to visit the impressive bearded fig, a massive tree with unruly roots that droop from the branches like whiskers from the face of an unshaven man. Historians think early Portuguese explorers named the island *Los Barbados* because of these bearded trees that once flourished along the shore.

As you make your way through the gardens, watch for territorial hummingbirds that aggressively protect their turf, mongooses and lizards that rustle through the underbrush, and monkeys that appear most mornings to gather a breakfast of hibiscus flowers. If you have time, pick up a snack at the on-site **Hibiscus Café** to enjoy on a shady bench overlooking the ocean, and browse among the souvenirs for sale in the **Best of Barbados** gift shop.

Andromeda Botanic Gardens is open daily, 9 am-5 pm. Adult admission is B$12, children five and over pay B$6, and children under the age of five enter at no charge. ☎ 246-433-9261.

The east coast highway continues down from Andromeda Botanic Gardens to **Tent Bay**, the landing area for the local fishing fleet. There's not much of a beach here, but you may enjoy watching the fishermen return with their catch.

Balconies of the old, weather-beaten **Atlantis Hotel** overlook the bay. Built in 1880, the rather drab building shows its age, and the eight guest rooms are nothing more than basic. However, the inexpensive Bajan-style food served on the restaurant's ocean-side terrace is a local tradition well worth trying. Sunday's buffet lunch offers a variety of West Indian dishes and is especially popular. Don't show up without a reservation. ☎ 246-433-9445.

Bathsheba

Continuing along the winding coastal road, you come into the picturesque fishing village of Bathsheba. (The locals say BATH-shaba.) It sits on a prime surfing bay with fat hang-ten-type waves crashing to shore in an area known as the **Soup Bowl**. Experienced surfers will have a great time, but the waves and currents are too rough for swimmers, and large oddly shaped rocks create dangerous conditions for novice surfers.

Bathsheba has gained favor with wave-riders from around the world, and its rural quiet is shattered when Barbados plays host to international surfing competitions. At other times, the quaint little

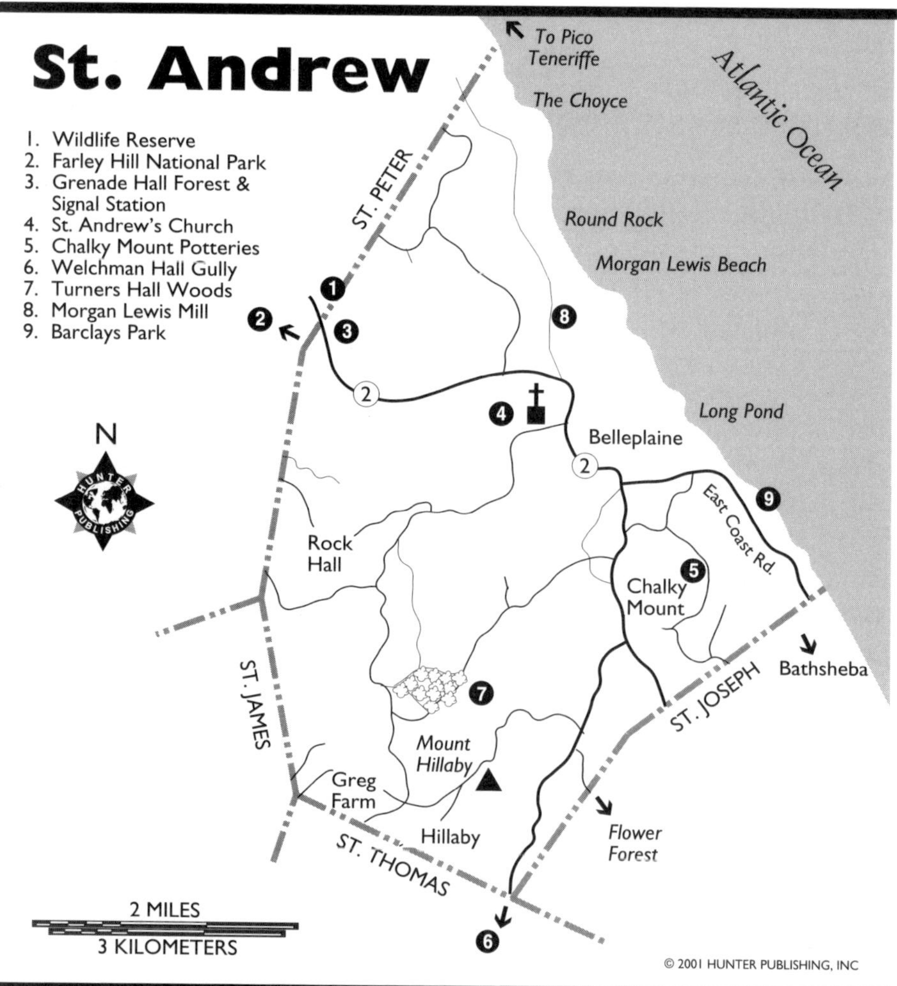

village snoozes in the sun, with more goats and roosters than visitors roaming its narrow streets. Bathsheba is wonderfully photogenic. Bring your camera. Wander aimlessly along the shore. Sit on a cliff and look out to sea. Enjoy the tranquility.

Belleplaine

The **East Coast Road** hugs the shoreline as it meanders northward from Bathsheba toward Belleplaine, about a mile inland in St. Andrew Parish. It follows the old right-of-way for the railroad tracks, which were in use from 1881 to 1938. At that time, the train brought picnic-toting, rum-sipping travelers from Bridgetown to Bathsheba – the island's most popular vacation spot – and Belleplaine, which had the distinction of being the end of the line. Passengers were entertained en route by a snappy band, and danced at the last stop while they waited for their turn on Belleplaine's primitive two-horse carousel.

There are a couple of interesting side trips on this road. The first is to the potteries of **Chalky Mount Village**, on Coggins Hill off Highway 2, east of Haggatt's Orchards. For a terrific view, carefully navigate the tight hillside road that snakes through the village, park at the dead-end, and hike up 550-foot **Chalky Mount**. Remote areas of the east coast are visible from the top.

Residents of Chalky Mount Village have been utilitarian potters for over 300 years, and they welcome visitors. Don't expect fancy workshops or exquisite *objets d'art,* but the centuries-old craft is interesting to watch. Potters turn lumps of clay taken from their hillside into ochre-colored monkey jars (used to keep drinking water cool) and *connerees* (used to keep meat from spoiling). You won't have trouble finding the potters' houses in the small village, but ask at Chalky Mount Bar if you have any doubts.

The second side trip is to **St. Andrew's Church**, a lovely graystone Anglican structure that survived two hurricanes before being condemned and rebuilt in the mid 1800s. Find it just past Belleplaine on Highway 2, between Chalky Mount and **Walker's Sand Dune** (a towering mound that provides the island with building sand). You may not be able to get inside the building, but the front tower looming over the green lawn is interesting to architecture buffs. Besides, a church with such tenacity deserves a visit.

■ North to South - The Best Attractions

St. Lucy Parish stretches coast to coast across the northern curve of Barbados. It possesses some of the island's most stunning scenery. The untamed countryside is sparsely populated and only a few tiny communities are scattered among fields of sugarcane.

At the most northern point on the island's ocean-battered coast, you'll find a dramatic span of stark, rocky terrain punctuated by the amazing and somewhat eerie **Animal Flower Cave.** The cavern got its name from the resident sea worms, or sea anemones, which look like flowers blooming when they extend the tentacles. Very few anemones still live inside the cave, but you may spot some of the tiny yellow or purple marine invertebrates growing in the rock pools. They are short, flexible, worm-like tubes with a central mouth surrounded by thin tentacles lined with stinging cells that paralyze their prey. A capture is fascinating to watch.

The cave was created over thousands of years by ocean waves beating against the limestone shore. If the surf is rough, you may not be able to go inside because salty spray breaks over the 60-foot bluffs, and water rushes into the hollowed-out cliff side with great force. On calm days, a guide will escort you down a short flight of wooden stairs to the slippery-wet cavern floor, where you can explore the vast underground rooms that are lighted by sun streaming through a large, jagged, window-like gap in the rock wall that opens directly to the sea. Stalactites hang from the ceiling, stalagmites grow from the floor, and sinkholes and tidal pools harbor tiny marine animals and plants.

Animal Flower Cave is open daily, 10 am-4 pm. Call ahead to be sure the seas aren't too rough to allow admittance into the cave. The entrance fee is B$7 for adults, B$3.50 for children, and guides appreciate a small tip. ☎ 246-439-8797.

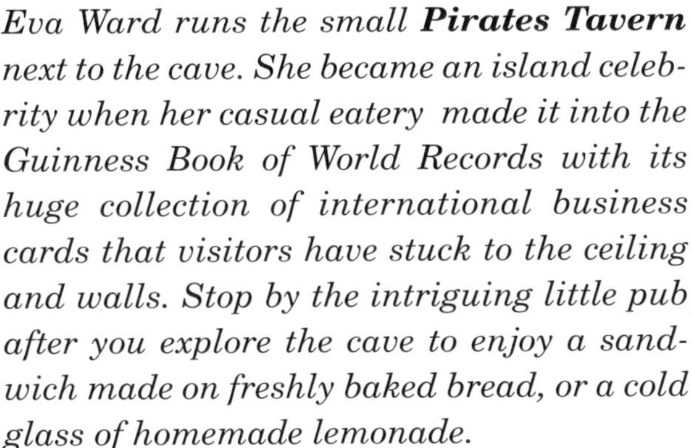

*Eva Ward runs the small **Pirates Tavern** next to the cave. She became an island celebrity when her casual eatery made it into the Guinness Book of World Records with its huge collection of international business cards that visitors have stuck to the ceiling and walls. Stop by the intriguing little pub after you explore the cave to enjoy a sandwich made on freshly baked bread, or a cold glass of homemade lemonade.*

The terrain surrounding the cave has been beaten down to bare rock by wind and salt spray, but take the time to walk along the cliffs and look out across the miles of endless ocean. In the past, this barren soil produced acres of valuable sugarcane on a spread known as Animal Flower Plantation.

Side Trip: The Spout & River Bay

It's well worth detouring a bit off the main highways to visit the far northeast coast – one of the most unchanged regions of Barbados.

Reach the scenic spot of **River Bay** by following the road from Animal Flower Cave south, then taking left turns toward the east until you reach the coast. Bajans come to this barren but picturesque area because of the swimming cove and picnic facilities. Underwater currents are erratic and often strong, so be cautious about swimming, and don't go in at all unless you see residents in the water. The bay gets its name from a stream that flows through the hilly valley and empties into the ocean here.

You can hike less than a mile north along the rugged coast to some salt ponds, then on to a rocky promontory that juts toward the ocean. Here, saltwater shoots up to 100 feet in the air through gaps in the coral cliff, causing a phenomenon called **The Spout.** This spectacle can be seen from a distance, if you don't want to walk out to the bluff.

Cove Bay (Gay's Cove on some maps) and **Little Bay** are farther south. Neither is good for swimming, but the views are fantastic and the ocean has carved interesting sculptures into the limestone cliffs. Hikers will want to travel along the coast on foot, but you can reach the bays by car, if you prefer.

At **Pie Corner**, a village where Arawak and Carib artifacts recently have been unearthed, watch for the sign that directs you toward the coast, past a horse stable and windmill, to Cove Bay. The view from the top of the cliff known as **Paul's Point** is breathtaking. **Pico Teneriffe** is the white 260-foot cliff that juts seaward immediately to the south.

Reach **Little Bay** by turning to the left (north) just before Cove Bay. You may be lucky enough to have this secret spot all to yourself. Again, the beach is too rocky and the water is too turbulent for swimming, but you can climb around the cave-riddled cliffs, explore the tidal pools, and enjoy incredible east-coast views.

The Barbados Wildlife Reserve

Barbados Wildlife Reserve, off Highway 1C in St. Peter Parish, is one of the most interesting attractions on the island. It's set on four acres of lush forest at the top of Farley Hill, across the road from Farley Hill National Park, next to Grenade Hall Forest. It serves as a habitat for a large population of uncaged creatures and gives visitors the uncommon opportunity to observe them at close range.

The **Barbados Primate Research Centre** began the reserve in 1985 with the intent of studying the island's green monkeys, descendants of those brought over as pets from Africa around 1650 by slave traders. Later, developers enlarged the project to include other animals in order to draw visitors. Now, many species reside harmoniously together in a natural environment without cages and go about their activities as if they were living in the wild.

Since nothing prevents them from leaving, the monkeys often go next door to the Grenade Hall Forest to hang out during the day. The best time to catch them at home in the reserve is late in the afternoon, when the staff brings out buckets of fruits and veggies for dinner.

Keep an eye on your possessions. The mischievous primates will steal anything from cameras to backpacks whenever they get a chance.

The world's largest population of **West Indian tortoises** also lives at the refuge. Experts say they are endangered, but you'll question that when you see a great number of them lumbering along the footpaths. During mating season, they are quite conspicuous and totally indiscreet. You can hear them snorting lustfully, like foraging pigs, throughout the compound.

Other species here include **hares** and **mongooses**. You probably won't see the hares, since they sleep during the day, but mongooses are plentiful, and you'll spot the ferret-like mammals scurrying about, just as they do outside the reserve. Don't mistake them for the **agoutis**, which look more like guinea pigs and spend most of their time in underground tunnels. Another similar rodent, the **hutia conga**, is more rabbit-like and also lives in burrows at the refuge.

The agoutis, *hutia congas*, and other non-native animals were donated to the Wildlife Reserve by neighboring islands, England, and the United States. The most interesting are shade-loving **brocket**

deer, **spectacled caimans** (similar to alligators), endangered **iguanas**, and adorable small-clawed **otters**. The only caged creature is a non-poisonous 10-foot **reticulated python** that eats only once a month.

A variety of **birds** perch in trees throughout the forest and Reserve, and several rare species live in a walk-through aviary, including cockatoos, macaws, parrots, and toucans. Brown pelicans and pink flamingos feed on fish in the two lily ponds.

This tropical sanctuary is open daily, 10 am-5 pm, with feeding time scheduled at 4 pm. Ticket prices include admission to nearby Grenade Hall Forest and Signal Station and are priced at B$23 for adults and B$11.50 for children under 12. For additional information, contact the Barbados Primate Research Centre and Wildlife Reserve, ☎ 246-422-8826, fax 422-8946.

Grenade Hall Forest, with its **Signal Station**, is right next door, so you may walk over. Your ticket to the Wildlife Reserve will get you through the gate of this eco-heritage park. The deep forest is accessed via moss-covered coral-stone pathways that loop between towering trees. Green, numbered placards along the way ask trivia questions about the nearby plant or tree labeled with a corresponding number (answers are revealed when you lift a cover). Sage, thought-provoking quotes attributed to Chief Seattle, Charles Darwin, and other astute men are posted here and there throughout the woods, and a description of traditional "bush medicine" is located near the entrance.

The restored signal station at the top of Farley Hill offers a stunning view across the island. Bring binoculars and a camera. Some of the 6,000 pre-Columbian and 19th-century artifacts unearthed during the renovation are displayed on the lower level of the watchtower. Various exhibits explain the use of flags and lights to communicate cross-island before the invention of radios and telephones. The facilities, including a snack bar and souvenir stand, are open daily, 9 am-5 pm. ☎ 246-422-8826, fax 422-8946.

Wear shoes with tread to prevent slipping on the slick stone path.

Farley Hill National Park

Farley Hill National Park, with the ruins of its greathouse, is directly south of the Wildlife Reserve and signal station. Again, the views from the 984-foot cliff are dazzling. The plantation house was restored in 1956, when it served as the setting for Hollywood's production of *Island in the Sun,* starring Harry Belafonte. However, the entire thing went up in smoke a short time later, destroying everything except the stone exterior.

The Parks and Beaches Commission is slowly reviving the grounds, planting new gardens, and clearing the underbrush, but the once-grand mansion is still a burned-out ruin. Originally named Grenade Hall, the oldest section of the imposing house was built around 1818, a date inscribed over an interior archway. Sir Thomas Graham Briggs, a Bajan merchant, moved to the estate in 1856 and renamed it Farley Hill.

Today, the shady grounds are the highlight of the hilltop park. It makes an excellent site for a picnic, and you can roam around the haunting ruins. The park is open daily, 8 am-6 pm. Admission is free, but there's a B$3.50 parking fee.

Side Trip: St. Nicholas Abbey

Not an abbey at all, this 1650-era Jacobean-style greathouse has, of all things, four fireplaces. No one can positively explain either the name or the fireplaces. Historians think the original owner probably insisted on the unnecessary feature simply because the homes of aristocratic Englishmen always had such comforts. However, it's possible that the builder had no imagination and, therefore, followed the British architect's plans without considering the absurdity of constructing heat-producing devices in the tropics.

The name "Nicholas" has two possible explanations. Some say it can be traced to Charles Nicholas, who married Suzanne, the daughter of John Berringer. It was John Berringer's father, Colonel Benjamin Berringer, who constructed the stone mansion on his plantation in the mid-1600s. Others say the name can be attributed to residents of St. Nicholas Parish in England, who occupied the property in the early 1800s. Those who don't mind guessing say "abbey" was added on a whim by a past owner who merely fancied the sound and image of the word.

Visitors are guided through the first floor of the three-story gabled mansion, which is furnished with 18th-century antiques including a Sheraton sideboard and a grandfather clock. A home movie, shot in the 1930s and run twice daily, shows a previous owner and his family on the plantation grounds and in Bridgetown. Rustic buildings behind the main house include a bath house, outhouse, and stables. Other sites on the 420-acre estate are a windmill and watermill used to grind sugarcane during plantation days.

St. Nicholas Abbey is north of Farley Hill and Morgan Lewis Sugar Mill near Cherry Tree Hill. It is open to visitors Monday-Friday, 10 am-3:30 pm. A B$10 entrance fee is charged, and guests may purchase snacks, lunch, and afternoon tea in the small Calabash Café. ☎ 246-422-8725.

Morgan Lewis Sugar Mill

Morgan Lewis Sugar Mill is the only intact windmill remaining from the hundreds that once dotted the countryside. The mills were used from the 17th through the 19th centuries to crush juice from cane to produce sugar. The Morgan Lewis mill has been restored with sails and points on all the arms and is fully functional; once a month, between December and June, the public is invited to watch the mill in action under the power of full sails. During windier months, the sails are removed to prevent damage.

Dutch Jews introduced wind-driven mills to Barbados in the 1600s, a technology they learned in Brazil, and the Morgan Lewis mill was probably built about 1776. However, the mill's working parts were made in England in 1908, most likely to repair and update the original machinery. The structure was added to the World Monuments List in 1996 as one of the most endangered sites on earth.

You'll spot the windmill on a hillside as you follow road signs east from Farley Hill Park, or southeast, through the mahogany trees on Cherry Tree Hill, from St. Nicholas Abbey. All along the way, and after you reach Morgan Lewis Sugar Mill, you'll have sweeping views of the east coast. Visitors are admitted at a charge of B$10 for adults and B$5 for children, Monday-Saturday, 9 am-5 pm, ☎ 246-422-7429.

Follow Highway 2 south to the **Flower Forest**, in St. Joseph Parish, a 50-acre former plantation with hundreds of indigenous and imported trees, shrubs, and flowers. Winding paths lead past thriving vegetation that has been allowed to grow almost untamed, and signs give each species a Latin and common name and designate its country of origin.

Most likely, monkeys will swing from the trees as you follow the mapped trail into the fragrant forest. Benches are scattered about so that you can sit and enjoy the sights, sounds, and scents of nature. Some of the highlights include bearded fig trees, dozens of varieties of palms, colorful orchids and hibiscus, and an interesting collection of medicinal plants.

Refreshments are available from the snack bar beside the main building, and you may want to spend a few minutes browsing through the adjacent Best of Barbados shop. Admission to the Flower Forest is B$13.80 for adults and B$6.90 for children, and visitors are welcome daily, 9 am-5 pm. ☎ 246-433-8152, fax 433-8365.

***Mount Hillaby**, the highest point on Barbados, is a quick detour to the north off Highway 2. Turn toward the west at **Baxters**, and follow the road up White Hill to the village of Hillaby. A left turn at the T-junction next to a church puts you on a narrow road that goes most of the way to the top, a height of 1,160 feet. Of course, the views are fantastic, and you can hike up to the windy peak for even more spectacular views-especially over the hills and ravines to the east.*

Welchman Hall

Welchman Hall Tropical Forest Reserve (formerly Welchman Hall Gully), in St. Thomas Parish, is one of the top natural attractions on Barbados. It's a three-quarter-mile ravine that was once part of a vast network of underground tunnels and caves that cracked

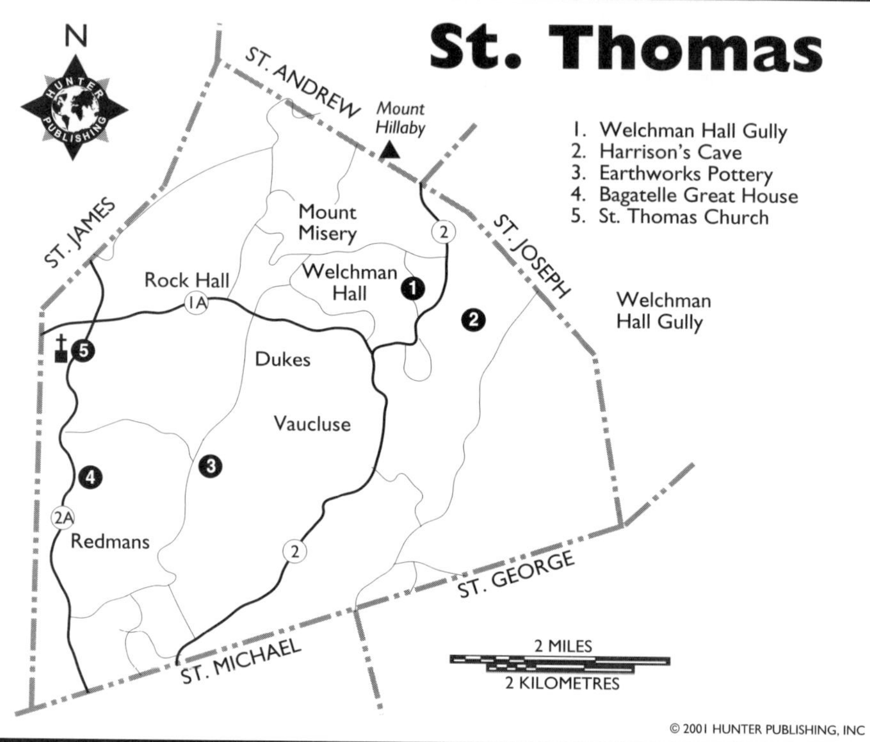

through the island's limestone cap. The steep-sided gully resulted when the roof of one of these caves collapsed.

The ravine was named for an early Welsh settler, General Williams, who originally owned the land. It is home to more than 200 species of plants and trees. The Barbados National Trust now manages the property and has labeled about 50 of the plants that grow along an easily navigated path through the shaded reserve. A stroll through the dramatic, spice-scented passageway will give you an idea of the lush vegetation that grew on the island before it was cleared for cultivation.

During early morning and late afternoon, watch for green monkeys romping through the underbrush and swinging from the trees. Bats live in small caves carved into the limestone walls of the ravine, and a variety of birds nest in the jungle-like trees. Plan to take the time to sit for a while on one of the shaded benches that are placed in particularly lovely spots along the trail.

Park at either the north or south ends of the reserve, which is off Highway 2A near Harrison's Cave. Welchman Hall is open Monday-Saturday, 9 am-5 pm, and admission is B$12 for adults and B$6 for children. ☎ 246-438-6671.

Harrison's Cave, just south of Welchman Hall Tropical Forest Reserve, is an immense underground cavern with waterfalls, lakes, and narrow tunnels connecting secondary chambers. Visitors tour the cave on an electric tram and wear protective helmets, but you'll get an opportunity to get out and take pictures several times during the 45-minute trip.

Locals knew about the caverns for many years, but in 1970 a cave specialist from Denmark discovered a new entrance into an unexplored section. This sparked the attention of the National Conser-

vation Commission (Codrington House, St. Michael, ☎ 246-425-1200), and an effort began to open the spectacular cave to the public – a feat that took over a decade of work.

You'll see only about a mile of the three-mile cavern, including the sensational Great Hall, a split-level 2,500-square-foot room 120 feet underground. The Cascade Falls plunge 40 feet into a pool in one of the smaller chambers, and throughout the cavern, still-developing stalactites and stalagmites form intriguing figures that are illuminated by indirect lighting. At one point in the tour, all the lights are turned off, plunging you into total darkness.

A short nature trail runs behind the visitors' center, which houses a snack bar and gift shop. Reservations are accepted for tours that are conducted daily between 8:45 am-4 pm. Call early during busy tourist season, when busloads of visitors arrive throughout the day. Tickets are B$17.50 for adults, B$8.75 for children. ☎ 246-438-6640.

Orchid World

Farther south, in the middle of the island, Highway 3 leads to **Orchid World** in St. George Parish, a dazzling display of colorful flowers located in a rain-prone area more than 800 feet above sea level. T-Bert Allman and his staff of orchid lovers tend the dainty blooms in a gorgeous setting of waterfalls and grottos.

Exact growing conditions are provided for the thousands of flowers in several houses and shaded gardens. A path winds through the lovely grounds, and information boards identify the many types of orchids. Facilities include a snack bar and gift shop. Visitors are welcome daily, 9 am-5 pm. Admission is B$13.80 for adults and B$6.90 for children. ☎ 246-433-0306.

Gun Hill Signal Station

Follow signs from Orchid World south on Highway 3 to Fusilier Road and Gun Hill Signal Station. It was built in 1818 on a hill 700 feet above sea level to serve as a strategic link in the military's chain of communication stations. The restored stone and brick structure presents an incredible panoramic view that extends north over the hills of St. Thomas Parish and southwest to the harbor at Bridgetown.

A restaurant near the entrance to the landscaped property serves Bajan snacks. When you leave, notice the lion carved of white stone at the base of the hill. It was crafted in 1868 out of a block of limestone by Henry Wilkinson, the adjutant-general of the British forces stationed on the island. A Latin inscription on a nearby rock translates: *It shall rule from the rivers to the sea, and from the sea to the ends of the earth.* Some say Wilkinson was referring to the lion, others believe he meant to proclaim England's power. Gun Hill Signal Station is open Monday-Saturday, 9 am-5 pm, and tickets are B$9.20 for adults and B$4.60 for children. ☎ 246-429-1358.

Francia Plantation House

Francia Plantation House is directly south of Gun Hill. Watch for signs directing you along a rough road to the landscaped gardens that surround the lovely, privately owned plantation house that's been featured in several international publications. Descendants of the original owner still live in the mansion, but visitors are welcome to tour the ground floor and vast English-style gardens.

Built around 1900 by Frenchman Rene Mouraille, the red-roofed structure features a dramatic front entrance with a broad staircase leading to a porch framed by three archways. Inside, the focal point is the dining room with its grand chandelier, long antique mahogany table, and extensive collection of silver and china. A finely furnished living area opens onto a covered veranda overlooking a garden, where guests are served a cool drink. Be sure to notice the antique maps dating back to 1522 that hang in the foyer and main room.

Spend a few minutes walking the grounds to see the well-tended fountains and flowers. Francia Plantation House is open to visitors Monday-Friday, 10 am-4 pm, at a cost of B$9 for adults and B$4.50 for children. ☎ 246-429-0474.

Adventures

On Water

With 70 miles of coastline, Barbados has enough sandy beaches and deserted coves to meet every vacationer's dream of paradise. The Caribbean side has long stretches of fine, gold-tinted, white sand fronting calm water. As you round the southern curve, the water becomes a bit more active, and the coral-flaked sand has a pink blush. On the windswept east coast, small strips of sand and rocky shore are tucked between boulders that lie below towering, jagged cliffs bearing the scars of huge Atlantic breakers crashing against their limestone facades.

Generally, swimmers, snorkelers, and water skiers gravitate to the west coast; windsurfers take to the breezier waters off the south shore; and experienced surfers tackle waves on the east side.

Pick up a complimentary copy of **Sporting Barbados** *at hotels and sports-oriented locations around the island for current information about all types of Bajan sports. Some information is available online at www.sportingbarbados.com.*

■ Beaches

All beaches are public, and public right-of-ways are government mandated along private-property lines. However, only guests may use the lounge chairs, towels, and facilities of waterfront hotels and restaurants.

Vendors are showing up more and more frequently on Bajan beaches, but, for the most part, they're polite entrepreneurs who quickly accept "No, thanks" as your final answer. You may run into young men who offer to show you the way to remote coves or sites outside the main tourist areas. Of course, they expect a tip, and you

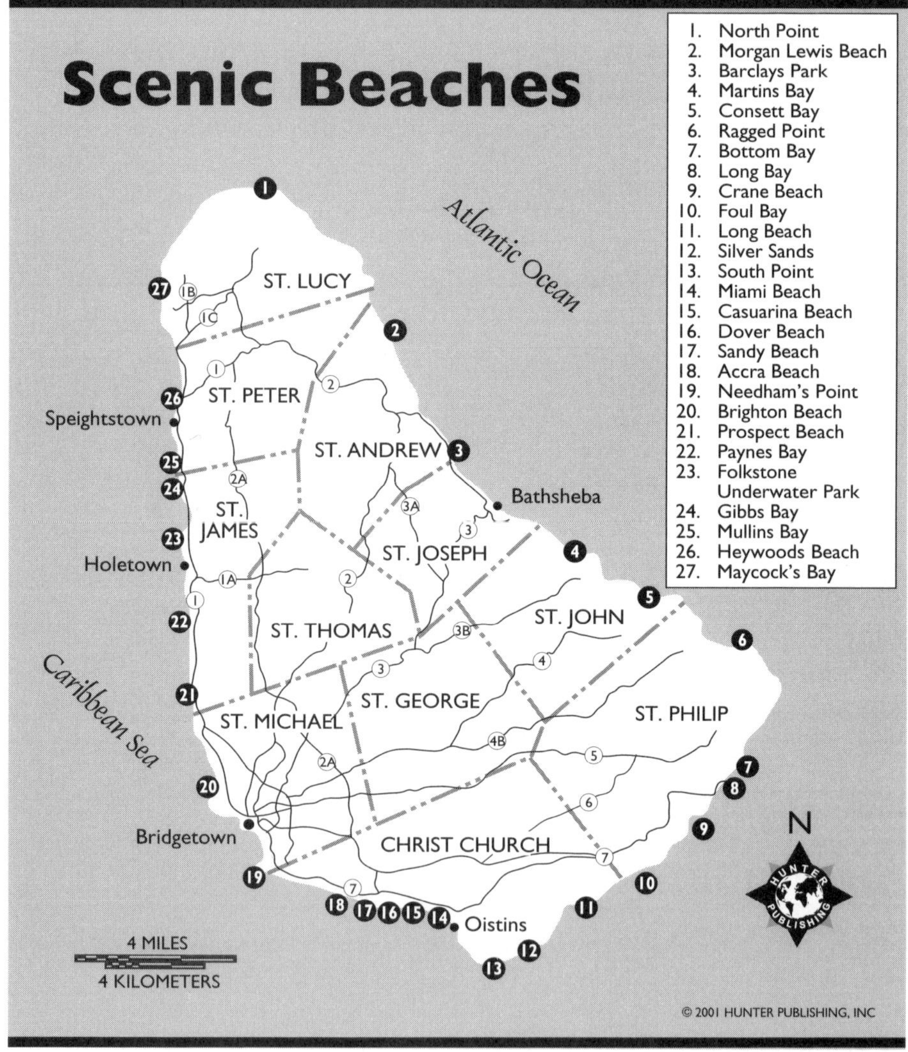

Opposite: Andromeda Gardens

Above: Chattel Village (Cottage Shops), Holetown
Opposite: Beach at Sam Lord's Castle
Below: Sam Lord's Castle

Above: Sunbury House
Opposite: Bathsheba Beach
Below: Gun Hill Signal Station

Above: Cobbler's Cove Resort
Opposite: North Coast from Animal Flower Cave
Below: Catamaran Along the Gold Coast

usually don't need their services, but accept their help, if you want. Just take the usual safety precautions.

Watch for red warning flags that alert swimmers to strong currents and rough seas. Unsafe conditions most often occur along the north and east coasts, but choppy waves and undertows occasionally make swimming dangerous in other areas.

There are no nude beaches on the island, and Bajans have a strong sense of modesty and propriety.

Watersports equipment is available on many western and southern beaches.

Be sure that you know whether rates are in US or Barbados dollars. Rates are sometimes negotiable, especially on a slow day during the off-season.

Snorkel in roped-off or secluded areas. Every year, a few tourists are injured by boats or jet-skis while snorkeling in busy open water. Remember that you're almost invisible to people enjoying motorized watersports.

West Coast

You will find excellent beaches from Bridgetown, in the south, to Speightstown, in the north. The most popular are:

Brighton Beach, site of **Malibu Beach Club**, is just north of the deep-water harbor at the edge of Bridgetown. Cruise-ship passengers often head here, so expect a crowd. Malibu offers watersports, full meals from the grill, drinks at the bar, and tours of the **West Indies Rum Distillery**. ☎ 246-425-9393.

Prospect Beach to **Paynes Bay** is home to a string of hotels and good seaside restaurants. Watersports equipment is available, and you can park near the Coach House and Bombas or farther south near Il Tempio at Fitts Village.

The beaches north and south of **Holetown** offer good snorkeling and swimming, and a variety of places to pick up a snack or drinks. The area directly off the beach in front of the **Lone Star Restau-**

Opposite: Earthworks Pottery

rant is a favorite turtle-spotting site. **Folkestone Underwater Park** is just north of Holetown. It includes a two-mile marine reserve with an artificial reef and terrific beach facilities.

Gibbs Beach and **Mullins Beach** are separated by a close-in underwater reef on a superb stretch of picture-postcard sand. You'll find shady areas, uncrowded eateries and shops, and a few places to rent watersports equipment. This is a fairly quiet area with expensive private homes and a few pricey resorts. Look for parking right on Highway 1, toward the northern end of Mullins Beach.

If you're in the **Speightstown** area, you'll find calm water and a good beach behind **Mango's Restaurant.** North of town, the highway bypass runs past Almond Beach Village on **Heywood Beach**, and the new Port St. Charles residential compound. Just past the cement plant, on the main highway, turn left at the junction with Highway 1B to **Maycock Bay**. Two steep paths lead down to a long, narrow strip of sand and the ruins of a fort.

South Coast

Carlisle Bay runs south from the **Careenage** in Bridgetown for about a mile to **Needham's Point** in the **Garrison** area. Cruise-ship passengers and locals crowd the beach, but there are plenty of places to eat, shop, and rent watersports equipment. You can rent lounge chairs, and snorkeling equipment at the **Boatyard Bar.**

There are good beaches with wonderful surf, one after another along the southern coast of huge Christ Church Parish from **Hastings** to **Oistins**. This was the first area to draw large numbers of investors during the island's initial tourist boom, so the network of affordable services along Highway 7 is excellent.

The beaches, marine life, and offshore reefs have suffered somewhat, but, unless you visited many years ago, you're unlikely to notice. The Bajan government has conservation measures in place to protect and rebuild the beaches. Artificial reefs are beginning to grow and harbor aquatic life – and tourists just keep coming.

If you're a watersports enthusiast, you can hardly choose a bad beach along this coast. Some to try:

Accra Beach has a parking lot off Highway 7 near the Chefette Restaurant. The waves are about right for body surfing, and you can rent or buy almost anything you need for a perfect day at the beach. Expect a crowd, especially on weekends.

Sandy Beach has a good stretch of white sand and calm, shallow water, making it popular with locals and the many tourists who stay in the **Worthington** area. Park on one of the little side streets off Highway 7.

Dover Beach is the site of **Charles' Watersports**, which rents all kinds of equipment. Restrooms and eateries are available, and you can park in the lot off Dover Road, which runs south from Highway 7.

Casuarina Beach is a tropical dream beach in the Maxwell area, with parking off Maxwell Coast Road. You'll find excellent facilities, a wide white-sand beach, and turquoise water that is often perfect for both swimming and beginner level windsurfing.

Miami Beach, at Oistins, is wide, breezy, and extremely popular with locals late on weekday afternoons and throughout the weekends. Beginner and intermediate windsurfers enjoy the flat side-shore winds.

Southeast Coast

From South Point, the coast turns northeastward, and the watersports turn more lively. Turn south off Enterprise Coast Road to get to the following:

Silver Sands Beach offers some of the best conditions for windsurfing in the Caribbean. Wave sailors show up daily from November through July to take advantage of the windy season, and both participants and observers hang out at the beach bar of the popular **Silver Rock Resort**.

Long Beach extends over a mile east from Inch Marlowe Point. This is a lovely, but less visited, stretch of sand with few facilities. Bring your own equipment and snacks.

Foul Bay is another lightly touristed beach, but not at all foul. It got its name from British sailors who found the area too blustery for good anchoring. A signed road leads down to a parking area near the water that is bordered by a wide, windswept swath of sand fringed with sea grape vines. You'll likely see more colorful fishing boats than people, but locals picnic here on weekends.

Crane Beach is the site of **The Crane**, the oldest hotel on Barbados, and one of the most photographed beaches in the West Indies. If you want to go through the hotel to the beach, you'll have to pay a B$10 fee, which can be redeemed in food or beverages at the bar. You can also park on a side road, south of the hotel, and take the stairs down to the beach. Either way, you'll love this marvelous place. The fine sand is flecked with pink coral, and the water is perfect for swimming and body surfing. Watersports equipment, lounge chairs, and refreshments are available.

Long Bay, below Sam Lord's Castle, and **Bottom Bay**, just to the north, are beautiful. Both have fine, palm-shaded sand that stretches between rugged cliffs and azure waters. The beaches are just right for naps and picnics, and rolling waves make for good body surfing.

East Coast

From **Ragged Point** to **North Point**, the east coast is lined with rugged cliffs that tower over fabulous bays. With very few exceptions, this is an area for serious surfers and adventurous explorers – but not swimmers. Strong currents, jumbo-sized boulders, and crashing surf create dangerous conditions for all but the most advanced wave riders.

The cliff over **Consett Bay** provides a gorgeous panoramic view, the fishing village at **Martin's Bay** is quaintly picturesque, and **Bathsheba** is the best place to watch champion surfers tackle the **Soup Bowl**. Farther north, **Barclays Park** offers showers, toilets, and a restaurant, but the water is still too rough for most people. It is, however, a good place to picnic and stroll.

Morgan Lewis Beach, north of Barclays, is about three miles of undeveloped coast. Find it by taking a turn toward the coast onto an unmarked, overgrown road at the south end of Boscobelle, and following it downhill to the beach. This is an ideal area for long walks, unhurried picnics, and leisurely explorations.

■ Scuba Diving & Snorkeling

Barbados' underwater attractions are as captivating as those on land. Reefs and wrecks harbor abundant marine life, and the crystalline waters provide superb visibility for divers and snorkelers.

Hawksbill turtles and other large sea animals live along the barrier reefs a mile or two from shore. Closer in, dense plant life growing on fringe reefs that parallel the shore serve as habitats for sea horses, eels, and frog fish. Hundreds of wrecks in Carlisle Bay and along the west coast shelter everything from small tropical fish to barracuda.

With nothing more than a mask and snorkel, you can spot colorful fish feeding around rocks and among healthy corals, sponges, and sea fans along shallow sections of the fringe reefs. Certified divers spot large corals, sea whips, and gorgonians during boat dives to pristine barrier reefs. Thousands of small fish swarm the barriers and attract larger pelagic fish. Visibility is dependably 40 to 70 feet year round, and increases to 100 feet during the summer months. The water temperature averages 80° year-round.

Experienced divers consider Barbados' underwater wrecks some of the best in the Caribbean. Three of the most popular lie in **Carlisle Bay Marine Park** near Bridgetown. This historic bay was the site of 300 years of maritime defense, and the waters are littered with several ships and their antique memorabilia. The ***Berwyn*** (or Berwind) is in only eight to 25 feet of water, making it ideal for beginners. It's a 70-foot French tug boat that sank mysteriously in 1919.

The MV *Eillon* is near the *Berwyn* in 15 to 53 feet of water. It was impounded by the Barbados Coast Guard in 1990 because it was carrying illegal drugs, and intentionally sunk (without the drugs) in 1996. Close by, a 46-foot fishing boat called the ***C-Treck*** or ***Sea Trek*** lies in 43 feet of water. Its concrete hull shelters eels and a variety of other aquatic wildlife.

Folkestone Marine Park, near Holetown, is interesting for both snorkelers and divers. Some coral and associated fish lie in only five feet of water, but the premier dive site is the SS ***Stavronikita***, found in 70 to 130 feet of water. The 365-foot Greek freighter is one of the largest wreck dives in the Caribbean. She was intentionally sunk in November 1978 to create an artificial reef and now sits upright on the ocean floor.

Other west coast wrecks include the *Lord* ***Combermere***, in Batts Rock Bay, and the ***Pamir*** in 50 feet of water off Heywoods, near Almond Beach Village. Experienced divers will want to visit her sister ship, ***Friars Craig***, in 165 feet of water in Carlisle Bay.

Among Barbados' reefs, **Bell Buoy** and **Shark Bank** provide coral variety and interesting sea life off the southwest coast. Named for its dome shape, Bell Buoy sits in 20-60 feet of water, and has throngs of fish feeding on its forests of brown coral. Shark Bank is better known for sea turtles and parrotfish than sharks, and experienced divers enjoy descending to depths of 145 feet. Farther north on the island's Caribbean side, **Dottins** is the place to feed turtles and observe thousands of tropical fish. Several coral reefs in **Maycock Bay** draw rays and barracudas.

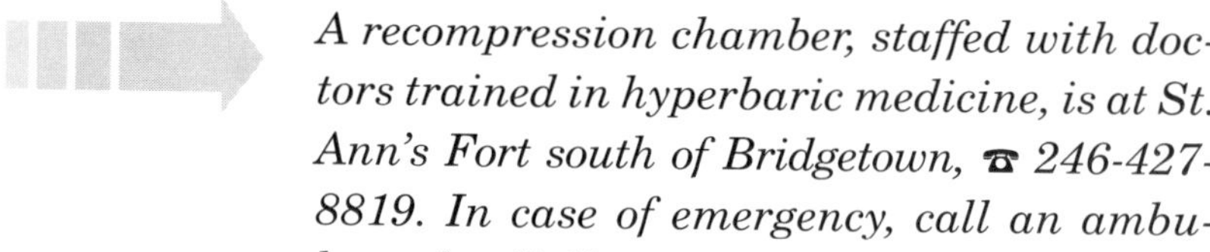

A recompression chamber, staffed with doctors trained in hyperbaric medicine, is at St. Ann's Fort south of Bridgetown, ☎ *246-427-8819. In case of emergency, call an ambulance by dialing* ☎ *115.*

Expect to pay around US$70 for a resort course geared toward strong swimmers with no dive experience. One-tank dives run about US$55-US$60 with equipment, US$40 without, and two-tank dives cost approximately US$85-US$90 with equipment, US$70 if you have your own gear.

Prices vary greatly among dive shops, and you may be able to negotiate lower prices during slack tourist season – which, ironically, is summer, the best time to dive Bajan waters.

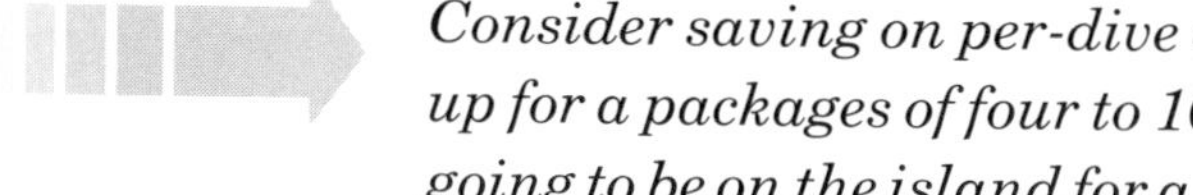

Consider saving on per-dive costs by signing up for a packages of four to 10 dives, if you're going to be on the island for a week or more.

All divers must purchase a **Rescue the Reef** dive pass at a cost of US$5. Most operators include this fee in the price of their dive packages, but ask when you call for reservations. Occasionally, the additional charge is tacked on to the quoted rate.

Dive Operators

Dive Barbados arranges dive vacations through several hotels using local dive operators. Call them for details on current packages. ☎ 800-513-5845 or 954-467-3173. Contact **The Professional As-**

sociation of Dive Operators for a listing of Bajan members, ☎ 246-426-4043.

The following dive shops are staffed by PADI instructors and dive masters who offer certification at various levels and lead scuba trips to the island's best reefs and wrecks. Most also provide snorkeling trips or allow snorkelers to go along on dive trips.

West Side Scuba Centre
Baku Beach, Holetown, St. James
☎ *246-432-2558, fax 432-2558, e-mail peterg@sunbeach.net*

This is an eco-dive shop that ties up to mooring buoys to avoid dropping an anchor near delicate reefs. Baku Beach facilities include two restaurants, a bar, restrooms, and a swimming pool.

Hightide Watersports
Coral Reef Club, St. James
☎ *800-513-5763 or 246-432-0931, fax 432-0931*
www.divehightide.com; e-mail hightide@sunbeach.net

Divers go out in small groups on a custom-outfitted boat with medic-trained PADI instructors and dive masters to explore wrecks and reefs. Drift and night dives are also available.

Exploresub Barbados
St. Lawrence Gap, Christ Church
☎ *246-435-6542, fax 435-8214, e-mail x-sub@caribsurf.com*

Barbados' Blue and Gold Dive Team offer scuba and underwater photography courses along with orientation dives to some of the best dive sites. They also arrange underwater weddings performed by a licensed minister. Trips go out on a 44-foot Super Cat Jet Drive catamaran equipped for diving.

The Dive Shop
Pebbles Beach, St. Michael
☎ *800-693-3483 or 426-9947, fax 426-2031, www.caribnet.net/diveshop*

Check with this shop for package vacations that include hotel and unlimited daytime boat dives. The operator has been in business for more than 30 years, and offers unhurried one- and two-tank dives for small groups each day at 10am, noon, and 2:30 pm. Twice a week, east-coast dives are available.

Bubbles Galore Dive Shop
Sandy Beach Island Resorts, Worthing, Christ Church
☎ 430-0354, fax 436-8806, e-mail bubbles@caribsurf.com

PADI instructors conduct certification courses and take divers on one- and two-tank dives to a variety of sites aboard a 31-foot Bertram equipped with a toilet and changing facilities. The staff speaks English, German, and Dutch.

Coral Isle Divers
The Careenage, Bridgetown
☎ 246-434-8377 or 432-1219 (after hours), fax 431-9068

Coral Isle offers four scheduled dives daily to a variety of dive sites off both the south and west coasts. Their catamaran, *Bubbles*, has twin 240 turbo-charged diesel motors and is the most spacious and comfortable dive boat on the island.

Dive Boat Safari
Grand Barbados Beach Resort, Aquatic Gap, St. Michael
☎ 246-427-4350 or 429-8216 or 426-4000, ext. 7631

This facility schedules three dive trips to reefs and wrecks on the south and west coasts each day. Night dives and special-request dives can be arranged.

Reefers & Wreckers Inc.
Kings Beach Hotel, Road View, St. Peter
☎/fax 422-5450 or 424-6343 (after hours)
e-mail scubadiving@caribsurf.com

The name says it all. Check out this operation south of Speightstown for two-tank dives that go out each morning. Amateur and semi-professional underwater cameras may be rented for spectacular photo ops.

*For diving and snorkeling equipment, swimsuits, and beach accessories at duty-free prices, check out **Hazell's Water World & Divers Supply**, in the Boatyard Complex on Bay Street in Bridgetown. ☎ 246-426-4043 or 228-6734, fax 436-5726, e-mail braemar@sunbeach.net.*

Atlantis Submarine and **Atlantis Seatrec** offer high-tech adventures for those who want to explore underwater sites without getting wet.

The 65-foot air-conditioned submarine accommodates 48 passengers and has 26 large viewports that allow excellent visibility. During the 45-minute tour, the sub descends to about 150 feet to allow guests to see colorful reefs, marine plants, and sea creatures along a sunken shipwreck.

Seatrec is an air-conditioned semi-submersible vessel with an above-water deck and underwater viewports that allow passengers a closeup look at shallow coral reefs and shipwrecks. Snorkeling tours with a PADI-certified diver last 1½ hours.

For information and reservations, contact Atlantis Submarines, Shallow Draught Harbour, Bridgetown, ☎ 246-436-8929.

■ Surfing & Windsurfing

Bajan supestar Brian Talma, one of the top wave performers in the world, touts his island's surfing attributes around the globe. And rightly so, since Barbados is ranked among the world's best windsurfing destinations. Its southeast coast enjoys a superb combination of excellent trade winds and challenging reef conditions that draws international sportsmen and big-prize competitions, including the Barbados Cup, an annual pro sailboarding event.

Even beginners enjoy riding the soft swells and gentle reef breaks off the south coast from Worthing's Sandy Beach to Oistin's Miami Beach. Advanced windsurfers head for **Silver Sands**, on the eastern side of South Point, where they find a steady row of waves slowly breaking over a deep reef. Surfboard experts tackle the pounding Atlantic in the world famous **Soup Bowl**, off Bathsheba's rugged shore.

Soup Bowl got its name in the 1960s when spectators noticed that wiped-out surfers struggling in the frothy waves off Bathsheba looked like veggies bobbing in a boiling broth.

Adventures

If you're interested in dedicating a large portion of your vacation to windsurfing or surfboarding, several hotels and tour companies offer package deals. Check with **Sailboard Vacations: Barbados**, ☎ 800-252-1070, fax 781-829-8809, e-mail sbv@ix.netcom.com; **Silver Sands Resort**, Silver Sands, Christ Church, ☎ 246-428-6001, fax 428-3758; **Silver Rock Adventure Sports Resort**, Silver Sands, Christ Church, ☎ 246-428-2866, fax 428-3687.

Equipment and instruction for every type of surfing are available from the watersports centers at both Silver Sands Resort and Silver Rock Resort (see above). Group lessons run about US$40-US$65 per hour, and equipment rents for US$25-US$35 per hour, US$75-US$90 per day, and US$285-US$350 per week. Both of the following shops offer well-maintained equipment at good rates: **Charles Watersports**, Dover Beach, Christ Church, ☎ 246-428-9550, fax 428-9550; and **Club Mistral**, Maxwell, Christ Church, ☎ 246-428-7277, fax 428-2878.

■ Parasailing & Paragliding

The view couldn't be better than from high in the sky over Bajan waters. You'll spot parasailing boats along the beaches on the west and south coasts, and the watersports centers at major hotels sometimes make arrangements for you. If you don't connect with the right people, contact **Skyrider Parasail** on Bay Street in St. Michael Parish, ☎ 246-435-0570, or the **Barbados Paragliding Association**, ☎ 246-423-8976, fax 246-424-3425.

Expect to pay about B$50-B$75 for a quick lesson and 10-minute ride. You'll get the best rates outside of tourist season.

■ Boating & Sailing

Barbados hosts an active yacht-racing season highlighted by the **Mount Gay Regatta** in May. Beginning in January and continuing through September, Bajan and international competitors vie for bragging rights and prizes in a series of events organized by **The Barbados Yacht Club**, ☎ 246-427-1125.

If you're arriving by private boat, check in with Customs and Immigration at the Deep Water Harbour on the northern edge of Bridgetown. The main anchorage is Carlisle Bay, near the Careenage in the center of the capital. An assortment of boat-related goods and services is provided at **The Boatyard,** ☎ 246-436-2622.

Since Barbados is almost a hundred miles from its nearest neighbor, it's not a popular port for boats touring the Eastern Caribbean. However, there's no shortage of locally based operators who offer day and evening cruises around the island.

The view of Barbados from the water is spectacular. You'll get an offshore look at natural attractions and glimpse celebrity mansions, secluded villas, and dazzling resorts that can't be seen from the road. Stops offshore allow snorkeling or swimming with sea turtles and colorful fish above marvelous coral reefs. Party boats feature unlimited drinks and booming reggae music. Evening cruises emphasize leisurely romance.

Rates and activities vary, but most cruises leave out of Bridgetown's Shallow Harbour and provide unlimited drinks. Many also include transportation from major hotels, lunch, snorkeling equipment, and some type of entertainment.

Cruise Operators

Limbo Lady

☎ 246-420-5418, fax 420-3254, e-mail limbolady@sunbeach.net

The entertaining and knowledgeable captain of this 44-foot CSY yacht is Patrick Gonsalves. He customizes daytime and sunset cruises for individuals and small groups that include a leisurely sail up the west coast. A full catered lunch and unlimited drinks are included in the daytime cruise. Sunset trips include champagne, hors d'oeuvres, and live entertainment.

Secret Love

☎ 246-432-1972

Small groups swim with turtles or snorkel over the *Berwyn* wreck before enjoying a meal or snacks and drinks aboard this 41-foot Morgan yacht with a roomy deck that offers both sun and shade. Private charters allow passengers to celebrate a special event at a secluded cove.

Small Cats

☎ *246-421-6419 or 231-1585, e-mail smallcats@sunbeach.net*

No more than 12 passengers go along on each sailing of this 30-foot Stiletto catamaran. Three- and five-hour cruises make stops to feed a family of turtles in a secluded bay and snorkel over a coral reef. The longer trip includes lunch, and all cruises have complimentary drinks and snorkeling equipment.

Rubaiyat

☎ *246-435-9913*

Scheduled trips on this 50-foot catamaran range from five-hour lunch and four-hour dinner cruises to three-hour sunset sails. The most popular charter is the longest trip that includes a barbecue buffet, open bar, and two stops for snorkeling and swimming.

Why Not

☎ *246-230-3792 or 429-8580 (after hours), fax 427-6007*

Captain Ron takes passengers on two- to five-hour private or small-group cruises aboard his beautiful 36-foot catamaran. Choose a snorkeling trip to a secluded cove, a lunch or dinner excursion, or a moonlight sail. The bar opens when the boat turns toward home port.

Stiletto III,

☎ *246-231-3829, fax 429-8967*

Stiletto IV

☎ *246-230-3495, fax 418-0002, e-mail stiletto@funbarbados.com*

The Allen brothers run these sister cats with spacious sun-and-shade decks. Peter, captain of III, and Graham, captain of IV, are friendly, experienced guides who take small groups to swim with the sea turtles. The five-hour lunch cruise features an on-board buffet and drinks. The intimate sunset cruise sets sail with no more than 10 couples, each supplied with their own bottle of champagne, for a leisurely trip up the coast. Hors d'oeuvres and open bar are included.

Heat Wave

☎ *246-423-7871, fax 430-0293*
e-mail hwscb@caribsurf.com

Passengers have plenty of room on this 57-foot catamaran. Trips up the west coast include complimentary drinks, a barbecue lunch, and stops to snorkel and swim with the turtles. The popular Wet 'n'

Wild cruise features banana boat rides, and use of jet skis, kayaks, and windsurfers.

Tiami Cruises
☎ *246-430-0900*

Swim and snorkel from the deck of this luxurious catamaran during a champagne breakfast cruise, lunchtime buffet excursion, or romantic sunset sail. The friendly crew takes care of all the details so passengers can relax and enjoy the trip. Special requests for entertainment, customized meals, and favorite watersports can be handled for private charters.

MV *Harbour Master*
☎ *246-430-0900*

This huge 100-foot boat has the largest floating bar in the Caribbean. With four decks, freshwater showers, air-conditioned areas, and a built-in retractable semi-submersible, the Harbour Master is the only vessel of its kind in the world. For that reason alone, you should try it. But, it has other compelling temptations, as well. The upper Sky Deck has room for sunning and relaxing, the chef prepares magnificent buffets, and the boat stops in a secluded bay for swimming and snorkeling. Starlight cruises feature live entertainment by popular Bajan bands.

Jolly Roger
☎ *246-436-6424*

It's party time all the time on this wooden schooner built to resemble a 300-year-old pirate ship. Of course, only a robust lunch would do for this reveling horde of rum-spiked swashbucklers. During a stop off the coast of Holetown, passengers swing from the yardarm, jump from the poop deck, and dance to the pounding beat of hot island music. If someone decides to get married under the skull-and-crossbones sail, an authentic pirate will step forward to carry out the formalities.

■ Fishing

Fishing for food and profit has been a way of life for Bajans for centuries, and once tourists began arriving, fishing for sport caught on in a big way. The very good possibility of pulling a monster out of the calm azure waters off Barbados's west coast is enticing, even for those who don't ordinarily care for deep-sea adventures.

Several powerboats and sailing vessels run half- and full-day charters geared toward both novices and experts who want to try their luck at reeling in big-game fish. Catches include barracuda, kingfish (wahoo), marlin, tuna, and dolphin (dorado).

Recent records set by fishermen competing in tournaments sponsored by the Barbados Game Fishing Association (BGFA) include a 505-lb blue marlin, a 78.25-lb sailfish, and a 167.5-lb yellow fin tuna. But the big-daddy of them all hangs at the Grantley Adams Airport : a 910-lb blue marlin caught in 1996 by Graham Manning.

If you want to head out to the deep blue sea to watch or participate in a few hours of exhilarating big-game fishing, contact one of the outfitters listed below. Most charter rates include tackle, bait, snacks, drinks, and transportation from your hotel. Full-day excursions usually include lunch and cost around US$700 per boat. Half-day charters run about US$350, but don't include lunch. Some operators allow you to keep the fish you catch, others don't, so ask before you book. If you're interested in sharing a charter, check around for a company that will match you with other fishermen.

Barracuda Too

☎ *246-426-7252, fax 429-4148, e-mail steve_burke@themutual.com*

Captain Steve Burke and his tournament crew hold the record for a couple of big-game catches made on the 41-foot *Barracuda Too*. Anyone who books a charter is challenged to break an official BGFA record and win a free day of fishing.

Cannon Charters

☎ *246-424-6107, fax 421-7582*
e-mail cannon@sunbeach.net, www.fishingbarbados.com

This family run company takes passengers on a 42-foot Hatteras convertible powered by twin 430hp engines. Equipment is top-of-the-line and the crew has 30 years of deep-sea experience.

***Blue Marlin* Charters**

☎ *246-436-4322 or 230-3515 (cellular), fax 435-6655, e-mail bluemrln@caribsurf.com, www.barbados.org/fishing/bluemrln/index.htm*

Idyll Time, a 42-foot Post sportfishing boat, *Freedom*, a 19.5-foot light-tackle boat, and *Blue Marlin*, a 36-foot tournament-rigged custom-built boat, make up the fleet of this family owned business. All vessels are outfitted with quality equipment and the experienced crew is committed to customer success.

Blue Jay
☎ *246-429-2326, fax 429-2326, e-mail burke's@caribsurf.com*

Callie is the captain of this 45-foot twin-diesel Sports Fisherman outfitted with creature comforts for four anglers and a fly bridge for spectators. Four- and eight-hour charters go in search of an assortment of game fish.

Honey Bea III
☎ *246-428-5344*

Twin diesel engines power this 41-foot Avenger Sports Fisherman captained by Ashton Small. Charters speed out to deep waters for fishing or cruise leisurely up the coast to a calm bay for frolicking with a family of sea turtles.

Billfisher II
☎ *246-431-0741*

Winston White, who is better known as "The Colonel," captains this 40-foot Pacemaker. With more than 25 years of fishing and boating experience, he's an expert at finding ideal spots for hooking a variety of big game. Full-day charters include a hot lunch featuring Bajan specialties. If you don't have your own fishing buddies, he'll help you find some to share the boat.

On Foot

■ Hiking Tours

Barbados has some of the best countryside in the Caribbean for brisk hiking, purpose-oriented walks, and leisurely strolls. Gullies, beaches, cliffs, and forests are best explored on foot, and there are routes to suit every level of fitness.

Organized hikes are led by guides from the **Barbados National Trust** on Sundays and cover a different area of the island each week. Participants split into fast, moderate, and slow groups and learn about Bajan history, geology, architecture, and horticulture as they trek along at an exercise or sightseeing pace. Hikes are free and begin at 6:30am and 3:30 pm. You can get a schedule of planned routes by contacting the National Trust; ☎ 246-426-2421, fax 429-9055, e-mail natrust@sunbeach.net.

Another popular guided hike is along the recently developed award-winning **Arbib Nature and Heritage Trail.** Named for Martin Arbib, a Bajan business man who generously provided much of the funding, the trail includes two itineraries – either an easy walk through historic Speightstown or a more vigorous hike through Whim Gully, Warleigh Plantation, Dover Fort, and along Heywoods Beach.

Islands Magazine *awarded Arbib Trail the 1999 eco-tourism award for its unique emphasis on culture and history mixed with natural wonders.*

Both the energetic three-and-a-half-hour **Whim Adventure** and the gentle two-hour **Round de Town Stroll** leave from the Arbib Nature and Heritage Trail kiosk on the main highway in Speightstown Wednesdays, Thursdays, and Saturdays at 9 am and 2:30 pm. Tickets for either route are priced at B$15 for adults and B$7.50 for children between the ages of five and 12. The trail isn't recommended for younger children. Make a reservation before 3 pm the day before you want to hike by contacting the National Trust; ☎ 246-426-2421, fax 429-9055, e-mail natrust@sunbeach.net.

Highland Outdoor Tours conducts hiking tours across private land. You can choose from several scheduled treks through former plantation land in the hilly Scotland District or along the dramatic cliffs on the east coast of the beautiful Parish of St. Thomas. The company also offers horseback riding and mountain biking, with lunch included in longer outings. Contact Highland at their headquarters in Canefield; ☎ 246-438-8069, fax 438-8070, e-mail cowflowers@sunbeach.net.

Hotel Peach & Quiet, ☎ 246-428-5682, fax 428-2467 (see page 176), offers a **Walking Week** package which includes daily excursions that involve hiking and scenic driving tours.

■ Hiking on Your Own

If you want to head out on your own, you'll find large tracts of undeveloped countryside in the center of the island and wild terrain along the east coast. Deserted roads in these areas often provide excellent hiking routes. Leisure strollers may prefer a walk through

Bridgetown early on a Sunday morning or a slow saunter along a remote beach.

Hiking Tips

Visitors in good health who walk, hike, jog, or run on a regular basis in their hometown can handle the same level of activity in the Caribbean heat and humidity by taking a few commonsense precautions.

- Plan to hike soon after sunrise or late in he day to take advantage of the coolest hours of daylight.
- Map out routes that include beaches for refreshing dips in the ocean, and forests for cool breaks in the shade.
- Wear sensible shoes with good traction.
- Carry and drink more water than normal to prevent dehydration.
- Stick to short routes along level terrain for the first day or two.
- Don't set overly ambitious goals, and stop as soon as the hike becomes more work and effort than fun.

A passenger train ran from Bridgetown to Bathsheba from 1881 until 1938, and one popular hiking route follows the track's obsolete right-of-way. Pick it up in **Cattlewash**, north of Bathsheba, and follow it south along the coast to **Bath**. A less strenuous stroll is along the beach below the cliffs at **Bathsheba**. You will find all kinds of interesting things washed up onto the sand during low tide.

Fit hikers may want to tackle 550-foot **Chalky Mount** in the Scotland District west of Barclays Park between the East Coast Road and H2 in St. Andrew Parish. A narrow road snakes through the village of Chalky Mount, and hikers can continue up the hill on foot.

Highway 2 heads southwest from Chalky Mount into a valley, where it splits. Take the right fork (west) through the community of Baxters, then turn right at the first exit. Drive to the top of **White Hill**, and take a left turn toward Mose Bottom, then a second left toward **Mount Hillaby**, which is in the parish of St. Andrew, near the St. Thomas boundary. A short, but steep, trudge from the top of

White Hill to the 1,160-foot summit of Mount Hillaby, the highest point on the island, rewards panting hikers with dazzling vistas of both coasts.

Turners Hall Woods, directly north of Mount Hillaby, provides an undeveloped tropical forest to explore. Anyone in good health can ramble for hours in the 46-acre patch of towering trees and dense vegetation imagining how the entire island looked to the early settlers. The forest is located west of H2 on a secondary road that branches off the highway and leads to the settlement of St. Simons, south of the village of Belleplaine.

Gullys such as **Whim**, **Sailor's**, and **Welchman Hall** are ideal places to walk, climb, and explore. These overgrown ravines stay pleasantly cool, while paths at Welchman Hall and roads at Whim and Sailor's make hiking easy.

Whim Gully is near Speightstown. Get there by turning south off H1 onto a secondary road soon after the highway forks onto H1B (the coast road) and H1 (the inland road) at the north end of Speightstown. While it's possible to drive through the gully's thick foliage, hikers may prefer to travel on foot. The same secondary road continues east from Whim Gully to **Sailor's Gully**, which has limestone caves and vine-covered cliffs.

Welchman Hall Tropical Forest Reserve (formerly Welchman Hall Gully) is off H2 in St. Thomas Parish, approximately nine miles northeast of Bridgetown, near Harrison's Cave (see page 143). If you have time to explore only one of the island's natural gullies, choose this one. The tropical plants and trees are superb, and the Barbados National Trust has installed benches along cleared paths in the three-quarter-mile ravine.

From **Morgan Lewis Beach**, you can walk north along the coast, then turn inland toward the hills for magnificent views. Get there by taking an unmarked, overgrown road that leads to the coast just south of the village of Boscobelle. For a shorter hike with the same view, start at the top of **Cherry Hill** and drive down. When you reach the bottom, turn left, then take the first right. Park when you run out of road and walk along the dirt path for less than a third of a mile.

Check with the Barbados National Trust (☎ 246-428-6001 or 246-436-9033) for additional hiking suggestions.

A book by David H. Weeks titled *Walking Barbados* is published by the Barbados National Trust and available at bookstores on the island. It's a bit out of date, but dedicated hikers may want to pick up a copy to use as a general orientation tool.

Consider buying a detailed 1:50,000-scale map of Barbados at the Public Buildings across from National Heroes Square in Bridgetown, or ask for an Ordinance Survey map at local bookstores.

■ Tennis

While tennis is catching on with Bajans, especially among school-age youths, the truth is, locals are more interested in cricket. Residents do enjoy **road tennis**, a sport that got its start in small communities more than 50 years ago when participants devised a game using makeshift equipment and rural-road courts.

Today, visitors may see Bajans playing on brightly-painted 20-foot by 10-foot courts marked off in parking lots. They use a wooden paddle instead of a racket, and an old tennis ball with little bounce. Scoring and rules are similar to table tennis. Crowds gather to watch the best players compete in tournament games. For information about scheduled tournaments, contact the Road Tennis Association, ☎ 246-436-6127.

Public Courts

West Side Tennis at Sunset Crest, next to Chattel House Village in Holetown, has public tennis courts. The center is open daily, 7 am-9 pm (☎ 246-432-5760, fax 432-5167). Additional facilities are in the **Barbados National Tennis Centre** at the Sir Garfield Sobers Sports Complex in the Bridgetown suburb of Wildey. International tournaments are hosted there, and the multi-purpose gym has changing rooms and showers (☎ 246-437-6016).

Hotel Courts

Many of the best resorts have excellent tennis courts. Registered guests play free of charge, and non-guests may book playing time when courts are available. Fees range from US$6 to US$20 per hour. Call the hotel's reception desk to inquire about reserving a court. See *Where to Stay*, page 157, for additional information on these hotels.

Cobbler's Cove (west coast) . . . . ☎ 246-422-2291
Royal Pavilion (west coast) . . . . ☎ 246-422-5555
Royal Westmoreland (west coast). . . . ☎ 246-422-5959
Bougainvillea (south coast) . . . . ☎ 246-428-7141
Club Rockley (south coast). . . . . ☎ 246-435-7880
Southern Palms (south coast) . . . . . . ☎ 246-428-7171
Crane Beach (southeast coast). . . . . . ☎ 246-432-6220
Sam Lord's Castle (southeast coast). . . ☎ 246-423-7350

■ Golf

Barbados is well on its way to realizing its dream of becoming the number-one golfing destination in the Caribbean. In addition to the two new 18-hole courses designed by Tom Fazio at Sandy Lane Resort, the island boasts a magnificent 27-hole course designed by Robert Trent Jones, Jr. at Royal Westmoreland, a newly designed 18-hole course at the Barbados Golf and Country Club, and a planned 18-hole signature course at Apes Hill, just inland from Royal Westmoreland.

Sandy Lane's original nine-hole golf course remains open during reconstruction of the resort facility and creation of two new 18-hole courses. This challenging course, which opened in 1961, was designed by Robertson Ward as an executive course for estate homeowners. Later, it was enlarged to an 18-hole championship course, and quickly became one of the Caribbean's premier golf facilities. Highlights include mature mahogany trees that line the fairways, small wooded ravines that challenge play, and magnificent views of the Caribbean-side coast. Call for a tee-time no more than 48 hours in advance, ☎ 246-432-1311, fax 432-2954.

During Sandy Lane's closure, **Royal Westmoreland Golf and Country Club** seized the honor of being the island's foremost golfing facility. Its 27-hole championship course is considered the best of Robert Trent Jones, Jr.'s designs. The US$30-million course opened in 1994 on land that was formerly a limestone quarry and sugarcane plantation. Evidence of the past is seen on greens bordered by attractive, but mercilessly unforgiving, stone. Untamed and unplayable forest grows right up to the manicured fairways in some spots, providing grandstand seating for monkeys that enjoy keeping a watchful eye on play. Additional challenging attributes include par-three holes that pros consider to be among finest in the world, and par-fives that often can be reached in two precise strokes due to the delightful trade winds. It all adds up to one of the finest golfing facilities in the Caribbean, one that every serious golfer will want to play. Reserve a tee time through your hotel, or contact the Royal Westmoreland pro shop for additional information at ☎ 246-422-4653. (Because it is part of a 500-acre private residential community overlooking the west coast, only club members, Westmoreland villa renters, and guests of select hotels may reserve a tee time.)

The new **Barbados Golf Club** is a recently redesigned and reconstructed course on the site of the original Barbados Golf and Country Club, which opened in 1974 and closed for renovation more than 20 years later. The new 6,805-yard, par-72, PGA-sanctioned Championship course was designed by Ron Kirby, and is laid out on lush terrain that includes mature trees and two lakes. Greens fees run US$47.40 for nine holes in the off season to US$115 for 18 holes during high season. For information and tee times contact the pro shop at ☎ 246-428-8463, fax 420-8205, e-mail bgc@caribsurf.com, website http://barbadosgolfclub.com.

The nine-hole executive golf course at the all-inclusive **Club Rockley Resort,** on the south coast, is a 2,800-yard, par-36 course. A second nine holes is playable from varying tee positions on the simple layout. Guests of the resort play without charge, and the 18-hole fee for non-guests is US$92. Check with the resort for additional information and reservations at ☎ 246-435-7873.

The Almond Beach Village Resort features the par-three, nine-hole, **Heywoods Golf Course** that can be played quickly with nothing more than a nine iron, a sand wedge, and a putter. Guests of Almond Beach Club and Almond Beach Village play free of charge. Contact the resort for more information at ☎ 246-422-4900, fax 422-0617, www.almondresorts.com, e-mail info@almondresorts.com.

Barbados Academy of Golf and Public Driving Range located in Christ Church Parish is the place for lessons, practice, and a fun round of miniature golf. A landscaped, 18-hole mini course is the focal point, but the 23 covered bays at the driving range get plenty of action. Coach Denny Foster gives instruction to perfect your swing or hone your putting skills, and beginners can sign up for a series of lessons. The clubhouse features a full bar, satellite TV, and a restaurant. Open daily, 8 am-11 pm; two-for-one prices are offered Monday-Friday, 10 am-5 pm. ☎ 246-420-7405, fax 420-7406, e-mail bagolf@sunbeach.net.

Sandy Lane Resort

This prestigious resort was closed for extensive redevelopment in 1998 and remains closed as this book goes into publication. Projected reopening dates have passed, but progress continues, so call to inquire about completion of the new tennis and golf facilities. Plans call for a tennis complex adjacent to the golf courses, with eight regular-play courts and an exhibition court.

Despite the closing of the resort itself, the original nine-hole golf course has remained open during construction of an additional 36-holes, and the greens are in excellent condition. Renowned golf-course architect, Tom Fazio, designed the two new 18-hole courses that are expected to be the best golf facility in the Caribbean. The **Molyneux Course**, with cascading waterfalls and groves of mahogany trees, will be open to guests of Sandy Lane and other resorts. The **Green Monkey Course** will be reserved for homeowners living in private villas surrounding the greens.

For tee-times on the original nine-hole golf course, or information about the new tennis and golf complex, contact Sandy Lane Resort, ☎ 246-432-1311, fax 432-2954.

On Horseback

Several stables give lessons and conduct guided tours through scenic areas of the island that aren't easily accessible by car. It isn't necessary to be an accomplished rider, since the horses are well trained and gentle.

Guides at the centers listed below match your skills and comfort level with an appropriate horse.

Rides vary from hour-long jaunts around abandoned plantation grounds to all-day outings to remote beaches. Prices range from B$50-B$65 per hour to B$250-B$300 per day, and most include transportation from your hotel.

Stables

Highland Outdoor Adventure Tours
Canefield, St. Thomas, ☎ 246-438-8069, fax 438-8070

Caribbean International Riding Centre
Auburn, St. Joseph, ☎ 246-422-7433

Brighton Riding Stables
Black Rock, St. Michael, ☎ 246-425-9381

Beau Geste Farm
St. George, near Gun Hill Signal Station, ☎ 246-429-0139

Ye Olde Congo Road Stables
Congo Road, St. Philip, ☎ 246-423-6180

Horse racing (see Sports, *page 144) has been called the sport of kings, and Bajans give the equestrian tradition royal treatment. The season runs throughout the year, with short breaks, and you can watch both thoroughbred and Creole horses compete for large purses at the Garrison Savannah. Contact* ***The Barbados Turf Club*** *for information on racing packages that include meals, drinks, tickets, and transportation. Call them at ☎ 246-426-3980, visit their website, www.barbadosturfclub.com, or e-mail them at barturf@sunbeach.net.*

On Wheels

Pedal power is an excellent fuel for Bajan sightseeing. Lightly traveled back roads running over flat or gently rolling terrain provide an ideal track for even marginally fit leisure cyclists. Unfortunately, there aren't many places to rent equipment, and only one tour company specializes in biking adventures. Truly serious bikers should consider bringing their own bikes from home.

Highland Outdoor Adventure Tours (see contact information on page 141) conducts mountain bike tours along paved roads and dirt tracks that wind through the island's interior and along undeveloped stretches of the east coast.

Bicycles are available for rent through a few shops, including one at the Cruise Ship Terminal in Bridgetown. Expect to pay about B$15-B$18 per day for a single-speed bike and around B$20-B$25 per day for a multi-speed model. Weekly rates usually work out to be a bargain and run approximately B$80-B$100 for a multi-speed bike.

Check with the following companies for rentals. Both will deliver to your hotel.

Flex Bicycle Rentals
☎ *246-422-8000*

M.A. Bicycle Rentals
☎ *246-427-3955*

Sports

Cricket

Bajans love a good game of cricket. In fact, it's the most popular sport throughout the West Indiesd. Barbados has produced several championship players, including five knighted stars. Even if you don't understand the game, try to catch one of the world-class matches held at **Kensington Oval** off Spring Garden Highway, east of the Deep Water

Harbour in Bridgetown. Call the Barbados Cricket Association for a schedule of events. ☎ 246-436-1397.

A team known as **The Wanderers** is the island's oldest team. British soldiers introduced the game to islanders in the 1800s and **The** Wanderers organized in 1877. Visitors are welcome to watch the weekend games played at the club's field on Dayrell's Road, north of Hastings and east of the Garrison Savannah in Christ Church Parish.

If you don't know a wicket from a pitch, just sit and watch. It won't take long for you to get caught up in the spirit of competition. Basically, the game is much like American baseball. It is played by two teams, each made up of 11 players, on an oval patch of mowed grass, which is called a pitch. A 28-inch high by nine-inch wide wicket, consisting of three vertical stumps and two horizontal bails, stands at either end of the pitch.

The batsmen (two members of the side at bat) defend the wicket, while members of the fielding team take turns to bowl (propel without bending the elbow) the ball, which is a 5.5-ounce round chunk of cork and string covered in red leather. Each batsman tries to prevent the ball from hitting the wicket by smacking it with his bat. If the ball is hit far enough, the batsman tries to score a "run." A run is scored when both batsmen run to the opposite wicket before the fielders get the ball back to the wicket.

The fielding team can get a batsman out by hitting his wicket with the ball, or catching the ball on the fly after it is batted. As each batsman is called out, another member of his team comes to bat, until 10 batsmen are out. The 11th can't come to bat alone; at that point, the batting team takes the field, and the fielding team comes up to defend its wicket.

When both teams have had a turn at bat, one inning is over. A complete game consists of one or two innings or a preset time limit, and the winner is the team that scores the most runs.

■ The Knights of Cricket

Sir Garfield Sobers was an international cricket champion who is still considered a national hero on Barbados. As captain of the winning West Indies team, he was called the greatest all-rounder in the world. In 1974 he retired from the game, and Queen Elizabeth II knighted him the following year in recognition of his outstanding contribution to the sport.

Other outstanding Bajan cricketers include **The Three Ws**, who were also knighted for their service to the game.

Sir Frank Worrell was the first black player to lead a West Indies team in competition abroad. He was born in Bridgetown August 1, 1924, knighted in 1964, and died in Kingston, Jamaica, on March 13, 1967.

Sir Clyde Walcott became the chairman of the International Cricket Council. He was born in Bridgetown on January 17, 1926, and knighted in 1994.

Sir Everton Weekes, who was born Everton de Courcy Weekes on February 26, 1925 in Bridgetown, was knighted in 1995. The right-handed player was known for his forceful striking and versatile fielding.

Horse Racing

Going to the races has been a national social event in Barbados since British military officers started the tradition in the 1800s. Soon residents began showing up to watch the soldiers race their horses around the Garrison parade grounds south of Bridgetown, and eventually wealthy landowners brought their own horses out to compete. At the turn of the century, Bajans were dressing in their finest clothes and bringing picnics to the track to watch the races, listen to the military band, and visit with friends.

In 1905, the **Barbados Turf Club** was founded to administer the Sport of Kings and organize the racing season. Today, residents and visitors turn out at the track, still located at the Garrison Savannah, on most Saturdays to enjoy the races and the festivities. The main events of the year are the 5000, in February; the Sandy Lane Gold Cup (formerly called the Cockspur Gold Cup), held in March; the United Barbados Derby, run in August; and the Heineken Stakes, which takes place on the day after Christmas.

Contact the Barbados Turf Club for information on racing packages that include meals, drinks, tickets, and transportation; ☎ 246-426-3980, e-mail barturf@sunbeach.net, www.barbadosturfclub.com.

Polo

If you're in Barbados between November and May, take in a polo match at the **Barbados Polo Club** grounds at Holder Hill in St. James Parish. Call for this year's schedule of events; ☎ 246-437-5412, fax 437-5414.

Auto Racing

Car racing is popular on Barbados and fans can see top international drivers compete in various events throughout the year. For information on dates and locations, contact the **Barbados Rally Clu**b, ☎ 246-432-1336; www.rallyclub.com; e-mail info@rallyclub.com.

Rugby

Head to the Garrison to see a rugby practice session or a match. Teams visit from other islands to compete in this popular sport. For event dates and information, contact The **Barbados Rugby Football Union**, ☎ 246-437-3836; fax 437-3838.

Hockey

Banks Beer hosts an annual **Hockey Festival** in August that draws teams from around the world. In addition, Bajans, both men and women, play regularly scheduled games during the May to November season. Check with event coordinator Mike Owen for information on the Banks Festival, ☎ 246-436-3911. The number for the **Barbados Hockey Federation** is ☎ 246-426-7347.

Squash

Feel up to a bit of squash? The **Barbados Squash Racquets Association** is quite active. Give them a call for details on upcoming events, ☎ 246-424-2613.

Running

One of the most popular athletic events of the year is the **Run Barbados Series**, which takes place annually in December. Some run for fun and some sprint seriously, but everyone, including the spectators, has a terrific time. Find out how to join in by contacting the Run Barbados Marathon, ☎ 246-427-2623.

Shopping

Duty-free shops are found in the center of Bridgetown, and uniquely Bajan wares are sold from trendy boutiques, craft stalls, art galleries, and gift shops across the island. Beach vendors set up on the most popular stretches of sand along the west and south coasts to offer swim wear, coverups, T-shirts, and handmade crafts.

Talented Bajan designers turn out high quality clothing using casual island styling, bright tropical colors, and silk-screened or hand-painted fabrics. You won't find anything like it in Europe or North America, so the well-priced apparel makes an ideal wearable souvenir. Other skilled artisans create sculpture, pottery, fine jewelry, intricate baskets, and colorful paintings.

Duty-Free

To qualify for duty-free prices, remember to take your immigration form when you go shopping. If you misplace or forget this document, which you receive when you clear immigration upon entering the island, take proof of foreign citizenship (a passport or birth certificate) and your return airline ticket.

Items in duty-free shops are marked with both the retail price and the tax-free price, and you can save 20 to 40% on imported merchandise, if you know what to look for and are familiar with prices in your hometown. Liquor and tobacco products must be sent to the airport or cruise-ship terminal for retrieval as you leave Barbados, and since there are duty-free shops at both points of departure, you may want to wait until you're ready to leave the island to buy these two items. You can take other purchases with you. You'll be required to give a copy of all receipts for duty-free merchandise to the customs agent.

See Customs & Duty-Free, *page 49, for regulations and information on bringing home merchandise bought while out of the US.*

Shopping Tips

Dress casually but conservatively. No swimsuits or skimpy outfits, especially when shopping in the capital.

Sales clerks are friendly, knowledgeable, and helpful. However, visitors may mistake their unhurried style and reserved British demeanor for disinterest or rudeness. Simply smile and be patient. Everyone's on island time here.

All major department stores and most other shops accept credit cards, travelers' checks, and both Barbados and US dollars. Independent vendors and out-of-the-way shops may deal only with Barbados currency.

Most shops in Bridgetown and shopping centers are air conditioned. However, it's still a good idea to shop early in the day when outdoor temperatures are lower.

You'll get the best prices on locally made products such as rum, jewelry, art, and crafts.

Most large stores will deliver purchases to your port of departure, free of charge. Take advantage of this service for heavy, fragile, or bulky packages.

Established stores have reliable after-sales service, and merchants sell only authentic brands and products, so expect the same guarantees that are offered in Europe and North America.

In & Near Bridgetown

Air-conditioned duty-free shops line **Broad Street** from the Nelson Monument at Heroes Square to the Mutual Building in central Bridgetown. Most of the stores are open Monday-Friday, 8:30 am-5 pm, and Saturday, 8:30 am-noon. Larger stores stay open until 6 pm on Fridays and until 4:30 pm on Saturdays. Some may stay open later during high season and when large cruise ships are docked at Deep Water Harbour, but don't count on shopping in the capital late on Saturday afternoon or any time on Sunday.

Cave Shepherd (☎ 246-431-2121) is a well-stocked Broad Street store that opened in 1906, and is the only true department store in the eastern Caribbean. You'll find almost anything you want to buy, including clothes by international designers, fine cigars stocked in a walk-in humidor, luxurious gemstone jewelry, imported china and crystal, and a collection of top-quality island-made products. Branch stores are located at Sunset Crest in Holetown, Grantley Adams Airport, and the cruise-ship terminal.

If you're looking for jewelry or watches, a walk down Broad Street will bring you to **Jeweler's Warehouse, Colombian Emeralds** (☎ 246-430-1310), **Diamonds International** (☎ 246-228-8990), and **The Royal Shop** (☎ 246-429-7072). **Diamonds In Paradise** is inside **Harrisons'** well-known flagship store (☎ 246-431-5500), which is filled with a good selection of luxury items from around the world. Exquisite crystal and china are tempting at **Little Switzerland** (☎ 246-431-0029), which is inside **DaCostas Mall** (☎ 246-430-4844), a converted historic structure that now houses more than 25 shops selling a variety of traditional and novel duty-free items.

The **Ganzee** (☎ 246-429-6762) stores at DaCostas Mall (☎ 246-430-4844), and Mall 34 (☎ 246-435-8800), both on Broad Street, sell 100% cotton T-shirts, bags, and hats featuring bold signature designs in bright tropical colors. (Other Ganzee stores are located at Chattel House Village, at both Holetown and St. Lawrence Gap.)

Across the street from DaCostas, **Cotton Harbour** (☎ 246-426-6658), in the Royal Plaza, offers a stunning selection of clothing for the whole family, which they advertise as "nautical wear with a tropical flair."

If you left your camera at home, stop in at **Louis Bayley** (☎ 246-430-4842) on the lower level of the DaCostas Mall. The staff knows everything about the latest cameras, and will guide amateurs and pros to the perfect tax-free purchase. The store also stocks filters, film, and all types of accessories for a broad range of cameras. **Flamboya** (☎ 246-431-0022) in the same mall, has gorgeous hand-painted, hand-appliqued, and hand-dyed clothing made of cool natural fabrics that are styled to move and flow. **Upbeat** (☎ 246-431-0713), at DaCostas and on Lower Broad Street, features casual wear for adults and children, including locally manufactured *Ripples* swimsuits.

The Verandah Art Gallery (☎ 246-426-2605), overlooking Nelson's statue in Heroes Square, is a large showroom displaying attractively priced top-quality art created by leading Bajan artists and sculptors. Shop Monday-Friday, 9 am-4:30 pm, and Saturday, 9 am-1 pm.

At the Bridge House on the Careenage waterfront, across the Chamberlain Bridge from the east end of Broad Street, **Colours of de Caribbean** (☎ 246-436-8522) is an exciting shop that promotes some of the best artisans in the Caribbean, including Nefertari designs. You'll find brightly colored clothing, decorative accessories, and jewelry designed to convey the ease and spirit of the tropical lifestyle. Nearby, the flagship store of **Soul Philosophy** (☎ 246-426-7769) offers mostly locally made apparel, jewelry, and home accessories that promote spirituality and ecology in an island setting.

On the Princess Alice Highway at the western edge of town, the **Pelican Craft Center** (☎ 246-427-5350) is home to some of the island's most talented artisans. You can visit their workshops and buy their products from stores arranged around a courtyard in the recently opened compound. The handsome, modern facility exhibits and sells only high-quality Bajan-made works that include sculpture, jewelry, batik, basketry, pottery, and paintings. Most shops are open Monday-Friday, 9 am-6 pm, and Saturday, 9 am-2 pm.

The Rasta Craft Village (no phone) at Temple Yard, on the west side of town between Lower Broad Street and Princess Alice Highway, is home to Rastafarian craftsmen who turn out high-quality goods made of straw, wood, clay, and leather. Individual businesses sell sandals, belts, jewelry, and decorative crafts.

The **Bridgetown Cruise Terminal** at the Deep Water Harbour has about two dozen vendors in chattel-house shops and stalls selling crafts, T-shirts, rum, and cigars. You will also find places to rent cars, bikes, and scuba equipment. You can arrange horseback riding and island tours inside the terminal as well, although cruise passengers may have already booked through the ship.

Local clay is used in all works at **Red Clay Pottery** (☎ 246-424-3800) on Fairfield Road between the ABC (Errol Barrow) Highway and Highway 1 north of Bridgetown. You can watch as craftsmen throw their pieces on the wheel, and tour the studio, which is set in a converted syrup-boiling house. Take home a genuine Bajan souvenir.

Medford Mahogany Craft Village (☎ 246-427-3179) is on Barbarees Hill, just a quick drive north and inland from Bridgetown (follow Baxters Road out of town). You can watch and photograph wood carvers as they turn huge mahogany-tree roots into lovely pieces of art. Dr. Reggie Medford, the owner, is a self-taught artist who oversees and works in the three-shop village. The showroom displays clocks, bowls, vases, and sculpture made from the beautiful wood, and everything is for sale, duty-free.

West Coast

Chattel House Village (☎ 246-428-2474) is a collection of brightly painted shops designed like traditional chattel houses on Highway 1 in Holetown. Don't miss **The Gourmet Shop** (☎ 246-432-7711). International food magazines give this epicurean boutique rave reviews for the vast selection of local and imported spices, hot sauces, preserves, cheese, fancy fruits, and freshly baked breads and pastries. You'll also find a great variety of wines, aged liquors, fine liqueurs, arabica coffees, and European chocolates.

Other Chattel House highlights include **Lazy Days & Island Waves** (☎ 246-432-5432), a popular beachwear and surf shop that features the famous Hawaiian brand, Jams World, as well as Reef sandals, Freestyle watches, and Oakley sunglasses. Surfers can pick up Morey Boogie and Custome X body boards or Pro-Shapes and Natural Art surfboards. **Mad Impulse** (☎ 246-432-5434) stocks lingerie, jewelry, shoes, and a good range of women's elegant and casual clothing, while **Splash** (☎ 246-428-4140) offers swimwear and T-shirts.

Gaye Boutique (☎ 246-432-1396) is a well-known shop owned and operated by Gaynor, Leonard, and Camille Asseling. Located in a quaint yellow-stone house on the main road in Holetown, the boutique carries casual resort wear, beachwear, and elegant evening clothes for adults and children. Imported designs are sold tax-free to visitors, so bring proof of foreign citizenship.

Several resorts in the Holetown area have **Gatsby Boutiques** (☎ 246-432-2205), which are owned by Karen Hopkin, a fashionable woman who travels widely to gather the latest designs for her shops. The emphasis is on chic, and the choices include evening wear, casual clothes, swimsuits, jewelry, accessories, and shoes. Look for Gatsby stores at upscale locations such as the Royal Westmoreland Golf Club, Royal Pavilion, and Colony Club Hotel.

Brazilian Gem Designs (☎ 246-432-5676) is also located in the Colony Club Hotel. Brazilian owner, Leila Beale, and her Bajan husband, John, import exquisite gemstones set in 18K gold direct from manufacturers in Brazil to sell duty-free. If they don't have exactly what you're looking for, you can have something custom designed. Expect prices to be at least 25% less than appraised values set by the British National Association of Goldsmiths.

At the south end of Holetown, **Sunset Crest Plaza** runs along the inland side of Highway 1. A variety of stores, including the large **Super Centre** food store (☎ 246-228-2020), sell basic necessities as well as souvenirs, T-shirts, and rum. **Le Caveau**, is a small gazebo inside the gourmet food shop, **The Emporium** (☎ 246-432-7472), which is on the north side of the Plaza. It stocks an extensive list of excellent wines and spirits and regularly sponsors wine tastings.

The modern **West Coast Mall** is directly south of Sunset Crest and houses a branch of **Cave Shepherd** department store as well as a fitness center, book store, bank, video rental shop, and several eateries and specialty shops.

The Art Foundry West (☎ 246-420-1366), across from The Cliff Restaurant on Highway 1 just north of Fitts Village in St. James Parish, is the second location of The Art Foundry at Heritage Park in St. Philip Parish. Like its sister gallery, Foundry West features fine work by internationally recognized Caribbean artists. Visit Monday-Friday, 10 am-6 pm, and Saturday, 10 am-2 pm.

Inland, on Highway 2A just east of Paynes Bay, you'll find a fascinating art gallery and restaurant set in an historic greathouse. **Bagatelle Restaurant's Great House Gallery** (☎ 246-421-6767) is the lovely creation of owners/artists Richard and Valerie

Richings. Paintings by the Richings and various Caribbean and British artists are well displayed on white walls with good lighting; most are for sale. Visit the gallery during restaurant hours Monday-Saturday, 11 am-2:30 pm, and 7 pm-9:30 pm.

Mango's Fine Art Gallery (☎ 246-422-0704) is part of Mango's by the Sea Restaurant on Queen Street in Speightstown. Artist Michael Adams produces vividly colored paintings and large hand-pulled silk screens that light up the room. He is internationally renowned and exhibits in Europe, Asia, Africa, and North America. Visit the gallery during restaurant hours Sunday-Friday, 6-9:30 pm, or call to see if someone will let you in if you're in the area during the day.

Walk up a flight of narrow stairs to get to the small **Gang of 4 Art Studio** (☎ 246-419-0051) located across from the CIBC Bank in the center of Speightstown. The artists may be at work, in which case you may watch, or you can discuss the displayed paintings and sculptures with whichever artists are around at the time. It's a very casual set up, but most of the works are high-quality and reasonably priced. Look for originals and reproductions by Azia, Sandra Headley, Sarah Venable, and Gordon Webster. The studio is open Monday-Saturday, 9 am-5 pm.

Southern Parishes

The towns of Hastings and Worthing have shopping centers and free-standing shops that carry a good variety of items, including local products. **The Sheraton Centre** (☎ 246-437-0970) in Sargeants Village off the ABC Highway (directly north of St. Lawrence Gap) has more than 70 stores and restaurants. Most shops are open Monday-Saturday, 9 am-9 pm, and Sunday, 9 am-1 pm.

Original art, fine ceramics, and limited-edition prints are the highlight at **The Kirby Gallery** (☎ 246-430-3032) in Hastings. Works by Bajan artists Darla Trotman, Vanita Comissiong, and Ann Dodson are featured, along with art by well-known artists from other Caribbean islands. The gallery is open Monday-Friday, 10 am-6 pm, and Saturday, 10 am-2 pm.

Ras Amica Creations (☎ 246-435-8068) is in Worthing, across from the Shell gas station near the traffic lights at the bottom of

Rendezvous Hill. Rastafarian Ras Amica crafts a large selection of shoes, handbags, and other items from leather and other natural materials. It's amazing to watch him work, and he will create sandals, belts, or bags just for you – usually in one day – if he doesn't have what you're looking for already made up. Prices are terrific. The shop is open Monday-Saturday, 10 am-10 pm.

The Yard (☎ 246-435-7068) at Quayside Centre at Rockley in Christ Church Parish is an explosion of colorful carvings, plaques, prints, ceramics, and jewelry. Owner Elaine Bowen roams throughout the Caribbean to gather the finest works for her shop, and the result is a banquet for the eyes. Stop in to browse among the well-priced items Monday-Friday, 10 am-5 pm.

Daphne's Sea Shell Studio (☎ 246-423-6180) on Congo Road in St. Philip Parish, is the 300-year-old plantation home and workshop of a talented artisan who makes picture frames, mirrors, ceramics, and other home accessories from lovely sea shells. A second shop is located next to Kitchen Korner on 2nd Street in Holetown, ☎ 246-432-7448, but try to visit the original location, if possible. Daphne and her family are charming, and visitors are amazed by the jewelry, Christmas ornaments, and other creations that fill the building behind the main plantation house.

Sandbox & Co. (☎ 246-418-0708), at Heritage Park in St. Philip Parish, offers hand-painted beachwear and home furnishings celebrating the natural beauty of Barbados. **The Art Foundry** (☎ 246-426-0714), also in Heritage Park, displays and sells contemporary art by internationally recognized Caribbean artists. Works include paintings, sculptures, and photographs. The park and shops are open Monday-Friday, 9 am-5 pm.

Wild Feathers Bird Art (☎ 246-423-7758), near Sam Lord's Castle in St. Philip Parish, contains the realistic works of Geoffrey and Joanie Skeet, along with their son, John, and his wife, Monica. Their detailed wood carvings of Barbados' native and migratory birds make excellent buys for collectors and visitors who want a souvenir that truly represents the island. The home-based studio is open Monday-Saturday, 9:30am-4:30 pm.

Walkers' Caribbean World (☎ 246-428-1183), near the Dover Beach Hotel at St. Lawrence Gap, exhibits a vast selection of regional products. Check out the Jill Walker prints in the Print Gallery. They make excellent gifts and souvenirs.

***The Best of Barbados Gift Shops**, owned by Jill Walker and her family, are scattered throughout the island. They carry first-rate arts and crafts created by skilled staff artisans, and offer the best products produced by freelance Bajan craftsmen. Look for these stores at Andromeda Gardens, the cruise-ship terminal, Chattel House Village, Flower Forest, Orchid World, and other popular tourist locations. For information, ☎ 246-420-8040.*

Elsewhere on the Island

Earthworks (☎ 246-425-0223) is a showroom and workshop for the pottery of mother-and-son artists Goldie and David Spieler. They work with a talented staff to create striking hand-finished dinnerware that is lead free, and dishwasher- , oven- , and microwave-safe. In addition to the colorful platters, bowls, and plates, they also create one-of-a-kind whimsical decorative pieces and custom-designed tiles for swimming pools, kitchens, and baths.

Next door at **Potters House** (☎ 246-425-2890), several artists create unique works in wood, glass, and metal, as well as clay. A few feet up the hill, **The Lunch Club** (☎ 246-425-2890) serves a choice of sandwiches and salads on a wide verandah overlooking the countryside. All three businesses are open Monday-Friday, 9 am-5 pm, and Saturday, 9 am-1 pm. The club is a challenge to find, especially if road signs are down or obscured by tree branches. You won't be sorry if you take the time to find this place. It's in Edghill Heights on Shop Hill in St. Thomas Parish. Take Highway 2 as if you're going to Harrison's Cave, and watch for small signs directing you north to Earthworks.

Where to Stay

Although Barbados is considered an upscale tourist destination, the island offers many types of accommodations in all price ranges. Location, facilities, and season determine the price you'll pay, with the best hotel suites commanding up to $2,000 in high season, and basic inns charging less than $50 for a double during the summer.

Many visitors prefer to stay on the island's magnificent west coast where lavish resorts line up alongside the splendid vacation estates of wealthy British families and international celebrities. Rates are exorbitant, especially during the winter, but guests are treated to the lifestyle of the rich and famous.

A growing group of tourists book rooms at mid-range hotels along the south coast, where there's more night life and a larger concentration of casual restaurants. Bargain hunters settle for small inland hotels, or retreat to hideaways on the lightly populated eastern and northern coasts.

Vacation Rentals

If you're staying at least a week, check out the possibility of renting a private home, villa, or condo with a kitchen. In addition to saving on restaurant meals, you'll enjoy added privacy, extra living space, and the fun of living like a resident. During high season, a private rental actually may cost less than a hotel room, and you'll be able to bring your children (some resorts do not allow children under 12 to stay during January and February).

Private rentals are available by the week or month, and Barbados has an abundance of choices. Even some of the former residences or current vacation homes of international celebrities are rentable. Search for a unit to meet your specifications on the Internet, starting with **www.gobeach.com**, **www.caribbeanway.com** or **www.islandtrips.com.**

The **Caribbean Villa Owners Association** has a toll-free number, ☎ 877-248-2862, and a website, **www.c-v-o-a.com**, that's worth checking out. At the same site, you'll find **Trade Wind Villas**, the upper upscale vacation homes of the super rich. Another source is the classified ad sections found at the back of travel magazines such as *Islands* and *Caribbean Travel & Life.*

You also may contact one of the following agents for information on their short-term rental listings.

Alleyne Aguilar & Altman Ltd.
Derricks, St. James,
Barbados, West Indies
☎ *246-432-0840, fax 432-2147*
e-mail villas@caribsurf.com, www.aaaltman.com

Property Management Services Ltd.
The Cays, Greenridge Drive
Paynes Bay, St James
Barbados, West Indies
☎ *246-432-6562, fax 432-5616, e-mail property@sunbeach.net*

Bajan Services
Seascape Cottage
Gibbs, St. Peter
Barbados, West Indies
☎ *246-422-2618, fax 422-5366, www.bajanservices.com*

Realtors Limited
Holetown, St. James
Barbados, West Indies
☎ *246-432-6930, fax 432-6919, e-mail realtors@sunbeach.net*

Big Mac
Bonanza Apartments
Dover, Christ Church
Barbados, West Indies
☎ *246-423-5829, fax 423-5830, e-mail bigmac@sunbeach.net*

Ernst & Young
Hastings, Christ Church
Barbados, West Indies
☎ *246-430-3790, fax 430-3789, www.eyrealestate.com*

Vacation Packages

Several companies offer combination airfare-accommodation packages with favorable pricing. If you shop around, you can often buy a package for the cost of airfare alone, and many deals include extras such as airport transfers, upgraded hotel rooms – even rental cars and island tours. Dollar-saving offers for honeymooners, scuba divers, and special-interest groups are another option.

Independent tour operators put together these great deals by buying in bulk at reduced rates. You benefit by paying one discounted price. But, compare prices and be sure you're comparing identical products. Some companies charge higher markups when they resell to the public, and others try to pass off inferior rooms or undesirable hotels as top-notch accommodations. So, spend a little extra time comparison-shopping, investigating your supplier, and reading the fine print to be sure what's included before you sign up.

The Internet is overflowing with travel offers and destination information. One well-respected site is **www.tourscan.com**, a company that analyzes deluxe package tours and categorizes them for easy comparison. They print two catalogs each year, and you can order either a summer or winter edition for $4 online, or at ☎ 800-962-2080.

If you're unsure about any feature of a tour, post a question on one of the Internet discussion boards. Someone is likely to answer with their unbiased opinion. Many travel sites have message boards. Try **www.caribtravelnews.com** or click on the ***Travelers' Opinion*** channel if you have access to *America on Line*.

Apartment Hotels

One of the best bargains on Barbados is the "apartel," a full-size apartment or small studio with some of the amenities of a hotel and the option of a short-term rental. Ranging from only-the-basics to quite-plush, they work well for travelers who want to settle in and live like a local with extra room and a place to prepare meals.

Expect to pay US$35-$50 per night for a studio in the summer, and around US$150-$200 per night for a two-bedroom apartment during the winter. Facilities, furnishings, and services vary greatly among individual apartment complexes, so ask to see a brochure or check out the website before you send a deposit.

The following listings have air conditioning, maid service, and pool. Others are featured on the Internet at **www.barbados.org**, **www.funbarbados.com**, and **www.barbados2000.com**.

Blythwood Beach Apartments
Worthing, Christ Church
☎ *246-435-7712, fax 435-6874*
e-mail camblys@caribsurf.com, www.barbados.org/apt/a64

14 units. Choose from studios to spacious two-bedroom apartments at this well-run complex on gorgeous Worthing Beach. If you splurge on the deluxe penthouse, you'll have a panoramic view of the ocean from your large private sun deck. Golf course, tennis courts, shops, restaurants, and nightclubs are within walking distance, and the public bus stops nearby. Bridgetown is a 10-minute ride west, and the airport is 15 minutes east.

Cacrabank Beach Apartments
Worthing, Christ Church
☎ *246-435-8057, fax 429-7267*
e-mail camblys@caribsurf.com, www.barbados.org/apt/a5

22 units. This south-coast hotel has many guests who return year after year to enjoy the spectacular ocean view from the private patio of their favorite apartment. Shopping and entertainment is close by; the public bus stops just outside the beautifully landscaped complex; and the friendly staff will book tours, car rentals, and watersports.

Alpha Services/Rockley Resort
Rockley, Christ Church
☎ *246-429-5349, fax 426-7530*
e-mail redspacker@hotmail.com, www.barbados.org/apt/alpha/index

The suites and apartments managed by Alpha Services are privately owned and managed by Barbara and Reds Packer, even though they're located within the Rockley Resort complex. Each cluster of apartments has a swimming pool and laundry facilities, and you can use the restaurant, golf course, and tennis courts at the resort. The beach, shops, and nightspots are nearby, and Bridgetown is six miles away.

Rival Cottages and Apartments
Sunset Crest, St. James
☎ *246-432-6457, fax 432-2422*
e-mail rival@caribsurf.com, www.barbados.org/apt/rival/a16fac

If you want to stay on the pricey west coast without paying the price, check out the detached cottages and bungalow-style apartments offered by Rival. The air conditioning is operated by a US$5 token that buys you 12 hours of refrigerated air, and each unit has a kitchen and daily maid service. The Baku Beach Club, within walking distance, offers a swimming pool, restaurant, bar, and beach access. Shops, banks, and nightspots also are within walking distance. You'll be 16 miles from the airport and six miles from Bridgetown.

The Legend Garden Condos
Mullins Bay, St. Peter
☎ *246-422-4369, fax 422-2056*

Eight units. Just south of Speightstown, this small complex offers casual west-coast accommodations and customized vacation options. Ideal for family reunions, wedding parties, and small business conferences. The former plantation house is a graceful old balconied building that sits on beautifully landscaped grounds with a swimming pool, restaurant, and shady patios. Each air-conditioned condo is individually decorated and has sitting areas and cooking facilities. Nearby Mullins Beach is popular for swimming and snorkeling. The Legend is 10 miles from Bridgetown and 20 miles from the airport.

Sea U
Bathsheba, St. Joseph
☎ *246-433-9450, fax 433-9210,*
www.funbarbados.com/lodgings/seau.cfm

Four units. No air conditioning. No swimming pool. But, this east-coast hideaway offers incredible scenery and total escape. Each little apartment has in-room cooking facilities, a ceiling fan, a queen-size bed, and a large patio that offers views of the fragrant gardens and the ocean 200 yards beyond. Surfers especially like this Atlantic-side location. Bathsheba is nearby, but the capital is more than eight miles away, and it will take you 45 minutes to drive the almost 20 miles to the airport.

Guest Houses & Inns

Another cost-saving alternative to high-dollar hotels is the folksy guest house or small inn. Don't expect air conditioning or plush furnishings, but do expect some of the lowest rates on the island.

The following offer simple, clean, double accommodations for around $50 in the summer and $80 in the winter.

Clairidge's Inn
Gibbs, St. Peter
☎ *246-422-2403, fax 422-2403*

12 rooms. Located near quiet Gibbs Beach on the Caribbean side, halfway between Holetown and Speightstown, this little inn offers nicely furnished rooms with private baths and patios, refrigerators, microwaves, and coffee makers. Guests may also use the inn's full-size kitchen and outdoor grill.

Villa Marie
Fitts Village, St. James
☎ *246-432-1745, fax 432-1745*

Six rooms and apartments. Guests at this super inn near the beach have large private baths and use of the inn's kitchen. Most everything you need is within walking distance, and the bus stops nearby. Spacious apartments sleep four, using a sofa sleeper and loft bedroom, and have a small cooking/dining area.

Kingsley Club
Bathsheba, St. Joseph
☎ *800-74-CHARM (in the US) or 433-9422 (locally), fax 433-9226*
e-mail kingsley@caribsurf.com

Eight rooms. Basic rooms in this small island-style inn have private baths and ocean views. Nearby Cattlewash Beach is one of the longest and quietest on Barbados, and an excellent choice if you want to escape the crowds on the west coast. The popular Kingsley Club Restaurant serves delicious West Indian meals.

Resorts & Hotels

Both the **Barbados Hotel and Tourism Association** (BHTA) and the **Barbados Tourism Authority** (BTA) publish brochures listing accommodations, facilities, and rates. If you want to make your own reservations, book well in advance for the popular winter season and during the Crop Over Festival, which takes place in late July and early August. At other times, rooms usually are available at the last minute. If you arrive without reservations, check with the tourist information desk at the airport for availability in your price range.

*See **Barbados A-Z**, page 215, for contact information for the BHTA and BTA.*

The resorts and hotels that follow were chosen as the best in their price group. Since Barbados isn't known as a budget destination, and doesn't cater to the backpacking set, you'll notice a lack of recommendations in the lower-price category. Those that are mentioned may be booked with confidence, since the island doesn't have many undesirable accommodations and even the least expensive rooms usually meet Euro-American standards for cleanliness and comfort.

If a well-known property is conspicuously absent, it may be an oversight, but is most likely an indication that the rooms, facilities, or services didn't measure up to expectations during a recent visit. However, keep in mind that with more than 200 properties registered by the tourist associations, an entire book could be devoted to accommodations. Some highly desirable options are not fully reviewed, but are listed with a brief description.

■ Pricing

The following scale is intended as a guideline to help you choose lodging to fit your vacation budget. It's based on the cost of a standard double room during high season, which runs from mid-December through mid-April.

The following scale is intended as a guideline to help you choose lodging to fit your vacation budget. It's based on the cost of standard accommodations for two adults during high season, which runs from mid-December through mid-April.

Keep in mind that a multi-room suite may be the standard accommodation at many Barbados hotels. In such cases, the price scale refers to a one-bedroom unit. When a resort requires purchase of an all-inclusive package, the price scale reflects the cost for two people sharing one room or suite.

Unlike restaurant menu prices, accommodation rates are given in US $, not Barbados $. Expect to pay an additional 7.5% government tax. Many hotels also add a 10% service charge, which takes care of tips for the staff.

All-inclusive resorts may be a better bargain than they appear. If you have a hearty appetite, figure in the cost of island-priced restaurant meals when you compare it to a room-only rate. In addition, consider the cost of car rental or taxi service if you must travel off-property for meals. On the other hand, Barbados has so many excellent restaurants, you may not wish to limit your choices. Keep in mind, also, that travel agents may try to oversell all-inclusives due to the increased commission they receive from your purchase.

Most hotels discount their rates during the spring and fall shoulder season, and give a more substantial reduction during the summer – in some cases as much as 50%.

ACCOMMODATIONS PRICE KEY	
Rates are per room, per night, double occupancy.	
$	Under US$100
$$	US$100 to $200
$$$	US$200 TO $300
$$$$	Over US$300

KEY TO MEAL PLANS	
AI	All-inclusive
MAP (Modified American Plan)	Breakfast & lunch or dinner
B	Breakfast
EP (European Plan)	No meals

Often, hotels that require or offer MAP also subscribe to a "Dine Around" program that allows guests to take some meals at other participating hotels or restaurants. Ask about such an arrangement and find out which properties are included when you make room reservations.

■ West Coast

The Gold Coast that stretches more than 10 miles along the western shore is popular for its velvety white-sand beaches and calm Caribbean-side water. You'll find most of the island's upscale hotels and restaurants in this area along the coastal highway (H1) that runs north from Bridgetown, the capital, through St. James Parish to the sleepy fishing village of Speightstown.

Cobblers Cove
Speightstown, St. Peter
☎ *800-890-6060 (in the US), 800-567-5327 (in Canada), 0181-7367-5155 (in the UK) or 422-2291 (locally), fax 422-1460*
e-mail cobblers@caribsurf.com, www.barbados.org/hotels/cobblers.htm
$$$$ EP (MAP with Dine Around Program available)

40 suites. Many discerning travelers consider Cobblers Cove the most luxurious hideaway on Barbados. International celebrities often check in for a few weeks of mindless escape, knowing that their privacy will be respected and their every whim will be fulfilled by the delightful general manager, Hamish Watson, and his attentive staff.

As one of only three Caribbean hotels selected to join the prestigious *Relais & Chateaux* organization of fine hotels, Cobblers Cove exceeds industry standards for the French consortium's Five Cs:

Character, Courtesy, Calm, Charm, and Cuisine. And, one might add, comfort, a quality missing from the association's charter, but foremost on the hotel's best-feature list.

A castle-like greathouse serves as the centerpiece of the three-acre property. Guests mingle in the beautifully decorated downstairs drawing room, which opens onto a patio surrounded by fragrant gardens. At the top of a sweeping staircase, two exquisite suites designed by renowned English decorator Prue Lane Fox offer uninterrupted views of the sea. The 2,000-square-foot Colleton Suite features four charming rooms, a luxurious marble bath with a double Jacuzzi tub, and a large veranda with a private plunge pool. The Camelot Suite is equally plush and has a spiral stone staircase that leads to a rooftop terrace and small private pool.

Standard suites spread across landscaped grounds in 10 two-level cottages. Each is decorated with island-style Bajan-made furniture and fine fabrics in sun-washed colors. Comfortable air-conditioned bedrooms open into a breezy living area with floor-to-ceiling shutters leading to a private patio furnished with cushy lounge chairs.

Mornings start with a hearty buffet breakfast at the award-winning open-air **Terrace Restaurant**, tucked snugly between the greathouse and the turquoise sea (see *Where to Eat.*) Later, guests lounge around the freshwater swimming pool, snorkel along the close-in reef off the quarter-mile-long white-sand beach, or sign up for complimentary watersports. Traditional English tea is served pool-side each afternoon, and guests dress up a bit for cocktails and candlelight dinner in the evening.

Lighted tennis courts, a well-equipped fitness center, and a colorful chattel-house-style gift shop are located on additional resort grounds across a narrow road from the hotel. The **Royal Westmoreland Golf Club**, designed by Robert Trent Jones Jr., is five minutes from Cobblers Cove, and extends preferred tee times and special golf packages to hotel guests. Island tours, sailboat cruises, scuba diving, and deep-sea fishing can be arranged through the reception desk.

Choose this intimate hotel for an exceptionally relaxing holiday or a romantic escape. Located on Highway 1, overlooking the Caribbean-side ocean, the resort is within walking distance of Speightstown and about 16 miles from the airport.

Almond Beach Village

Heywoods, St. Peter

☎ 800-425-6663 (in the Us) or 422-4900 (locally), fax 422-0617

e-mail info@almondresorts.com, www.almondresorts.com

$$$$ AI

330 rooms. All-inclusive packages at this sprawling resort truly include all. You never have to leave the 32-acre tropical-garden resort that backs up to a mile-long beach near Speightstown to find four restaurants, an ice cream parlor, a pizza shop, 10 swimming pools, a nine-hole golf course, five lighted tennis courts, two air-conditioned squash courts, a watersports center, and health club.

You can eat, drink, and play all day and every night without paying so much as a tip above the package rate. The resort even provides complimentary transportation to the airport at the end of your stay.

Once the site of a 19th-century sugar plantation, the grounds provide abundant space for the many scheduled activities. Infants through pre-teens enjoy the **Kids' Club** every day from 9 am until 5 pm, while the adults grab a nap on the beach, play a round of golf, or sign up for a shopping excursion into town. Watersports include everything from kayaking to catamaran sailing to snorkeling. All equipment is available, and guests never have to scramble for a lounge chair, towel, or float.

The resort offers a dine-around option, although there's plenty of variety at the Village. **Horizons** is a breezy continental restaurant that lays out a grand buffet breakfast each morning and changes the lunch and dinner à la carte menu daily. **Enid's** is a colorful café serving Bajan-style food. The elegant **La Smaritta** restaurant features gourmet dishes inspired by northern Italy. Most guests favor **The Reef**, which recently got a new deck right on the beach. Kid's have a special menu and adults enjoy seafood and a stars-and-candlelight atmosphere in the evening. A pizzeria, located next to The Reef near the water, serves designer pizzas and snacks all day.

Air-conditioned rooms are laid out around the freshwater swimming pools and outfitted with color satellite TVs, hair dryers, coffee makers, and safes. Standard rooms feature a private balcony with either a garden or sea view. For more space, consider either a superior room, which includes a sitting area, or a suite, which has a bedroom that can be closed off from a separate living room. Families or friends traveling together may want to book the Presidential Suite, a two-bedroom/two-bath unit with a large living and dining area. Sliding glass doors open onto a private balcony that overlooks the landscaped grounds and the sea beyond.

Choose this busy all-inclusive if you enjoy lots of activity. It's especially suited to families with young kids. Find it on west-coast Highway 1, north of Speightstown, 11 miles from the capital and 19 miles from the airport.

A free shuttle provides transportation between Almond Beach Village and Almond Beach Club and Spa. Guests at either resort may use the facilities of both.

Almond Beach Club and Spa
Vauxhall, St. James
☎ *800-425-6663 (in the US) or 432-7840 (locally), fax 432-2115*
e-mail info@almondresorts.com, www.almondresorts.com
$$$$ AI

161 rooms. The Beach Club and Spa is smaller than its sister resort, and nearer Bridgetown, the island's main city. Unfortunately, its beach is not as nice, and many guests go off-property to find a more pleasing stretch of sand.

Otherwise, the resort has much to offer, including the new Salud Spa, where you can enjoy a variety of hair, face, and body treatments. Like Almond Beach Village, everything is included, from meals and beverages to afternoon tea. There's no golf course, but guests may shuttle to The Village to play. On-site tennis courts, a watersports center, three swimming pools, and a fitness center provide plenty of activity for most vacationers.

Rooms are in seven three-story buildings and equipped with satellite TVs, radios, hair dryers, and coffee makers. Standard rooms are nicely decorated and fairly spacious, but don't have patios or balconies. Deluxe rooms are bigger and include a sitting area and private verandah. One-bedroom suites have separate bed and living areas as well as a private patio/balcony with a pool or sea view.

The **Continental Restaurant** serves a buffet breakfast with cooked-to-order eggs, and a varied selection of lunch and dinner dishes with a menu that changes every day. **Enid's**, like it's twin at The Village, serves tasty island-style food in a casual atmosphere. On recent visits, meals at The Village rated higher on the tasty scale, but both resorts strive to provide variety, freshness, and quality – a challenge for any all-inclusive.

Choose Almond Beach Club and Spa if you aren't bringing kids, want an all-inclusive vacation, and prefer pampering over nonstop activity. It's located on the west-coast Highway 1, six miles from Bridgetown and 14 miles from the airport.

Royal Pavilion
Porters, St. James
☎ *800-441-1414 (in North America), 0171-407-1010 (in the UK), or 422-5555, fax 422-3940*
e-mail royalpavilion@fairmont.com, www.cphotels.ca
$$$$ EP (B and MAP available)

72 rooms, one three-bedroom villa. Every glamorous room in this lavish 30-acre estate has a picturesque view of the sea from a large nicely furnished private terrace or balcony. Inside, the spacious, air-conditioned rooms have a comfortable king-size bed (two side-by-side twins may be requested), a stocked mini-bar, cable TV, radio, and an in-room safe. The marble dressing area and bathroom is equipped with a hair dryer and stocked with bathrobes, oversized towels, hand-milled soaps, and luxurious grooming products. Each room is individually decorated in soft tropical shades of sky blue, garden green, and Caribbean turquoise.

Royal palm trees line the drive leading to the soft-pink Mediterranean-style pavilion that houses the sumptuous reception area. The adjacent **Palm Terrace Restaurant** has an exquisite dining room open to cool breezes and sweeping ocean views with a gourmet menu featuring French cuisine accented by subtle Caribbean flavors. **Café Taboras** is the more casual open-air restaurant set near the water serving a mix of international and Caribbean dishes. Afternoon tea is served daily, and offers traditional scones, finger sandwiches, and pastries.

The health club is outfitted with treadmills, stair climbers, free weights, weight machines and computerized exercise bikes. Personal trainers and massage therapists are available for private sessions. Guests also may use the facilities at the more casual sister resort, Glitter Bay, which is next door. The two resorts together offer three freshwater swimming pools surrounded by gardens; a full watersports program including complimentary snorkeling, waterskiing, sailing, and windsurfing; lighted tennis courts; and privileged tee times at the exclusive **Royal Westmoreland Golf Course**.

Choose sophisticated and adult-oriented Royal Pavilion if you're traveling without children and want an elegant resort on a spectacular west-coast beach. It's about eight miles from Bridgetown and 18.5 miles from the airport.

Glitter Bay
Porters, St. James
☎ *800-441-1414 (in the US), 0171-407-1010 (in the UK), or 422-5555, fax 422-3940, www.cphotels.ca*
$$$$ EP (B and MAP available)

87 suites. The aristocracy in England at one time coveted invitations to visit the lavish Barbadian home of shipping tycoon Sir Edward Cunard. The former greathouse, which was built to resemble a Venetian palazzo, now serves as the centerpiece of captivating Glitter Bay. Guest accommodations are in white stucco Mediterranean-style buildings surrounded by 10 acres of manicured lawns and gardens set back from the half-mile-long beach. Each air-conditioned one- and two-bedroom suite is luxuriously decorated and features a king-size bed (two side-by-side twins may be requested) and a private patio or balcony. Larger units have kitchens, and some will sleep a family of four to six.

Traditional afternoon tea is served daily, and guests dine in the alfresco **Piperade Restaurant** in the evening. The more casual **Sunset Beach Bar** serves throughout the day, and often features live entertainment. Reciprocal dining privileges are arranged with Royal Pavilion, the next-door sister resort.

Glitter Bay has two freshwater swimming pools (one for adults, one for children), which are connected by a waterfall and footbridge. A well-equipped health club is outfitted with treadmills, stair climbers, free weights, weight machines and computerized exercise bikes. Personal trainers and massage therapists are available for private sessions, and groups participate in a variety of scheduled exercise classes.

Guests of Glitter Bay and Royal Pavilion have access to the facilities of both resorts, which together offer three freshwater swimming pools surrounded by gardens; a full watersports program including complimentary snorkeling, waterskiing, sailing, and windsurfing; lighted tennis courts; and privileged tee times at the exclusive **Royal Westmoreland Golf Course**.

Choose Glitter Bay for a first-class family or couples vacation on a stunning west-coast beach. It's eight miles from Bridgetown and 18 miles from the airport.

Coral Reef Club
Holetown, St. James
☎ 800-223-1108 (in the US & Canada), 0800-894-057 (in the UK), 246-422-2372, fax 422-1776
e-mail caribisles@aol.com, www.caribisles.com/coralreef
$$$$ EP (MAP with Dine Around Program available)

85 rooms and suites. The Coral Reef Club is a member of both the Small Luxury Hotels of the World and the Elegant Resorts of Barbados organizations. Much is expected of this intimate, family owned hotel, and much is delivered. Tucked into 12 acres of lushly landscaped gardens on a prime stretch of white west-coast sand, the recently renovated resort emphasizes privacy, serenity, and total relaxation for guests.

The O'Hara family opened the hotel, just north of Holetown, more than 30 years ago, and operate the property with the help of a friendly, dedicated staff. **Windward House**, the magnificent balconied centerpiece, encompasses a reception area, library/living room, restaurant, piano bar, and several elegant guest suites. Cottages scattered here and there among the tropical plants and towering trees contain a variety of accommodations, from one-person garden-view rooms to ocean-view luxury suites.

All units are air conditioned, individually decorated in bright tropical colors, and feature private balconies or patios, wall safes, ceiling fans, hair dryers, and small refrigerators. Singles may request one of the four small garden rooms with a double bed, and couples have a choice of suites or cottages with one king-size or two twin beds. For ultimate comfort, request a spacious luxury plantation suite with a four-poster or canopied bed, living area, oversized bathroom equipped with a shower and separate tub. Each of these suites opens onto a large terrace and swimming pool.

Meals are served in a gracious English-manor dining room, and guests gather in the adjacent bar to listen to music and sip specialty drinks. Amenities include a new swimming pool where guests relax on cushy lounge chairs, a lighted tennis court, and a watersports facility with complimentary snorkeling and windsurfing equipment. The knowledgeable staff at the front desk will arrange golf, sailing, island tours, waterskiing, and scuba diving.

Choose Coral Reef Club for an indulgent splurge on a choice west-coast beach near all the facilities of Holetown. The resort is best for couples, but accepts children except during February's busy high season. It's about seven miles from Bridgetown and 17 miles from the airport.

The Sandpiper
Holetown, St. James
☎ *800-223-1108 (in the US & Canada), 0800-894-057 (in the UK), 246-422-2372, fax 246-422-1776, e-mail caribisles@aol.com, www.caribisles.com/sandpiper/*
$$$$ EP (MAP with Dine Around Program available)

45 rooms and suites. Wayne and Karen Capaldi are charmingly fanatic about their delightful patch of paradise on St. James Beach. No detail escapes their attention, and guests' priorities are their priorities. Every Sandpiper room and suite is carefully appointed for casual comfort, which guarantees a coming-home atmosphere for returning guests, some of whom have been coming back year after year since they were children.

All rooms and one- or two-bedroom suites are air conditioned and have private terraces, where guests may enjoy room-service drinks and breakfast. Suites include spacious living areas that adjoin bedrooms. Some have full kitchens, while all accommodations are outfitted with small refrigerators, toasters, and coffee makers. Every roomy bath features an English-style tub.

Guests stay in traditional two-level island-style buildings set in fragrant gardens surrounding a pool-side restaurant that serves gourmet Mediterranean/Caribbean cuisine. The resort shares a long white-sand beach with neighboring Coral Reef Club, and two lighted tennis courts are on the grounds.

Choose the cozy and exclusive Sandpiper for an elegantly relaxing vacation. The Capaldis and their long-tenured staff will see to your every need. Located about seven miles from Bridgetown and 17 miles from the airport, the resort is within walking distance of Holetown.

The Lone Star
Mount Standfast, St. James
☎ *246-419-0598, fax 419-0597*
or 0181-977-6333, fax 0181 977-9444 (in the UK)
e-mail lonestargarage@caribsurf.com, www.thelonestar.com
$$$$ B

Four rooms. Recently, the popular ocean-front **Lone Star Restaurant** bought the building next door and turned it into a hotel with four 650-1,050 square-foot suites – two facing the ocean. Each casually luxurious air-conditioned unit opens onto a large patio, and has a spacious bathroom with a six-foot-square shower and a king-size bed. No expense has been spared on the gadgets. Every room has a TV, VCR, CD player, wet bar with a refrigerator stocked with complimentary items, hair dryer, safe, and a communications center with phone, fax, and e-mail service. Guests have use of complimentary watersports equipment on the wide white-sand beach that fronts the hotel.

Choose this prime location, just north of the Royal Pavilion, if you're a beach bum who demands high-class comforts and amenities. Families will enjoy the extra-large rooms, and kids will appreciate direct access to the beach, but the place actually seems more suited to romantic couples. It's located approximately eight miles from Bridgetown and 18.5 miles from the airport.

Other recommended west coast hotels:

Tamarind Cove Hotel
Paynes Bay, St. James
☎ *246-432-1332, fax 432-6317*
$$$$ EP

165 rooms. This large hotel on the beach features air-conditioned rooms, eight swimming pools, Jacuzzi pools, a restaurant, shops, a fitness center, and watersports equipment.

Coconut Creek Hotel
Derricks, St. James
☎ *246-432-0803, fax 432-0272*
$$$$ MAP (the MAP plan includes a dine-around program with other resorts)

53 rooms. Honeymooners like this intimate resort near Holetown, because it's secluded on a sandy beach, yet close to all the west-coast action. Many couples get married while staying here. Rooms

are air conditioned and outfitted with a mini-bar, telephone, and clock-radio. On-site amenities include a cliff-top Jacuzzi, swimming pools, watersports equipment, a bar, and restaurant.

Royal Westmoreland
Westmoreland, St. James
☎ *800-550-6307 (in the US) or 0171-292-5000 (in the UK) or 422-5959, fax 422-3473 (locally), e-mail villarentals@coronation.uk.com*
$$$$ EP

115 two- to five-bedroom villas. This ultra elegant residential/resort complex isn't for everyone, but it's excellent for those who demand the best and can afford it. During high season, rentals must be for a minimum of 14 nights. The larger villas have private pools and include the services of a cook and housekeeper. Guests may use the beach facilities and watersports at Glitter Bay and Royal Pavilion Hotels, but greens fees are charged for play at the 18-hole Robert Trent Jones, Jr. championship golf course.

Mango Bay Resort
Holetown, St. James
☎ *246-432-1384, fax 432-5297*
$$$$ AI

64 rooms. The cost of a double room at this attractive resort on the beach includes all meals, all drinks, transportation to shopping and attractions, and several excursions.

Sandridge Beach Hotel
Road View, St.Peter
☎ *246-422-2361, fax 422-1965*
$$ EP

58 rooms, studios and suites. Near Speightstown, this three-story beachfront hotel offers the best low-cost accommodations on the west coast. You'll get a large, clean room with air conditioning and a satellite TV. Facilities include a swimming pool, two bars, and two restaurants.

Sugar Cane Club
Maynards, St. Peter
☎ *246-422-5026, fax 422-0522, e-mail sugarcaneclub@caribsurf.com*
$ B (continental)

22 studios. Almost a mile from the nearest beach, this hilltop hotel near Speightstown is a real find for visitors who want to explore and relax. On-site facilities include a swimming pool, restaurant, bar,

and sauna. Each studio has a kitchenette, a private balcony or terrace, and ceiling fans. Room air conditioners are operated by tokens. Guests get free shuttle service to the beach and shops.

■ South Coast

The Parish of Christ Church on the south coast is home to most of the island's low- to mid-range accommodations, and some of the liveliest nightspots. Highway 7 runs from the capital along the shore, which is lined with sandy beaches that front calm aquamarine water. The area draws an active, informal group of visitors who keep the bars open late.

Time Out at the Gap
St. Lawrence Gap, Christ Church
☎ *246-420-5021, fax 420-5034*
e-mail timeout@gemsbarbados.com, www.gemsbarbados.com/timeout/
$$ B and MAP available

76 rooms. Fun dominates the amenities list at this jumping little hotel that advertises a stay as a week-long Saturday. Located in the heart of energetic St. Lawrence Gap, Time Out is walking distance from great beaches, good restaurants, and nightclubs featuring live entertainment by some of the most popular bands in the Caribbean.

Air-conditioned rooms are furnished simply, with one king- or queen-size bed or two double beds. For the little time that you spend in your room, there's a cable TV and a small fridge for snacks. Onsite facilities include a swimming pool, and the **Whistling Frog,** a pub-style restaurant and sports bar equipped with dart boards, pool tables, and a big-screen TV tuned to satellite sports. Public areas are decorated with whimsical wall murals of island life in knock-your-socks-off colors.

The beach across the street features a wide stretch of pinkish-white sand with inviting lounge chairs shaded by palm trees. All sorts of equipment is available at the watersports shop, and easy-going vendors offer bargains on clothes, hats, sunglass, and island-made souvenirs. Join in a game of sand volleyball or try your boogie-boarding skills.

Choose this high-energy hotel if you're over 18 years old, don't plan to rent a car, and won't spend much time in your room but need cool comfort for a good night's sleep. Time Out at the Gap is on the south coastal road off H7, six miles from the airport and four miles from Bridgetown.

Accra Beach Hotel & Resort
Rockley, Christ Church
☎ *246-435-8920, fax 435-6794*
or 201-902-7878, fax 201-902-7707 (in the US & Canada) or 01142-476293, fax 0142-476883 (in the UK and Europe)
www.funbarbados.com
$$ EP

122 rooms and six penthouse suites. In its newly refurbished and expanded state, Accra gets high reviews from vacationers. The deluxe rooms are air conditioned and have modern extras such as ceiling fans, voice mail, satellite TV, and computer terminals. Ask for a pool- or ocean-view room well away from the noisy street. Wooden shutters in these preferred rooms open to private patios with spectacular views.

Guests enjoy watersports on the busy beach and have use of a huge swimming pool that appears to be constructed of rock and has a bridge, lounging area, swim-up bar, and hot tub. Other facilities include a well-equipped gym, two squash courts, and a snack bar that serves light meals all day.

Choose the moderately priced Accra Beach Resort if you want to be near shopping and restaurants on the popular south coast. The airport is about 15 minutes away by car, and you can be in Bridgetown in 10 minutes.

Hotel Peach and Quiet
Inch Marlow, Christ Church
☎ *246-428-5682, fax 428-2467*
$ EP

21 rooms. Spacious, clean, and simply furnished garden- and ocean-view rooms at this *Peach* of a hotel are indeed *Quiet,* and that's the point. If you're eager to write a great novel or paint a masterpiece, this is the dramatic location for creative inspiration. When you want to take a break, the oceanside pool awaits, and the hotel staff will suggest interesting day trips, excellent restaurants, and a variety of activities. Special packages can be arranged to include buffet breakfasts and other meals, a rental car, and guided tours.

Choose Peach and Quiet if you're traveling without children, prefer an out-of-the-way location, and are content with simple pleasures –

especially when they come at a bargain price. The hotel is less than three miles from the airport and about nine miles from the capital.

Bagshot House
Worthing, Christ Church
☎ *246-435-6956 or 435-9000, e-mail bagshot@caribsurf.com*
$ B (MAP available)

16 rooms. Andrew Gomes and his son run this small bed-and-breakfast hotel located on the main south-coast road. You can save by booking a room with a shared bath, but even a double room with a private bath is less than US$100 off season. All guests enjoy a complimentary continental breakfast, and an excellent full breakfast and dinner can be added for a reasonable cost.

Named for the 19th-century plantation that originally occupied this land, Bagshot House is a place for traditional, old-Caribbean hospitality. You'll feel as though you're visiting relatives as you relax in the shady garden and enjoy a dip in the sandy cove. The on-site **Sand Dollar** serves delicious food, and the restaurants of St. Lawrence Gap are within walking distance. Choose Bagshot House for gracious hospitality and simple accommodations in a good location at a budget rate. Bridgetown is about four miles away, and it's just under seven miles to the airport.

Barbados Beach Club
Maxwell, Christ Church
☎ *246-428-9900, fax 428-8905*
e-mail wibh@cariaccess.com, www.barbados.org/hotels/bdosbeachclub
$$$ AI

110 rooms. Rates are surprising low at this all-inclusive resort on a nice stretch of sand off the Maxwell Coast Road. While accommodations aren't luxurious, they aren't bad, and guests have the advantage of relaxing and exploring without worrying over plans for dinner.

Rooms are air-conditioned, spacious, equipped with a TV and hair dryer, and overlook the ocean or swimming pool. While the food can be bland and monotonous, it is filling, and guests are allowed a few nights of à la carte dining at various restaurants. Live entertainment is featured most nights, limited watersports are available, and St. Lawrence Gap is within walking distance.

Choose the Beach Club if you want an all-inclusive package and don't demand perfection. Everything here is average to good, but if you expect excellent, you'll be disappointed. This is an especially appealing place for young families on a budget. Bridgetown and the airport are just over five miles away, and you can walk or take the bus to most of the island's hot spots, attractions, and shops.

Bougainvillea Beach Resort

Maxwell Coast Road, Christ Church
☎ 800-988-6904 (in the US & Canada) or 01753-684810 (in the UK) or 418-0990, fax 428-2524, e-mail bougainvillea@sunbeach.net
www.funbarbados.com/Lodgings/bougainvillea
$$$ EP

100 suites. Part timeshare, part all-suites hotel, the Bougainvillea is an excellent value for renters who want extra space and cooking facilities. Options range from studio suites to two-bedroom units, all with air-conditioning and ocean views from private balconies and terraces. In addition, all rooms have ceiling fans, cable TV, safes, and microwave ovens. Larger units have full kitchens.

The beautifully landscaped grounds open onto a wide stretch of sandy beach where guests enjoy complimentary use of watersports equipment. A fully equipped fitness center has scheduled aerobic classes, guests may use the lighted tennis courts free of charge, and an energetic director sets up various free and fee-based activities to appeal to everyone, including families, singles, and newlyweds. Many vacationers spend most of their days and nights at the large freshwater pool, which has waterfalls and a swim-up bar.

Sand Acres (☎ 246-428-7141), the adjacent sister resort, has 38 spacious suites and shares Bougainvillea's resort facilities. Together, the hotels have two open-air restaurants: **Lanterns by the Sea**, which serves international cuisine, grilled fish and meats, and salads; and **Water's Edge Restaurant**, which opens early for breakfast and serves a mix of Bajan and international dishes for lunch and dinner.

Choose Bougainvillea or the smaller Sand Acres for a moderately priced vacation with plenty of activity. Restaurants and nightclubs at St. Lawrence Gap are within walking distance, and both Bridgetown and the airport can be reached by car in 15 minutes.

Casuarina Beach Club
St. Lawrence Gap, Christ Church
☎ *246-428-3600, fax 428-1970, e-mail info@casuarina.com*
$$ EP

158 studios and apartments; one three-bedroom villa. Although the Casuarina sits at the edge of the busy St. Lawrence Gap district, the resort itself is quiet and relaxing. Low-rise buildings are connected by shady walkways; a freshwater pool is lined with lounge chairs and umbrella-topped tables. Nearby, the landscaped grounds meet a long coral-sand beach with gentle waves, and guests have complimentary use of non-motorized watersports equipment. A playground, supervised playroom, and round, shallow children's pool keep kids occupied while adults relax, play a game of tennis on the lighted courts, or exercise at the nearby gym.

Each air-conditioned unit, ranging from studios to two-bedroom apartments, is colorfully decorated and features cool white-tiled floors, ceiling fans, cooking facilities, and cable TV. Paintings and sculpture by local artist blend with fine mahogany furniture in the lovely public areas. The **Dover Reef Restaurant** serves Bajan buffets, à la carte island specialties, and seafood feasts, while a quiet piano lounge features afternoon tea and cocktails.

Throughout the year, the activities director arranges entertainment and historical/cultural excursions. Guests may also participate in group pool aerobics, beach volleyball, billiards, and shuffle board.

Choose Casuarina if you're traveling with kids and want a great beach near, but shielded from, the hectic tourist activity along the south coast. This surprisingly inexpensive family run resort is 20 minutes from Bridgetown and 15 minutes from the airport.

Turtle Beach Resort
Dover, Christ Church
☎ *800-326-6898 (in the US) or 0171-495-5588 (in the UK) or 428-7131, fax 428-6089, e-mail CVanGilder@eleganthotels.com.bb*
$$$$ AI

167 suites. Popular with Europeans and tour groups. All-inclusive rates cover all meals and drinks (except bottled mineral water, champagne, and fine wines); watersports such as kayaking, surfing, sailing, and jet skiing; tennis; fitness classes in the well-equipped gym; and entertainment. There's a good program for chil-

dren, as well, but the ocean's surf tends to be a bit rough for younger kids. More individualized and tranquil than typical all-inclusive properties, this resort is well worth checking out.

Southern Palms Beach Club
St. Lawrence Gap, Christ Church
☎ *800-223-6510 (in the US & Canada) or 428-7171, fax 428-7175*
$$ EP

92 rooms and suites. A recently remodeled old-timer, this beachfront hotel is great for anyone who wants to be on a strip of nice restaurants along the St. Lawrence Gap. Amenities include two pools, watersports, miniature golf, tennis, a duty-free shop, and hair salon. Rooms are simple but clean and comfortable.

■ Southeast Coast

As the shoreline swings northward toward the Atlantic side of the island, the countryside becomes less developed and the sea turns more lively. Serious watersports buffs prefer the bigger waves and stronger winds that hit this coast. Accommodation choices are limited, but delightful. Most visitors rent a car for at least a few day, so they can explore other parts of the island and try the restaurants and nightspots along the west and south coasts.

Silver Rock
Silver Sands, Christ Church
☎ *246-428-2866, fax 420-6982, e-mail silver@gemsbarbados.com*
http://gemsbarbados.com/silverrock/h78acc.htm
$$$ AI

70 rooms and suites. Each of the air-conditioned rooms and suites in this old-Caribbean style resort has cable TV, a refrigerator, and a patio with views of windsurfers riding the wild waves. Guests enjoy swimming in the freshwater pool, relaxing on the shaded landscaped grounds, and hiking along the coral-studded beach.

The all-inclusive plan features buffet and à la carte dining at **Jibboom's Restaurant** and drinks at **The Wipeout Bar**, both overlooking the ocean. Most guests come to enjoy the excellent windsurfing, and international champions often train right in front of the hotel. The pro shop outfits experts and offers lessons for beginners. If you tire of riding the waves, you can get a preferential tee time at the 18-hole **Barbados Golf Club**, designed by Ron Kirby.

Choose Silver Rock if you're a waverider and adventure lover who wants a carefree vacation away from the main tourist areas. The resort is nine miles from Bridgetown and about five miles from the airport. You can take a bus or rent a car to get to the restaurants and shops around St. Lawrence Gap.

Crane Beach Hotel
Crane Bay, St. Philip
☎ *800-223-6510 or 423-6220, fax 423-5343*
e-mail cranebeach@sunbeach.net, www.crane.com
$$$ EP

18 rooms and one- or two-bedroom suites. Standing on a cliff overlooking one of the island's most spectacular beaches, the elegant Crane Hotel offers guests an intimate retreat on Barbados' dramatic southeastern shore. It was built in 1887 as the island's first hotel with world-class amenities, and is still ranked among the best resorts in the Caribbean. Today, it welcomes both timeshare owners and rental guests.

Deluxe suites feature canopied beds, gracious antique furniture, island-style mahogany shutters, and private terraces with ocean views.

You may recognize the swimming pool guarded by Roman-style columns. It's been a favorite with photographers for many years, and is often used as a background for fashion shots and wedding scenes.

If there's a drawback to this unique property, it's that non-guests are allowed to use the resort's amenities when they pay a US$5 entrance fee. This means that the pool, beach, bar, and restaurant are sometimes crowded with day trippers. Also, since the hotel has an interest in selling timeshares, you may be approached by a soft-sale hawker who simply wants to make you aware of the benefits of ownership. These minor annoyances are easily forgotten during an excellent candlelight dinner at the **Crane Restaurant** or a sunset stroll along the half-mile stretch of beach.

Choose the historic Crane if you plan to rent a car (the resort is some distance from everything on the island) and want to spend most of your time relaxing. You'll have a memorable experience at this gracious hotel 14 miles from Bridgetown and five miles from the airport.

Sam Lord's Castle
Long Bay, St. Philip
☎ *888-765-6737 or 423-7350, fax 423-5918*
e-mail castle@caribsurf.com, www.barbados.org/hotels/samlords
$$$$ AI

248 rooms and suites. The story behind this fabled resort is as fantastic as the accommodations and setting. Legends handed down for generations claim that Sam Lord built his greathouse with money stolen from ships that he coaxed into wrecking on shallow Cobblers Reef in Long Bay. (See the whole story on page 95.)

Today, visitors can stay in Sam's bedroom inside the greathouse or in low-rise buildings scattered about the landscaped 72-acre property that borders a sandy beach. A total of nine rooms are located in the exquisitely crafted main house. All are furnished with antiques, and some feature canopied beds. Rooms in the outer buildings are typical hotel-style with colorful fabrics, king-size beds, and wide sliding doors opening onto a patio or balcony.

The all-inclusive rate provides meals in the **Wanderer Restaurant**, **Seagrill**, or beach-side **Oceanus Café**, drinks at any of the bars, nightly entertainment, afternoon tea, and use of three swimming pools, six tennis courts, a fitness room, and watersports equipment on the private beach.

Choose Sam Lord's for the legendary fun of it. Even if you don't stay in the greathouse, you'll enjoy the sprawling beachfront splendor of the grounds, and the diversion of planned activities. However, be aware that conventions and tour groups love this place, and you may get lost in the crowd. You'll need a car to see island attractions, unless you plan to stick with guided tours. The resort is six miles from the airport and 14 miles from Bridgetown.

Silver Sands Resort
Silver Sands, Christ Church
☎ *246-428-6001, fax 428-3758, e-mail slvsnd@sunbeach.net*
$$ EP

130 rooms, suites and studios. Sitting on a long sandy beach known for good windsurfing, this simple, clean, air-conditioned hotel caters to tour groups made up of young families and couples. On-site

facilities include tennis courts, swimming pool, a hair salon, a mini-mart, and an activity center.

■ East Coast

Barbados' entire east coast can be considered off the beaten track. The stunningly gorgeous countryside is blessedly undeveloped and wild. Don't book a room on this side of the island if you need a lot of organized activities, a variety of eating and drinking options, or like to shop. However, if you crave a bit of seclusion, the mind-cleansing white-noise of ocean waves, and big gulps of fresh tropical air, you couldn't make a better vacation choice.

Edgewater Inn
Bathsheba, St. Joseph
☎ *246-433-9900, fax 433-9902*
e-mail reservations@edgewaterinn.com, www.edgewaterinn.com
$$ EP

20 rooms. Set on seven acres fronting a nine-mile beach near a tropical forest, this quixotic inn is an artist's dream, and a nature-lover's paradise. The friendly staff goes the extra step to guarantee your comfort and satisfaction, but most guests are content to just aimlessly explore and relax. Rooms are basic, with either two twin beds or one king, and the best amenities are the hammocks. Most guests do their swimming in the hotel pool, but experienced surfers tackle the huge Atlantic waves off the beach.

Choose the Edgewater if you're a good surfer, like an adventure, or want to spend a few days simply chilling out. New talent in the kitchen promises to upgrade the previously average food served in the hotel's restaurant, and Bonito's and Round House restaurants are nearby if you need a change. Bridgetown and the west-coast sites are less than 10 miles away, and it's almost 20 miles from the airport.

Atlantis Hotel
Bathsheba, St. Joseph
☎ *246-433-9445*
$ MAP

15 rooms. Some visitors have stayed at this isolated hotel for years and won't consider other options. They love the rugged scenery, the turbulent Atlantic Ocean, the simple rooms, the terrific Sunday

Bajan buffet, and the friendly Maxwell family who run the place. Ask for a room overlooking the rocky shore.

Choose this plain, but clean, hotel if you love nature, hate crowds, and want to escape TVs and telephones for a few days. It's located eight miles from the capital and almost 20 miles from the airport.

Villa Nova
St. John Parish
☎ *800-567-5327 (in Canada) or 433-1524, fax 433-6363*
e-mail villanova@sunbeach.net, www.villa-nova.com
$$$$ EP

28 suites. Villa Nova was built in 1832 and recently reopened as an ultra-luxurious home-away-from-home for travelers who demand excellence. It is being praised as a masterpiece of historical renovation. The elegant country manor is secluded on 15 acres of park-like woodlands 830 feet above the Atlantic coast, about three miles southeast of Bathsheba.

A new guest wing containing junior suites and one-bedroom suites has been added to the original coral-stone mansion. Each spacious air-conditioned unit is individually decorated, elegantly furnished, and has high molded ceilings, hardwood floors, and a large covered balcony or patio. Luxurious bathrooms feature bidets, showers, tubs, and double vanities.

Walkways meander through the lushly landscaped grounds past lighted pavilions, water fountains, a 650-square-foot swimming pool and two lighted tennis courts. Inside, the majestic villa features a library, sitting room, and billiard parlor. Guests have a choice of dining in the formal **Plantation Room** or **Nova Room**, where French cuisine is the highlight, or in **La Terrazza**, where Italian specialties are featured. Lighter meals are available at **The Verandah**, and morning coffee and afternoon tea are served at **The Pavilion**. A pool-side bar offers snacks and drinks.

Choose Villa Nova for the ultimate escape into old-world elegance. The former plantation manor is three miles from the beach, and just over seven miles from both Bridgetown and the airport. Complimentary transfer service is provided to and from the airport, golf courses, beaches, and shops.

Where to Eat

Barbados has a surprisingly large number of excellent places to eat. Talented international chefs are drawn to the island's natural beauty and the visitors' insatiable hunger for new and creative dishes. *Au courant* European and Pacific Rim twists turn local seafood, produce, and spices into an exciting treat for the taste buds.

Traditional Bajan food is delicious, too. Don't miss flying fish, saltfish cakes, cohobblopot, peas-'n-rice, and conkies. Most meals are spiked with a freshly made seasoning that includes finely chopped onion, garlic, red pepper, marjoram, parsley, thyme, salt, lime, and the blistering Scotch bonnet pepper. If you develop a fondness for this fiery flavor, you can buy a bottle of Bajan seasoning or pepper sauce at the supermarket to take home.

In general, the island's most luxurious restaurants are located along the west coast, while the majority of more casual eateries are found on the south shore. Exceptions to this generalization are widespread and increasing. The ever-expanding tourist market demands variety and excellence throughout the island, and diverse new restaurants open continuously.

■ Bajan Specialties

Fresh-from-the-water fish and seafood is the main ingredient in many special dishes served in Barbados' numerous restaurants. **Flying fish** is considered the national dish, and cooks often marinate the small, silver-winged fish with spices, onions, garlic, and red pepper before putting them into the frying pan.

It requires skill and a razor-sharp knife to fillet a flying fish, and Bajans make a contest of it at the annual **Oistin's Fish Festival**. Once the head, tail, and bones are removed, the fish can be cooked in various ways. Smoked flying fish is sometimes served with cream cheese and bagels. Steamed flying fish is delicious in curries.

Markets are filled with other delicious-tasting fish, and restaurants regularly feature barracuda, dolphin, kingfish, snapper, and tuna. Local lobster is popular, but the supply is limited, so unless they have a loyal supplier, restaurants serve it only at certain times of the year.

Fish is often served with **cou-cou**, a filling cornmeal and okra mix that tastes better than it sounds. The secret of preparing perfect cou-cou is stirring until all the ingredients are blended smooth as pudding, turning the mush over heat until it is thick and golden, then topping it with spicy gravy or butter sauce.

You'll see something in rum shops called a **lead pipe.** If you decide to try one, be careful. The long, thin rolls are hard as Bajan coral. **Rotis**, on the other hand, are so soft and fragile, they often must be eaten with a fork. Similar to an Indian *chipati* or Mexican burrito, they are made by wrapping flat bread around a curried meat or vegetable filling.

Conkies are harder to find on restaurant menus, but they are well worth the search. Pumpkin, coconut, and spices are mixed with cornmeal and folded into a banana or plantain leaf. The whole package is steamed and served piping hot.

Breadfruit is a round fruit, green on the outside and white on the inside, that is used like potatoes as a staple in the Bajan diet. You'll find it on menus of island-style restaurants cooked in a variety of ways. Often, it's part of a dish called **provisions**, which includes root vegetables such as yams and cassava, an ingredient in tapioca. Other popular fruits and vegetables include pumpkins with neon-orange meat that make excellent soup and fritters, and banana-like plantains that are served fried as a side dish.

Bakeries sell all sorts of breads, cakes, and pastries. Try the **coconut bread,** a sweet loaf cake that is particularly delicious sliced, toasted, and slathered with butter.

Since coconut bread is popular with locals, most bakeries sell out early, so plan to pick up a loaf first thing in the morning.

Beware of a dish known as **pudding and souse**. Bajans have passed the recipe for this dish down through many generations, and families typically eat the delicacy on Saturdays. The pudding part is a benign mix of grated and spiced sweet potato, which is turned into sausage when it is stuffed into a pig's intestines and steamed. The souse is lime-and-pepper pickled pig's head and feet. You may prefer the **cohobblopot**, also called **pepperpot**, a fiery stew traditionally made with finely chopped pig's tails, snouts, heads, and feet.

Island-Wide Fast-Food

A chain called **Chefette** is popular around the island for its freshly prepared roasted chicken, pizza, rotis, and hamburgers. **Barbecue Barn**, part of the same chain and adjoined to select Chefette Restaurants, offers barbecued fish, chicken, ribs, and steaks served with baked potatoes and make-your-own salads. Both types of eateries are located on the main roads in towns and villages throughout the island. All are open for lunch and dinner, some stay open late (the Warrens location is open non-stop on weekends), and about half the restaurants have drive-through windows. In addition, their **Pizza Hotline** will deliver anywhere, ☎ 246-436-6000.

Chefette Restaurants:

Harbour Road, Bridgetown . . . . ☎ 246-430-3385

Broad Street, Bridgetown . . . . ☎ 246-430-3420

Marhill Street, Bridgetown . . . . ☎ 246-430-3440

Fairchild Street, Bridgetown . . . . ☎ 246-430-3460

Warrens, St. Michael . . . . ☎ 246-417-8552

Oistin's, Christ Church . . . . ☎ 246-418-8750

Rockley, Christ Church . . . . ☎ 246-430-3402

Six Cross Roads, St. Philip. . . . . ☎ 246-430-3480

Holetown, St. James. . . . . ☎ 246-419-8652

The Lunch Club has a couple of sandwich-bar locations on the island: Chattel House Village in Hastings, Christ Church Parish, (☎ 246-228-3649), and next to Earthworks Pottery on Edghill, St. Thomas Parish (☎ 246-425-2890). They make wonderful gourmet sandwiches on freshly baked breads, salads, homemade soups, and homemade pastries. Both are open Monday-Saturday, 9 am-4:30 pm, and prices are inexpensive.

■ Price Scale

The following price scale is based on the US dollar. However, most restaurants list prices on their menus in Barbados dollars. Simply multiply the US numbers by two to see the Barbadian equivalent. If you think in sterling, remember that a British pound is worth roughly three Barbados dollars, so divide menu prices by three. It's a bit more complicated for Canadians, since two Barbados dollars equals about 1½ Canadian dollars. Perhaps the easiest method is to divide menu prices by two, then add back 50% of the remainder.

Use the price scale as an indication of the average cost of a full dinner for one person, excluding drinks. Lunch, snacks, and light meals will be less expensive.

RESTAURANT PRICE KEY	
The average cost of a full dinner for one person, excluding drinks.	
$	US$10 or less
$$	US$11 to $20
$$$	US$21 to $35
$$$$	Over US$35

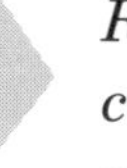

Restaurants often change their hours or close for extended periods during low season, so call to check.

Dining Tips

■ Dinner reservations are suggested and often required at many restaurants, especially during high season.

■ If you plan to hit the bars after dinner or drink a bottle of wine with your meal, leave the rental car at your hotel and take a taxi. Driving on the left side of Barbados' roads requires a clear head, even in daylight.

■ Prices at most restaurants include the Value Added Tax (VAT) and a 10% service charge. You may want to leave an additional 5-10% tip for especially good service, but it's not required.

■ Drinking water, straight from the tap, is pure and tasty, so bottled water isn't necessary, but it's available at most restaurants.

■ Swim wear and skimpy attire should be reserved for the beach and swimming pool. Barbadians expect visitors to dress as they do, which means shirts, shoes, and coverups inside all restaurants during the day. In the evening, Bajans dress up a bit to go out for dinner or to nightclubs. Polo-style shirts with long pants are appropriate for men in all but the most elegant restaurants. Women wear sundresses or lightweight slacks.

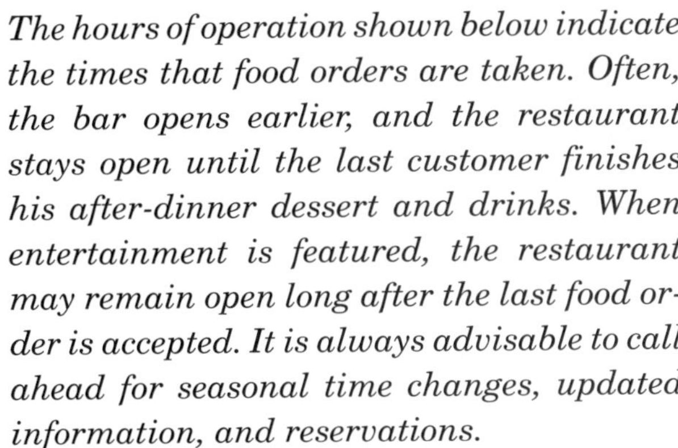

The hours of operation shown below indicate the times that food orders are taken. Often, the bar opens earlier, and the restaurant stays open until the last customer finishes his after-dinner dessert and drinks. When entertainment is featured, the restaurant may remain open long after the last food order is accepted. It is always advisable to call ahead for seasonal time changes, updated information, and reservations.

■ In & Near Bridgetown

Waterfront Café
Bridge House, Careenage, Bridgetown
☎ *246-427-0093*
Seafood / Caribbean, $$$
Monday-Saturday, 10 am-12 pm
Credit cards accepted
Reservations required

Located in a former warehouse preserved by the National Trust in the historic Careenage area, Waterfront offers a spectacular view of National Heroes Square (previously called Trafalgar). Seating is either indoors or on the wide dockside walkway. The menu includes several seafood entrees as well as a selection of traditional Bajan fare. Make early reservations for the popular Tuesday night Caribbean buffet, which features a steel-drum band to get you in the mood. Space also books up fast for Dixieland-band Night held every Thursday.

The Rusty Pelican
Bridge House, Careenage, Bridgetown
☎ *246-436-7778*
Seafood / International, $$$
Daily, 10 am-late
Credit cards accepted
Reservations suggested; essential on Friday nights.

Rocking music booms from this spirited restaurant most evenings. The converted historic warehouse is a perfect waterfront venue for coal pot cooking, zippy spiced shrimp, tandoori chicken, and grilled fish. Drinks are strong and creative. The staff is energetic and reasonably attentive. Decor is rustic and nautical. If you're looking for a good party or just want to hang out, this is the place.

The Boatyard
Bay Street, Bridgetown
☎ *246-436-2622*
Mediterranean, $$
Daily, 11 am-late
Credit cards accepted
Reservations suggested for dinner

Carlisle Beach is less than a five-minute walk south from the Careenage, and is popular with cruise-ship passengers and shoppers who want to enjoy a nearby strip of sand. During the day The Boatyard, located directly on the beach, serves as a casual bistro and bar serving salads, sandwiches, and flying fish. As the sun goes down, the **South Deck**, built a step above the sand, draws locals and visitors looking for good Mediterranean food, and the **Boatyard Bar** caters to a lively crowd that lingers late into the night. Some type of live entertainment and bar specials are featured most evenings.

Brown Sugar
Aquatic Gap, Garrison Savannah area, St. Michael
☎ *246-426-7684, fax 427-2329*
On-line reservations: reservations@brownsugarrestaurant.com
Bajan / Seafood, $$$
Sunday-Friday, noon-2:30 pm; daily, 6 pm-9:30 pm
Credit cards accepted
Reservations recommended

You can walk to Brown Sugar from Bridgetown in 10 minutes, and you'll be in a whole other world once you get there. The classy old-Bajan-home atmosphere is enhanced by lush vegetation, covered patios, waterfalls, rattan tables lighted by hurricane lamps, tiled floors, and white lattice work. A generous lunchtime buffet features local specialties such as pumpkin soup, cou cou, macaroni pie, and flying fish. In the evening, à la carte meals include creole dishes, garlic pork, spiced fish, and a selection of appetizers and homemade desserts. The band "Azure" plays jazz on Tuesday, Thursday and Sunday nights.

Boucan Wine Bar & Restaurant
Savannah Hotel, Garrison, St. Michael
☎ 246-228-3800
Continental, $$$$
Daily, 7 am-11 pm
Credit cards accepted
Reservations recommended for dinner

"Boucan" is a word used to describe a method of cooking over open fire used by Carib Indians, and this hotel restaurant features a central grill to turn out mouth-watering fish, lamb, pork, chicken and beef. All entrees are garnished with creative side dishes such as sweet potato shavings and wild rice pancakes. Arrive early for a drink at the lovely mahogany bar.

Weiser's on the Bay
Brandons Beach, St. Michael
☎ 246-425-6450, fax 435-0424
Caribbean/International, $$$
Daily, 9 am-midnight
Credit cards accepted
Reservations requested

During the day, Weiser's is a great beach bar just north of the capital on the coastal Spring Garden Highway, where you can enjoy watersports, have a salad or sandwich for lunch, and take a nap in the shade. As the sun sets, the casual open-air restaurant becomes a casually romantic place for a seafood dinner. Stay afterwards to enjoy special rum drinks and live entertainment by steel-drum and reggae bands. Expect a crowd when cruise ships are docked at Bridgetown. The port is three minutes away by taxi, and customers can redeem the fare in drinks at the bar.

■ West Coast

The Fathoms

Paynes Bay, St. James
☎ 246-432-2568
International, $$$
Daily, noon-3 pm and 6:30 pm-10 pm
Bar service, 11:30am-late
Credit cards accepted
Reservations recommended

Candlelight dinners feature exotic dishes such as Moroccan-spiced lamb kebab with almond, honey and raisin sauce or pan-roasted dolphin-fish steak with Hunan-style sauce. Lunch is as impressive with crab-and-shrimp étouffée or lamb-and-eggplant moussaka. The surroundings are casual with service outdoors on a shady wooden deck a step above the sandy beach or inside the stucco house at tables surrounded by plants and island-style pottery. Fathoms is the laid-back sister of the elegantly romantic Carambola Restaurant.

Carambola Restaurant

Derricks, St. James
☎ 246-432-0832, fax 432-6183
On-line reservations: wdville@caribsurf.com
French/Asian, $$$$
Monday-Saturday, 6:30 pm-9:30 pm
Credit cards accepted
Reservations highly recommended

Dress up a bit for dinner at this romantic al fresco cliff-side restaurant that dresses up for you with white table linen and candle light. The menu is almost secondary, but outstanding nonetheless. You'll have a choice of French-inspired cuisine with delightful Caribbean and Asian touches. Freshly caught fish is the star attraction, but duck, lamb, and beef play supporting roles. Special creativity is seen in the sauces and side dishes made from local produce. Choose a fine wine to go with your meal, and save room for one of the excellent desserts.

Mango's by the Sea
Speightstown, St. Peter
☎ *246-422-0704*
International, $$$$
Sunday-Friday, 6 pm-9:30 pm
Saturdays, December-April 6 pm-9:30 pm
Credit cards accepted
Reservations recommended

Canadians Gail and Pierre Spenard own and operate this outstanding restaurant facing the main road and overlooking the sea in eatery-deprived Speightstown. If you're staying in or north of Holetown, you may request shuttle service, which gives you an idea of the restaurant's level of service. The art-filled interior (See *Shopping* for details) is quixotic with candlelight, the sound of lapping waves, a well-stocked wine cellar, and unobtrusively friendly service. Lobster lovers will enjoy the grilled offerings here, and the finely seasoned lobster bisque makes an excellent appetizer or light meal. Fresh-catch choices are brought in each day by local fishermen, so you won't find a better selection anywhere on the island. If you're tired of seafood, try the grilled filet mignon or barbecued ribs. Both are excellent. Finish the evening with a homemade dessert and a perfect cup of cappuccino.

Angry Annie's
Holetown, St. James
☎ *246-432-2119*
Eclectic, $$$
Credit cards accepted

Look for the brilliant purple, pink, and yellow colors decorating this lively restaurant and bar, run by Annie and Paul Matthews, off the main highway in Holetown. The menu lists Rasta Pasta, grilled chicken, and blackened fish, but Annie's is known for outstanding barbecued ribs and zesty curries. If you call ahead, you can order Nan bread to go with your meal. Eat inside or out, or order take-out to enjoy on your own patio.

Cobblers Cove
Highway 1, St. Peter
☎ *246-422-2291*
On-line reservations: cobblers@caribsurf.com
International, $$$$
Dinner daily, 6 pm-9:30 pm
Credit cards accepted
Reservations required

This award-winning Relais & Chateaux hotel restaurant caters to overnight guests but welcomes outside dinner reservations. You'll dine by candlelight on a covered terrace facing the sea and feast on superb specialties created by talented chefs who use local produce to devise new-style cuisine from old-favorite recipes. Choose from the à la carte menu, or order the prix-fixe five-course table d'hôte meal that features a selection of imaginative dishes.

La Maison
Holetown, St. James
☎ *246-432-1156, fax 432-5858*
French, $$$$
Tuesday-Sunday, 11:30am-2:30 pm and 6:30 pm-9:30 pm
Credit cards accepted
Reservations required in high season, recommended at other times

Elegance reigns over this coral-stone house surrounded by towering casuarina trees on Payne's Bay. The lobster in lime sauce is particularly popular, and the dinner menu includes grilled snapper, sautéed shrimp with mango salsa, and herb-crusted rack of lamb. At lunch, the choices are grilled items, salads, and sandwiches. Since this is a French restaurant, treat yourself to chocolate soufflé served with white chocolate ice cream for dessert.

Bagatelle Great House
Highway 2A (three miles east of Paynes Bay), St. Thomas
☎ *246-421-6767*
On-line reservations: gourmand@sunbeach.net
French / Caribbean, $$$$
Tuesday-Sunday, 7 pm-9:30 pm
Sunday buffet lunch 11 am-2:30 pm
Credit cards accepted.
Reservations recommended

An Insignificant Trifle

Barbados' first governor, the Earl of Carlisle, built this coral-stone plantation house around 1645, and gave it to Lord Willoughby in 1651 to settle some debts. Willoughby, who was named governor of the island due to his loyalty to King Charles II during England's civil war, called the plantation "Parham," after his estate in Britain. Sometime during the 19th century, the manor took on its current name after the owner referred to his grand home as *a mere bagatelle* (an insignificant trifle) upon losing it to a rival during a poker game.

This outstanding greathouse surrounded by five acres of forest is a magnificent setting for a gourmet dinner. Artists Richie and Val Richings own the historic home now and display original paintings by great Caribbean talents on the well-lighted white walls of the high-ceilinged rooms.

Sunday lunch in the **Buffet Room** has become popular recently, but dinner is more elegantly romantic. The menu changes frequently but always features imaginative appetizers such as chicken-and-duck pâté, and entrees such as grilled seafood topped with a sauce made of herbs and Cabernet Sauvignon served on a bed of linguini. On Sunday evenings, enjoy Fresh Lobster Night. Homemade desserts round out every meal.

Lone Star
Mt. Standfast, St. James
☎ *246-419-0599, fax 419-0597*
On-line reservations: lonestargarage@caribsurf.com
Eclectic/International, $$$$
Daily, 7:30am-10:30 pm
Saturday and Sunday, brunch 11 am
Credit cards accepted
Reservations recommended for dinner and brunch

The dining deck of this fantastic restaurant stretches almost to the water's edge on Alleynes Bay, just north of the Royal Pavilion Hotel. Stylish black and white decor adds to the sophisticated atmosphere, and the innovative menu choices lure diners to return again and again to sample intriguing dishes. Andy Whiffen and his European-trained local chefs prepare traditional sandwiches and salads, but are better known for spicy Indian curries, tandoori-style shrimp, garlicky moules, and Thai chicken. Seafood choices include imported oysters, freshwater crayfish, crab legs, and lobster as well as local fish and shellfish. Breakfast and lunch are informal affairs, but dinner is elegantly casual, so dress up a bit.

Ile de France
Settlers Beach Hotel, Holetown, St. James
☎ *246-422-3245, fax 432-0507*
On-line reservations: martine@indl.net
French, $$$$
Tuesday-Sunday, 11:30am-2:30 pm and 6:30 pm-9:30 pm
Credit cards accepted
Reservations recommended at dinner

You will think you're on the coast of France rather than the coast of Barbados when you dine at this *très chic* award-winning waterfront restaurant. French chef Michel Gramaglia, his wife and hostess, Martine, and Peter, the knowledgeable sommelier, aren't satisfied unless your meal and dining experience is magnifique. Fresh local produce and delicacies flown in from Martinique combine in flavorful traditional dishes such as foie gras, escargot de Bourgogne, and thinly sliced fish carpaccio. The popular Fisherman's Platter includes four types of seafood, which leaves little room for the rich crême brûlée that's featured on the dessert menu.

The Cliff
Highway 1, Derrick, St. James
☎ *246-432-1922*
International, $$$$
Monday-Saturday, 6:30 pm-10 pm
Credit cards accepted
Reservations required in high season, recommended at all times

The fabulous Cliff restaurant is so popular and internationally acclaimed that it seems unnecessary to say more about it. However, lest you assume that the establishment has become too full of itself to care about maintaining the attributes that made it famous, let me assure you that such is not the case. Indeed, Chef Paul Owens and his staff are trying harder than ever to impress and please.

The restaurant's physical appearance is nothing short of dazzling. Multi-level dining areas are built on a cliff so that all tables have a view of the water. In the evening light you see everything in a golden glow – coral-stone pillars, flickering candles and torches, rich terra-cotta tile – all open to the sea breezes and moonlight. Enchanting. Imaginative dishes include grilled fish and steaks topped with various sauces, sushi with wasabi on the side, and curried seafood and chicken. Select an excellent wine to accompany your meal, and indulge in one of the superb desserts. Unpretentious, but polished, service adds to the casually relaxed ambience.

Other Recommended West Coast Restaurants

Kitchen Korner

2nd Street, Holetown, St. James
☎ 246-432-1684
Eclectic, $$
Daily, 7:30am-10 pm
Credit cards accepted

Casual fare in a casual setting. Good for lunch and evening takeout.

Olives Bar & Bistro

2nd Street, Holetown, St. James
☎ 246-432-2112
Mediterranean / Caribbean, $$$
Daily, 6 pm-10 pm (bar open later.)
Credit cards accepted
Reservations required in high season, recommended at other times

See the review in *Nightlife*. The restaurant is quite popular; servings are large, and the choices extensive.

Bombas

Paynes Bay, St. James
☎ 246-432-0569
Vegetarian / Caribbean, $$
Daily, 11 am-10 pm (high season) or 11 am-6 pm (low season)

This casual beach bar serves inexpensive sandwiches and rotis during the day and offers a more substantial menu in the evenings during the winter.

■ South Coast

David's Place
Main Road, Worthing, Christ Church
☎ *246-435-9755*
Bajan, $$$$
Tuesday-Sunday, 6 pm-10 pm
Credit cards accepted
Reservations recommended

Check out this black-and-white cottage on the bay at St. Lawrence for upscale Bajan meals. Owners David and Darla Trotman provide all the ingredients for a fantastic meal: soft music, waves lapping against the shore, candles flickering on tables grouped on a plant-filled covered terrace, an extensive wine list, and smooth service from the friendly staff. Flying fish and Arawak pepperpot stew are the specialties, but the menu includes vegetarian choices, steaks, lobster, and fresh fish. Everything comes with outstanding cheddar cheese bread, and you can order a fresh-baked dessert such as cassava pone or carrot cake topped with rum sauce.

Bellini's Trattoria
Little Bay Hotel, St. Lawrence Gap, Christ Church
☎ *246-435-7246, fax 435-8574*
On-line reservations: lbay@sunbeach.net
Northern Italian, $$$$
Nightly, 6 pm-10:30 pm
Open for lunch during high season
Credit cards accepted
Reservations recommended

Enjoy soft music on a moonlit balcony overlooking the sea at this informal restaurant. Start with antipasto, then try a gourmet pizza or one of the meat dishes served with fresh pasta, and finish with tiramisu. The signature drink from the bar is, of course, a Bellini (champagne or sparkling wine with a touch of peach schnapps or fruit nectar), and there's a good selection of wines to accompany your meal.

Pisces
St. Lawrence Gap, Christ Church
☎ *246-435-6564, fax 435-6439*
On-line reservations: pisces@sunbeach.com
Seafood / Caribbean, $$$$
Daily, 5:30 pm-9:30 pm
Credit cards accepted
Reservations recommended

Herbs and fruit from the restaurant's private garden flavor the freshly caught fish specialties at this open-air eatery on the waterfront. If you don't care for seafood, the menu offers chicken, beef, and pork, and vegetarians can make a meal of homemade soups, crisp salads, and a sinfully rich dessert. Look for the simple wooden building on the bay.

Josef's
St. Lawrence Gap, Christ Church
☎ *246-435-8245, fax 435-8248*
On-line reservations: joes@caribsurf.com
Caribbean / International, $$$$
Daily, noon-2:30 pm and 6:30 pm-10 pm
Credit cards accepted
Reservations recommended

Austrian chef Josef Schwaiger oversees this well-known restaurant set in a seaside garden in St. Lawrence Gap. Recent renovations and a new dining deck that overlooks the bay add fresh sparkle to a reliably good eatery. The menu, with a wide variety of cooking styles and ethnic touches, is characterized by dishes such as chicken teriyaki served with soba noodles and crispy spinach; grilled dolphin with mango salsa, garlic whipped potatoes, and wok vegetables; and pecan-crusted rack of lamb served with thyme-roasted potatoes, grilled christophenes glazed with tamarind and sweet red onion confit.

Sunbury Plantation
Off Highway 5, near Six Cross Roads, St. Philip
☎ *246-423-6270, fax 423-5863*
On-line reservations: sunbury@caribsurf.com
Continental, $$$$
The Courtyard Restaurant and Bar, daily, 9:30 am-4:30 pm
Call for information and times of scheduled lunch and dinner tours
Credit cards accepted
Reservations required well in advance

The Candlelight Plantation Dinner in the stunningly beautiful dining room of this historic greathouse is an occasion to remember. Guests begin with cocktails in the courtyard, then enjoy a five-course meal with wine at the exquisite 200-year-old mahogany table in the grand dining room. Afterward, everyone adjourns to the drawing room to savor coffee and liqueurs. The cost is B$150 per person, which includes tax and service charge.

At noon, lunch guests pay B$40 to tour the house before sitting down to a Bajan-style meal that includes rum punch.

Other recommended south coast restaurants:

Champers
Hastings, Christ Church
☎ *246-435-6644*
International, $$$
Monday-Saturday, noon-3 pm and 6 pm-10 pm
Credit cards accepted
Reservations recommended for dinner in high season

Set right on the water, patrons drink downstairs and eat upstairs. Great place for a hearty lunch. Seafood is excellent at dinner. Lots of good wines from around the world.

Roti Hut
Worthing, Christ Church
☎ *246-435-7362*
Rotis / burgers, $
Monday-Thursday, 11 am-10 pm
Friday-Saturday, 11 am-11 pm

The name says it all – this is the best place on the island for a variety of large, inexpensive rotis – but you also can get burgers, fried chicken, and a few other snacks.

Café Sol
St. Lawrence Gap, Christ Church
☎ *246-435-9531*
Mexican, $$
Daily, 6 pm-11 pm
Happy hour 6 pm-7 pm and 10 pm-11 pm
Credit cards accepted

This is the place to go for good Tex-Mex food, lively entertainment, and great margaritas. (See *Nightlife* for additional information.)

■ East Coast

Atlantis Hotel
Bathsheba, St. Joseph
☎ 246-433-9445
Caribbean / Creole, $$
Daily, 11:30 am-3 pm and 7 pm seating for dinner
American Express accepted
Reservations required

Owner-chef Enid Maxwell and the Atlantis Hotel are famous for two things: mouth-watering buffet lunches and breathtaking ocean vistas. The weather-worn hotel, which opened in 1945, sits at the edge of the Atlantic Ocean and offers sweeping views of the east coast. Visitors join locals to enjoy the home-cooked Bajan specialties that are laid out buffet-style at lunchtime. Many return in the evening for the fixed-price dinner. Favorite dishes include spinach cake, fried flying fish, pepperpot stew, macaroni pie, and pumpkin fritters. It'll be difficult, but top off this feast with a slice of homemade coconut pie.

Bonito Beach Bar & Restaurant
Bathsheba, St. Joseph
☎ 246-433-9034
Bajan, $$
Daily, 10 am-5 pm
Credit cards accepted
Reservations requested for groups

The Worrell family owns this sunny second-floor restaurant that specializes in home-cooked meals made with fruits and vegetables from their own garden. The hearty buffet lunch that's served from noon until 3 pm is popular with locals and tourists, so call ahead to ask if a tour group is expected on the day you want to visit. The east coast views are great from the open louvered windows, and a sea breeze keeps the dining area cool and comfortable. You'll usually find Raymond Parris behind the bar making his special fruit punch (available with or without rum). His mom manages the kitchen and is often seen scurrying around behind the buffet table refilling plates with fried fish, baked chicken, and various vegetables and salads. Save room for cake or pie with ice cream for dessert.

Round House
Bathsheba, St. Joseph
☎ *246-433-9678*
Bajan, $$
Tuesday-Sunday, 11:30 am-2:30 pm and 6 pm-10 pm
Reservations requested

This attractive 19th-century house with panoramic views of the pounding Atlantic surf is owned by Robert and Gail Manley, who ensure top-quality meals and friendly service. The menu emphasizes upscale Bajan specialties such as flying fish pâté, blackened snapper, and baked brie with nut-rum sauce. Lighter fare includes sandwiches and salads. The Mount Gay label rules over a bar that stocks more than 60 rums from around the world. Live entertainment is provided on Tuesdays, Wednesdays, Saturdays, and Sundays.

Nightlife

Barbados knows how to entertain after the sun goes down. Many bars and restaurants kick off the evening by discounting drinks during Happy Hour, which begins around four or five in the afternoon. Several boats run romantic sunset sails and all-you-can-drink party cruises. A dozen or so hot-spot clubs are popular for their live bands, and a couple of dinner shows get excellent reviews.

A free publication called *Visitor* is widely available around the island and lists current shows, specials, and happenings. Also, your hotel's reception or activities desk may post flyers about local events and featured entertainment. Perhaps the best way to find out what's popular at the moment is to stop by a busy bar for a drink and ask the bartender or local patrons for suggestions.

Whatever you do, expect music to be part of the evening. Bajans love music, especially calypso and soca, but also jazz, steel pan, and tuk. Local bands and lead singers have won regional and international recognition for innovative sounds with a jump-up beat.

Bajan Music

Calypso was started by slaves in Trinidad in the 18th century as a way to entertain themselves while they worked. The lyrics were sung in slave jargon so the white masters couldn't understand the scathing insults that were being sung about landowners and field bosses. Bajans still use calypso as a means of spreading social commentary, spoofing politicians, and directing the course of civic issues. The lively beat is meant to move the feet. The clever words are meant to move the mind. Bajan-born forms of calypso include **ring bang** (a local form of tuk), and ***ragga soca*** (created by Red Plastic Bag, a legendary calypso musician who played a vital part in setting Bajan music apart from other Caribbean sounds).

Soca puts soul into calypso to create an upbeat, heavy-on-the-bass sound that first became popular in the 1970s. Several Bajan bands currently write and perform this type of popular music.

Steel Pan got its start in the 1940s on Trinidad when the bottoms of old steel oil kegs were hammered out to create drums with various pitches. This sound is instantly associated with the islands and is as popular on Barbados as in the rest of the Caribbean. Bajan bands are improving on the quality of steel-pan music, but Trinidad still turns out the best drums in the world.

Tuk got its name from the *boom-a-tuk* sound made by the huge log drum that the main musician wears on a strap around his neck. These drummers, accompanied by a banjo or flute, or both, play a spirited beat that often sounds similar to tunes played by military marching bands, but may shift to a feverish African beat as the crowd warms up. Spontaneous tuk bands started as roving musicians going from village to village on holidays. People dressed up in crazy costumes and followed the band as it moved along the streets. Today, every special occasion and parade calls for a tuk band complete with stilt-walkers, clowns, and men dressed in women's clothes.

Calypso and all the other Caribbean beats are heard everywhere on Barbados. Boomboxes blast it on street corners, live bands perform it at festivals, even the churches rock with lively songs of praise on Sunday mornings. Along with the music, comes the dancing. Bajans are crazy about dancing. And, the wild gyrations of African slaves long ago overtook the sedate ballroom steps of European landowners.

Casual parties with dancing, music, and a lot of rum and beer often take place in communities around the island on weekend nights. As a visitor, you probably won't be involved in these jump-ups or fêtes, where Bajans work-up to contagious beats. You're more likely to join in the fun of one of the annual festivals, such as **Crop Over**, which runs from mid-July until the first Monday in August (see page 47). Trendy clubs feature popular Bajan and Caribbean bands, but the best way to see and hear a variety of music and dance is to attend a colorful production at a dinner theater.

Dinner Shows

1627 and All That
Courtyard of the Barbados Museum
Garrison, St. Michael
☎ *246-428-1627*

In 1627, you'll remember, the first English settlers landed at what is now Holetown. This buffet dinner and cultural show traces the island's history and traditions from that year to the present through music, dance, and storytelling. Performances are Thursday and Sunday nights beginning at 6:30 pm at the Garrison in St. Michael Parish. Tickets are B$115, including transportation from your hotel, a crafts market, cocktails and hors d'oeuvres, dinner, and drinks. If you prefer to skip dinner, and simply enjoy the show, ask about non-diner tickets when you call for reservations.

The Plantation Tropical Spectacular
Highway 7
St. Lawrence, Christ Church
☎ *246-428-5048, fax 420-6317*
e-mail plantationrest@sunbeach.net

You may have seen a review of this popular show on *CNN's Travel Guide Show.* It's billed as the island's number one dinner show, and there's no doubt it's a sensational extravaganza. Flamboyant costumes, pulsating music, and polished dancing make this slick presentation an enjoyable evening. You'll be treated to transportation from your hotel, a buffet featuring Bajan specialties, unlimited drinks, and dancing after the show to music by The Plantation Band. The all-inclusive cover charge is B$120, and you may purchase show-only tickets for B$55. Dinner is served at 6:30 pm Wednesdays and Fridays, followed by the show at 8 pm.

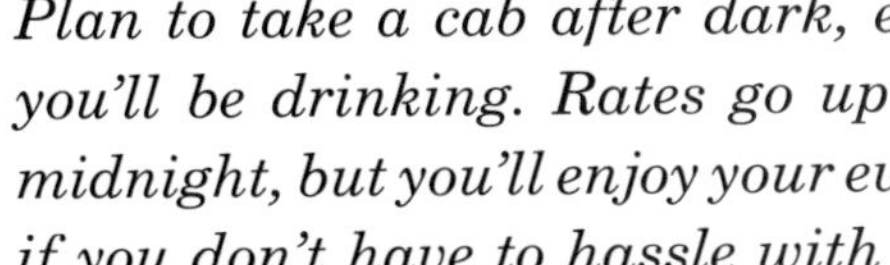

Plan to take a cab after dark, especially if you'll be drinking. Rates go up a bit after midnight, but you'll enjoy your evening more if you don't have to hassle with unfamiliar streets and hesitate about ordering an extra drink. *See* Getting Around, *page 57.*

Clubs and Bars

Certain areas of the island are known for their nightlife. Locals still hang out on **Baxter Road** in Bridgetown late on weekend nights. The *caf'* crawling goes on until all hours of the early morning, and it's supposedly a *saf' nuff* place for tourists. However, there are better areas for both locals and visitors.

*If you're a beer drinker, pick up a **Banks Beer Trail** placard (Banks is the national beer of Barbados) and follow the route to enough bars to earn a Banks prize.*

■ St. Lawrence Gap

The St. Lawrence Gap district is extremely popular. This strip of restaurants, bars, and street vendors is busy every night of the week, year-round. Start at either end of the road that dips seaward off Highway 7 between Worthing and Maxwell, and move from place to place as the mood and music inspires you. A few places to try:

After Dark
St. Lawrence Gap Main Road, Christ Church, ☎ 246-435-6547

Live bands play in the outdoor courtyard in back several times each week and the club draws big crowds with the island's most popular musicians. Inside, a huge bar stocks every liquor known to man, or so they claim, but you may be able to catch them without some drinkable brand, if you care enough to try. The action begins around 10 pm and goes strong until 3 am.

Ship Inn
St. Lawrence Gap Main Road, Christ Church, ☎ 246-435-6961

Top local bands play a wide variety of music in the pub at this well-known spot every night of the week. Sports are shown on satellite TV and the **Garden Bar** offers space for quiet conversation. **Barnacle Bill's All Night Grill** serves pub-style snacks and hot-off-the-grill burgers, steaks, and fish. More than half of the entertainment cover charge is redeemable in food or drinks. Two happy hours feature two-for-one drinks every day from 4 pm-6 pm and again from 10 pm-11 pm.

McBride's Pub and Cookhouse

St. Lawrence Gap Main Road, Christ Church, ☎ *246-435-6352*

Designed like an Irish pub, this casual place serves up non-Irish food and good drinks in a laid-back atmosphere. Expect a crowd most nights, but there's plenty of room everywhere except the dance floor. Two happy hours run daily, 6:30 pm-7:30 pm and 10:30 pm-11:30 pm. Entertainment ranges from local bands to karaoke, so call ahead to see what's going on while you're in town. If the music doesn't interest you, you can get up a game of pool or darts, or watch sports on the satellite TV.

Whistling Frog

St. Lawrence Gap Main Road, Christ Church, ☎ *246-420-5021*

Part of the *Time Out at the Gap* hotel (see page 175), this bar draws a crowd with a big-screen showing sports, pool tables, darts, and an upbeat and friendly staff. During jazz season, you often will find visiting performers playing in the bar.

Café Sol

St. Lawrence Gap Main Road, Christ Church, ☎ *246-435-9531*

While this is mainly a Mexican food restaurant, the bar serves 15 flavors of icy Margaritas. Happy Hours are nightly 6 pm-7 pm and 10 pm-11 pm.

■ Along Highway 7

Highway 7, which runs parallel to the south coast past a cluster of mid-priced hotels, is also home to a variety of popular night spots from Hastings to just west of Oistins:

39 Steps

Chattel Plaza, Hastings, Christ Church, ☎ *246-427-0715*

Among the chattel houses in Hastings, this wine bar and restaurant features a live jazz band every other Saturday night. Call to see if you'll be in town to enjoy it. Otherwise, stop by for a glass of wine Monday-Friday, noon-midnight and Saturday, 6 pm-midnight.

Carib Beach Bar

2nd Avenue, Worthing, Christ Church, ☎ *246-435-8540*

Sandy Beach in Worthing is the home of this popular bar that has live music on weekends. Kick off your shoes and relax with locals that come by to chat with James Meihuizen, the owner and well-known star of the Barbados Stars rugby team.

Lucky Horseshoe

Main Road, Worthing, Christ Church, ☎ *246-435-5825*

Just as its name suggests, this 24-hour saloon and steakhouse offers booze, bar games, slot machines, and a multitude of satellite TVs in an Old-West atmosphere. If you want to get away from the noise, try the upstairs lounge. Happy Yee Haw Hour is daily, 5 pm-6 pm. Kindly leave your spurs outside the front door.

Red Rooster Pub and Grill

Main Road, Rockley, Christ Church, ☎ *246-435-3354*

Owned by the daughter of a London pub proprietor, this English-style bar serves beer by the pint. Happy Hour begins at 5:30 pm daily.

Bubba's Sports Bar

Main Road, Rockley, Christ Church, ☎ *246-435-6217*

A dozen TVs and three 10-foot screens transmit all the top sporting events from around the world via two satellite dishes. Patrons can enjoy well-priced meals and snacks while they watch the game and have drinks poured by some of the friendliest bartenders on the island.

Bert's Bar

Abbeville Hotel, Main Road, Rockley, Christ Church, ☎ *246-435-7924*

This well-established sports bar at Abbeville Hotel in Rockley has a reputation for making terrific fruit daiquiris. Live sporting events are broadcast on satellite TV, and you can try your luck at the slot machines during timeouts.

***Oistins Friday Night Fish Fry** takes place every week in the stalls and parking lot of the town's well-known open-air fish market, located on the coast side of Highway 7. Recorded music and live bands play while folks browse the stalls for grilled or fried fresh fish with all the fixings. Drink and dessert kiosks sell beer, rum, pastries, and ice cream. Everyone eats family style at long picnic tables, so this is a great place to be limin' with the locals.*

■ Bridgetown

Bridgetown and the surrounding areas have a good selection of nightclubs and restaurant bars. Start at the Careenage on the waterfront and work your way south to the following beach-side hot spots off Bay Street (Highway 7).

The Waterfront Café
Bridgetown Marina, The Careenage, Bridgetown, ☎ 246-427-0093

Jazz is the music of choice at this trendy restaurant bar on the boardwalk at the Careenage. Tuesday through Saturday, live bands play a variety of music, but mostly jazz with an island accent. There's no cover charge, so stop in for dinner or a drink and enjoy the bistro-style atmosphere and lively sounds of a steel pan band or jazz musician.

The Boatyard
Bay Street, Bridgetown, ☎ 246-436-2622

Happy hour runs 6 pm-10 pm at this jumping beachfront bar and grill on Bay Street (Highway 7) just south of Bridgetown. The beach party goes all day, and after dark you can count on the action gearing up a notch or two. **Sunday Sunset Jam** features live entertainment as the sun goes down. **Tuesday** night is free drinks, shooter specials, live music, and a guaranteed good time from 8 pm-2am for a cover charge of B$30. **Wednesday** is dollar night, with drinkers paying full price for a souvenir glass, then refilling it for a dollar during the live entertainment from 8 pm to 3 am with a B$10 cover. **Thursday** is limbo and bonfires on the beach with no cover charge and festivities beginning around sunset. **Friday** features flying fish. Say it fast five times, then head out to join the locals at this end-of-week bash. No cover charge until 9 pm, but the live entertainment shows up about 8 pm. **Saturday** caps off the weekend with a free-drinks-and-great-bands party covered by a B$36 entrance fee. And Monday – well, on Mondays the staff locks the doors and takes a break.

Harbour Lights
Bay Street, Bridgetown, ☎ 246-436-7225

Known for its all-you-can-drink beach parties, this popular nightclub just south of the capital on Upper Bay Street (Highway 7), draws a dynamic 18-and-over crowd every night of the week. Monday night parties run B$78 for transportation from your hotel, buffet dinner, unlimited drinks, and dancing to the music of a live band. Other nights, the cover charge is B$12-B$30, depending on the entertainment and the number of drinks that are included. The oceanfront deck is the place to meet and mingle.

■ The West Coast

West Coast nightspots tend to be a bit more sophisticated than those found elsewhere on the island, but that doesn't mean Highway 1 goes dead after sunset. Much of the entertainment is found at glitzy hotel restaurants where well-dressed diners linger over a meal and drinks while enjoying light jazz or a solo musician. Check with hotels listed in the *Where to Stay* section for current entertainment schedules. Restaurants along 2nd Street in Holetown often turn into late-night bars with live entertainment after the diner hour. The following clubs, bars, and restaurants draw locals and tourist by featuring Bajan bands on a regular basis:

Coach House
Sandy Lane, St. James, ☎ 246-432-1163

An enduring favorite with locals and visitors, this pub-like bar features live local entertainment every night, dependably good food, and a friendly atmosphere. Happy hour runs 5 pm-7 pm, you can catch your favorite sports team on satellite TV, and the band fires up around 9 pm. A B$10 cover charge will get you B$6 worth of coupons for drinks at the bar. Look for the antique coaches and red phone booth outside the green house on Highway 1 at Paynes Bay, just south of Sandy Lane Golf Course.

The Casbah
Holetown, St. James, ☎ 246-432-2258

Guests at hotels around Holetown meet at this new Moroccan-style nightclub at Baku Beach. DJ-spun music plays and people lounge on silk throw pillows or mingle on the beachside boardwalk. There's a cover charge and casual-resort dress code to keep out the riff-raff. Enter through the **Baku Brasserie and Bar**, and if you stop to have dinner at Baku, you get into the Casbah free of charge.

Nico's Champagne Wine Bar
Main Road, Derricks, St. James, ☎ 246-432-6386

A smart crowd gathers in the air-conditioned bar of this casually chic restaurant. Most stay on for dinner in the courtyard, but some just stop in for a cocktail or glass of wine; at least a dozen wines are sold by the glass. You'll enjoy the friendly bartender, upbeat music, and informal atmosphere. Look for Nico's on the east side of Highway 1 across from The Cliff and Carambola restaurants in Derricks.

Olives Bar & Bistro
2nd Street, Holetown, St. James, ☎ 246-432-2112

The upstairs lounge in this graceful old balconied building in Holetown serves light meals and an excellent variety of well-priced wines and champagne.

Bourbon Street
Highway 1, Prospect, St. James, ☎ 246-424-4557

Known for their New Orleans-style cuisine, this beachside bistro features live blues and jazz on Wednesday, Friday, and Saturday nights.

The Mews
2nd Street, Holetown, St. James, ☎ 246-432-1122

Listen to live jazz on Friday nights beginning at 11 pm at this renovated balconied house in Holetown. Primarily popular for its international menu, the intimate bar, with its impressive wine and champagne list, has become a lively spot for after-dinner drinks.

Cobblers Cove Hotel,
Highway 1, St. Peter, ☎ 246-422-2291

The bar at this elegant country-house resort is famous for its Cobblers Cooler, a powerful mix of exotic fruit juices and local rums served in a tall glass. (Ask about manager Hamish Watson's challenge for any guest to drink five Coolers in one sitting.) Sit at the lovely mahogany bar adjacent to the poolside restaurant, or relax in the breezy plantation-style lounge area that looks out to the sea.

The Lone Star Beach Restaurant
Highway 1, Mount Stanfast, St. James, ☎ 246-419-0599

If you've changed out of your beach wear, you'll be welcomed at the trendy air-conditioned bellini and cocktail bar. All tropical cocktails, including the Italian bellini (peach schnapps and champagne), are outstanding, and the wine list offers selections priced from B$40 to more than B$400.

■ The East Coast

The East Coast is deliciously deserted and ideal for artistic loners, romantic honeymooners, and eccentric escapists. So, there's not much in the way of nightlife or after-dark entertainment – unless you count the billions of brilliant stars in the limitless sky or the melodic sound of waves crashing against limestone cliffs. If you must seek sustenance and diversion, head into the tiny town of Bathsheba (a half-hour drive from the west and south coasts) and try:

Round House
Coast Road, Bathsheba, St. Joseph, ☎ 246-433-9678

More than 70 types of rum from around the world, including the Bajan Mount Gay, go into a variety of drinks at this seaside bar.

If you're not having dinner – and you should – order an appetizer or dessert to accompany a bottle of good wine. Entertainment includes a guitar band on Tuesdays, a solo guitarist on Sundays, a reggae band on Saturdays, and a jazz band on Wednesdays.

Night Time Alternatives

■ Cruising

Enjoy a night on the high seas aboard the **MV *Harbour Master***, ☎ 246-430-0900. The dinner cruise includes a buffet, a floor show featuring comedy acts and dancers, and dancing to a popular Bajan band. Thursday night's all-inclusive price is B$123, and Sunday nights cruise-only price is B$55 (dinner and drinks may be purchased separately).

A more tranquil cruise is available on several boats that set sail around sunset. Expect rates in the B$75-B$120 range depending on the length of the trip and type of refreshments. Some vessels, such as *Secret Love* and *Limbo Lady*, are small yachts that take only a few passengers and offer a personal touch. You may be allowed to handle the boat or choose the sailing route, and there will be plenty of time to chat with the captain or sit alone on deck to watch the sun set.

Larger yachts, such as *Cool Runnings* and *Heatwave*, carry more passengers and offer the option of mingling or escaping to a secluded corner with the drink and a friend. Check with the following operators for details and rates:

Secret Love, a 41-foot Morgan Yacht, that takes guests snorkeling then finishes off with a sunset-and-drinks sail, ☎ 246-432-1972.

Limbo Lady**,** a 44-foot CSY Yacht captained by Patrick Gonsalves, one of the friendliest sailors in the Caribbean. Enjoy a glass of champagne while watching the day turn to night at sea. ☎ 246-420-5418.

Heatwave**,** a 57-foot catamaran, sails up the west coast just as the sun slips below the waterline. Join the gregarious crew on Thursdays and Saturdays for the three-hour trip. ☎ 246-429-9283.

Cool Runnings, a 54-foot catamaran, runs four-hour sunset cruises that leave early enough to snorkel before dark. ☎ 246-436-0911.

(See *Cruise Operators* on page 129 for additional cruise options.)

■ Underwater Wonders

Night diving is popular with many certified scuba divers, and most operators take groups on after-dark expeditions to reefs and wrecks. Check the listings under *Dive Operators* in the *Scuba Diving & Snorkeling* section of the chapter on *Adventures* for PADI-certified guides.

Atlantis Submarine, ☎ 246-436-8929, offers night voyages that allow you to see the mysterious underwater world at night without getting wet. The comfortable, climate-controlled vessel submerges, then shines 22 high-powered spotlights on the reefs and shipwrecks to bring out the brilliant colors of the corals, sponges, and fish. The marine gardens look amazingly different, and even more beautiful, in the artificial light.

■ Reel Ventures

Catch a movie at one of the island's two cinemas. The best one is **The Vista,** ☎ 246-435-8400, on Highway 7 at the bottom of Rendezvous Hill in Worthing, Christ Church. Tickets are B$8. The older **Globe Cinema**, ☎ 246-426-4692, is on Upper Roebuck Street in Bridgetown. Again tickets are B$8. If you miss the old drive-in theaters, head to **Globe Drive-In**, ☎ 246-437-0479, just east of the Sheraton Shopping Center north of Graeme Hall off the ABC Highway. You can see two movies for the B$8 admission price.

Barbados A-Z

Airline Phone Numbers & Websites

Air Canada, ☎ 800-776-3000 (US); 246-428-5077 (Barbados); www.aircanada.com

Air Jamaica, ☎ 800-523-5585 (US); 0181-570-7999 (UK); 420-7361 (Barbados); www.airjamaica.com

American Airlines, ☎ 800-433-7300 (US); 0345-789789 (UK); 246-428-4170 (Barbados); www.aa.com

British Airways, ☎ 800-247-9797 (US); 0345-222111 (UK); 246-436-6413 (Barbados); www.british-airways.com

BWIA, ☎ 800-538-2942 (US); 246-426-2111 (Barbados); http://bwee.com

Delta Air Lines, ☎ 800-221-1212 (US); 0800-414767 (UK); 246-420-9529 (Barbados); www.delta-air.com

LIAT, ☎ 800-468-0482 (US); 246-436-6224 (Barbados)

Virgin Atlantic, ☎ 800-862-8621 (US); 012937-747-747 (UK)

ATMs

Most banks, including the **Barbados National Bank** at the airport, have ATM machines.

Banks

Banks are open Monday-Thursday, 8 am-3 pm and Friday, 8 am-5 pm.

Branches of **Caribbean Commercial Bank** in Hastings and Sunset Crest are open Saturday, 9 am-noon.

The **Barbados National Bank** at the airport is open every day from 8 am until the last flight arrives or departs. The bureau de change at the airport is open daily, 8 am-midnight.

Caribbean Commercial Bank
Broad Street, Bridgetown, ☎ 246-431-2500.
Hastings Plaza, Hastings, ☎ 246-431-2450.
Sunset Crest, Holetown, ☎ 246-419-8530.
Six Cross Roads, St. Philip, ☎ 246-431-2544.

Scotiabank of Nova Scotia
Broad Street, Bridgetown, ☎ 246-431-3000.
Independence Square, Bridgetown, ☎ 246-436-6428
Highway 1, Holetown, ☎ 246-431-1662
Haggatt Hall, in the Julie 'N Complex, ☎ 246-430-3000 (main bank number).

■ Barclays Bank

Broad Street, Bridgetown, ☎ 246-431-5151.
Lower Broad Street, Bridgetown, ☎ 246-431-5000.
Sunset Crest, Holetown, ☎ 246-432-1472.
Speightstown Mall, Speightstown, ☎ 246-422-2194.
Highway 7, Oistins, ☎ 246-428-7444.
St. Lawrence Gap, ☎ 246-428-7452.

Mutual Bank of the Caribbean
Broad Street, Bridgetown, ☎ 246-436-8335.

Royal Bank of Canada
Broad Street, Bridgetown, ☎ 246-431-6700.
St. Lawrence Gap, ☎ 246-431-6565.

Barbados National Bank
Airport, ☎ 246-428-0921.
Broad Street, Bridgetown, ☎ 246-431-5700.
Fairchild Street, Bridgetown, ☎ 246-431-5700 (main bank number).
Speightstown Mall, Speightstown, ☎ 246-422-4104
Sam Lord's Castle, ☎ 246-423-8210

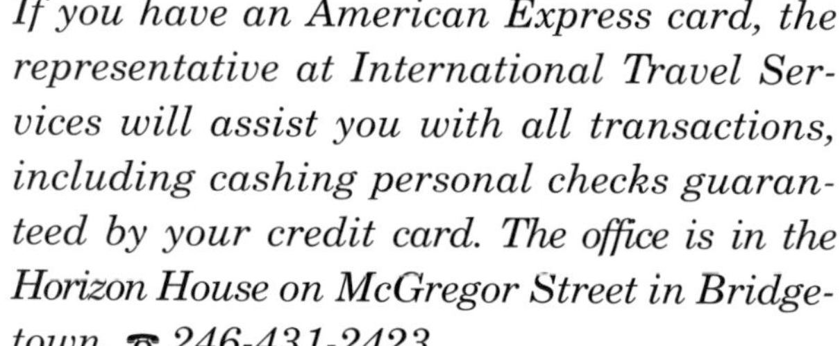

If you have an American Express card, the representative at International Travel Services will assist you with all transactions, including cashing personal checks guaranteed by your credit card. The office is in the Horizon House on McGregor Street in Bridgetown, ☎ 246-431-2423.

■ Book Stores

The Cloister Bookshop
Hincks Street, Bridgetown, ☎ 246-426-2662, fax 429-7269.

Brydens
e-mail asbretail@caribsurf.com
Victoria Street, Bridgetown, ☎ 246-431-2600.
Hastings Plaza, Christ Church, ☎ 246-435-8572.
Sheraton Center, Christ Church, ☎ 246-437-2646.

Days Books
Independence Square, Bridgetown, ☎ 246-426-9887, fax 436-5289.

Pages
Cave Shepherd Store, Broad Street, Bridgetown, ☎ 246-431-2159.
DaCostas West Mall, Sunset Crest, St. James, ☎ 246-419-3110.

■ Capital

Bridgetown

■ Churches & Religions

Bajans are primarily Christian, but more than 100 different religions are practiced on the island. Among the Christian churches, about 40% of the population is Anglican. The main Anglican church is **St. Michael's Cathedral** in Bridgetown. ☎ 246-426-2761.

A list of churches and times of services is listed in *Visitor,* a free publication that is widely available at hotels and tourist attractions around the island.

■ Climate

Year-round: eight to nine hours of sun, average low temperature is 75°F and the average high is 85°F. Average rainfall is 1.1 inches during the driest month of February, and 8.1 inches during the wettest month of November.

■ Credit Cards

Most restaurants and businesses accept credit cards. Charges are posted in Barbados dollars. Credit cards are preferred over traveler's checks by most businesses.

■ Decompression Chamber

Barbados Defense Force, Garrison, St. Michael, ☎ 246-436-6185.

■ Departure Tax

B$25 or US$12.50

US dollars usually are accepted without a problem. However, some official literature states that the tax must be paid in Barbados dollars. It is recommended that you have the exact amount in local currency, to avoid delays.

■ Driving

Traffic travels on the left side of the road. You must have a valid driver's license to purchase the required temporary Barbados license for B$10 from your car rental agency or any police station.

■ Electricity

All but a few older establishments use 110 volts, 50 cycles. American appliances run without converters or adapters. Dual-voltage British appliances run without adapters, but European devices require converters and adapters. Some hotels supply converters and adapters, but take your own to avoid inconveniences.

■ Embassies

Many foreign embassies are located in an area off H4 east of Bridgetown known as Pine Garden.

Australian High Commission
Bishop's Court Hill, St. Michael Parish
☎ *246-435-2834*

British High Commission
Lower Collymore Rock Street, St. Michael Parish
☎ *246-436-6694*

Canadian High Commission
Bishop's Court Hill, St. Michael Parish
☎ *246-429-3550*

US Embassy
Broad Street, Bridgetown
☎ *246-436-4950*

■ Emergencies

Police, ☎ 112

Fire, ☎ 113

Ambulance, ☎ 115

Dial ☎ 115 in an emergency, ☎ 246-426-1113 to summon a government ambulance or ☎ 246-426-4170 to request the private Lynghurst's Ambulance, if the situation is not an emergency.

■ Geographical Information

Location: Barbados is the easternmost island of the Lesser Antilles archipelago, 100 miles from St. Lucia and St. Vincent.

Population: Approximately 260,000.

Size: North to south, 21 miles; east to west across the widest southern expanse, 14 miles.

■ Government

Barbados is an independent nation under the British Commonwealth. The queen (or king) of Great Britain serves as the monarch of Barbados. An appointed Senate and an elected House of Assembly make up the bicameral legislature. The Prime Minister is normally head of the majority party in the House of Assembly, which is the third oldest parliament in the western hemisphere.

■ Hospitals

Queen Elizabeth, Martindale's Road, Bridgetown, ☎ 246-436-6450.

Bayview, St. Paul's Avenue, Bridgetown, ☎ 246-436-5446.

■ Language

English.

■ Maps

Barbados in a Nutshell is available free at tourist spots. *Holiday Map* and *Ordinance Map of Barbados* is for sale at bookstores in Bridgetown.

■ Metrics – Quick & Painless

- Temperature is converted from °C to °F by multiplying the Celsius temperature by nine, dividing the result by five and adding 32.

Too hard? Here's about all you need to know on Barbados:

15°C . . . . 59°F
20°C . . . . 68°F
25°C . . . . 77°F
30°C . . . . 86°F
35°C . . . . 95°F

■ At the market, if you want a pound of fruit, ask for half a kilo. When you buy gas, you'll need almost four liters to make a gallon. The real numbers work out this way:

1 kilogram = 2.2046 lbs

1 pound = 0.4536 kilograms

1 liter = 1.06 quarts or 0.264 gallons

3.8 liters = 4 quarts or one gallon

To convert imperial gallons to liters, multiply by 4.55

To convert liters to imperial gallons, multiply by 0.22

To convert US gallons to liters, multiply by 3.79

To convert litters to US gallons, multiply by 0.26

■ The distance from one town to the next may be 10 kilometers, but that's only a little over six miles. Do the math this way:

1.6 kilometers = 1 mile

To convert miles to kilometers, multiply by 1.61

To convert kilometers to miles, multiply by 0.62

■ Money

The rate of exchange is fixed to the US dollar so that one US dollar (US$1) equals two Barbados dollars (B$2). One British pound sterling (UK£) equals approximately three Barbados dollars (B$3). Both US dollars and pounds sterling can be used on the island.

Major credit cards and travelers checks are accepted by most businesses. Travelers checks in US$ denominations are easier to cash than other currencies. Small shops, restaurants, and gas stations often do not accept credit cards or travelers checks.

Prices on the island usually are quoted in B$, except for accommodations, which normally list rates in US$. Be sure to ask if prices are B$ or US$ before you pay for tickets or merchandise.

■ Newspapers

The Barbados Advocate (daily), ***The Nation*** (weekdays), and foreign newspapers are sold at newsstands, book stores, and large hotel gift shops.

■ Pharmacies

Cheapside Pharmacy
Cheapside, Bridgetown, ☎ 246-437-2004

Collin's Pharmacy
Broad Street, Bridgetown, ☎ 246-426-4515
Speightstown, ☎ 246-422-5319

Lewis's Drug Mart
Rockley, across from Accra Beach Hotel, Christ Church, ☎ 246-435-8090

Knight's Pharmacy
Southern Plaza, Oistins, Christ Church, ☎ 246-436-6120

■ Post Office

The main post office is at Cheapside in Bridgetown, ☎ 436-4800. It's open Monday-Friday, 7:30 am-5 pm. Each parish has a post office, which is open Mondays, 7:30 am-noon and 1 pm-3 pm; Tuesday-Friday, 8 am-noon and 1-3:15 pm. Phone the main number for information about branch locations.

■ Radio Stations

The Voice of Barbados broadcasts news and music 24-hours per day at 95.3FM and 100.1FM.

■ Tax

Most services, including hotels and restaurants, add a 15% Value Added Tax (VAT).

■ Time

Barbados is on Atlantic Time, which is one hour ahead of Eastern Time in the United States, and four hours behind Greenwich Mean Time in the winter. The island observes daylight-saving time. At noon in Barbados during Standard Time, it's 11 am in New York and 4 pm in London.

■ Tips

Most hotels and restaurants add a 10% service charge. If service is exceptional, many visitors leave an additional 5%. When no service charge is added to the bill, expect to leave a 10% tip.

■ Tourist Information Offices

In Barbados

Barbados Hotel and Tourism Association
4th Avenue
Belleville, St. Michael
Barbados, West Indies
☎ *246-426-5041, fax 429-2845*

Barbados Tourism Authority
PO Box 242
Harbour Road, Bridgetown
Barbados, West Indies
☎ *800-744-6244 (in the Caribbean) or 246-427-2623 (on Barbados), fax 426-4080, www.barbados.org*

In the United States

Barbados Tourism Authority
800 Second Avenue
New York, NY 10017
☎ *800-221-9831 or 212-986-6516, fax 212-573-9850*
www.barbados.org, e-mail btany@worldnet.att.net

Barbados Tourism Authority
3440 Wiltshire Boulevard, Suite 1215
Los Angeles, CA 90010
☎ *213-380-2198, fax 213-384-2763*
www.barbados.org, e-mail btala@worldnet.att.net

Barbados Tourism Authority
150 Alhambra Circle, Suite 1270
Coral Gables, FL 33134
☎ *305-442-7471, fax 305-567-2844*
www.barbados.org

In the United Kingdom

Barbados Tourism Authority
263 Tottenham Court Road
London W1P OLA, England
☎ *051-262081 or 0171-636-9448, fax 0171-637-1496*
www.barbados.org

In Canada

Barbados Tourism Authority
105 Adelaide Street West, Suite 1010
Toronto, Ontario M5H 1P9, Canada
☎ *800-268-9122 or 416-214-9880, fax 416-214-9882*
www.barbados.org, e-mail btapublic@globalserve.net

Barbados Tourism Authority
4800 de Maisonneuve W, Suite 532
Montreal, Quebec H3Z 1M2, Canada
☎ *514-932-3206, fax 514-932-3775*
www.barbados.org, e-mail btasmith@globalserve.net

Visitor Information Network
☎ *246-426-5017*

A voice menu will guide you to information on activities such as restaurants, nightclubs, tours, special events, and cruises.

Websites

www.barbados.org – The official website of the Barbados Tourism Authority. Almost everything you want to know about the island is found somewhere on this vast site. Start your trip research here.

www.insandouts-barbados.com – *Ins and Outs* is a publication found in hotel rooms filled with visitor information on shopping, dining, sightseeing, and activities. The online edition is easy to use and helpful for planning your trip. However, accommodations are not listed (since you are meant to be browsing the publication once you're already in a hotel room). Take a look to get into the island mood.

www.funbarbados.com – This website is similar to barbados.org, but not as extensive in some areas. It has information on accommodations, restaurants, tour operators, and special events. Well worth a hit.

Index